WAGING
RECONCILIATION

God's Mission in a Time of Globalization and Crisis

Edited by
IAN T. DOUGLAS

CHURCH

Church Publishing Incorporated, New York

Library of Congress Cataloging-in-Publication Data

Waging reconciliation : God's mission in a time of globalization and crisis /
ed., Ian T. Douglas.
       p. cm.
    Includes bibliographical references.
     0-89869-378-0 (pbk.)
      1. Episcopal Church--Missions. 2. Globalization--Religious aspects--
Episcopal Church. I. Douglas, Ian T.

BV2575 .W34 2002
261.8'088'23--dc21

                                                                    2002019985

Church Publishing Incorporated
445 Fifth Avenue
New York NY 10016

www.churchpublishing.org

5 4 3 2 1

CONTENTS

WAGING
RECONCILIATION

ACKNOWLEDGMENTS

It seems trite in these acknowledgements to thank all of the individuals "without whom this work would not have happened." In an edited book of collected addresses and papers, however, it is literally true that without the contributions of friends and colleagues a volume like this one would never have been published. I thus would like to take this opportunity to thank the folk who have made this particular book possible.

To begin with I want to thank the Presiding Bishop, Frank Griswold, for inviting me to assist him in planning both his June 2001 retreat with missiologists and the September 2001 meeting of the House of Bishops of the Episcopal Church. I am honored by the confidence and trust he has in me, and deeply appreciate his challenge of me to live into my "charism" as a missiologist. I am also indebted to the excellent staff of the Presiding Bishop, with whom it is a joy to work. Jim Griffiss, the Canon Theologian to the Presiding Bishop, helped to shape the initial plans for the retreat with missiologists. Barbara Braver, Assistant to the Presiding Bishop for Communication, has provided constant support and friendship to me throughout this journey. Carl Gerdau, Canon to the Presiding Bishop, ensured that all administrative details would be in good order. Susy Miller, the process consultant for the House of Bishops, challenged the presenters and me to "go deeper" in our offerings to the bishops and spouses. And Alfreda Barrow, Administrative Assistant in the Presiding Bishop's office, was an ever-helpful, calm, and organized presence in the midst of it all. To all of these fine co-workers, I owe much.

I am tremendously blessed with close friends and colleagues who also happen to be some of the brightest minds and most gifted theologians in the worldwide Anglican Communion. The fact that six incredibly busy individuals would immediately and without reservation offer so much time and energy to the House of Bishops is a testimony to their goodwill, generosity, and commitment to the church. To Grant LeMarquand, Valerie Batts, Richard Parker, Leng Lim, Denise Ackermann, and Christopher Duraisingh, I thank God for your vision, your leadership gifts, and your theological insights. I am honored and humbled by your friendship and collegiality.

I want to thank others who have contributed to this book in order to make it a fuller and more complete record of the September 2001 gathering of the "Community of Bishops and Spouses." Thank you to Gerry Wolf for your artistic gifts of prayer and sculpture that graced the worship space at the Vermont meeting. Thank you to David Gitari for offering your leadership and the contributions of sister and brother Christians in Kenya. And thank you to Karlah Gibbs and Cristina Daniels for agreeing to let us publish your reflections from the "spouses' program."

I would like to thank other colleagues who have supported the publication of this volume, directly and indirectly. To Frank Tedeschi, the Managing Editor at Church Publishing, I am deeply indebted to you and your staff for the immediate and never-failing efforts to bring this book out in a very short period of time. I want to thank my editorial assistant Jay Lawlor, who in the midst of his final year of seminary studies and the General Ordination Examinations, always found time to work through drafts, and then more drafts, of this manuscript with an eye for detail and the acumen of an economist. Thanks also go to the Theological Writing Fund at the Episcopal Divinity School that provided funds to pay for Jay's editorial assistance. I am deeply indebted to Arthur Walmsley for his guidance and direction offered to me personally over many years, as well as for his vision and energy given to the bishops' "reconciliation initiative" in its early months. These and many other colleagues at the Episcopal Divinity School, in the Episcopal Diocese of Massachusetts, and at St. James's Episcopal Church in Cambridge, are a never-ending source of inspiration, challenge, and collaboration.

Finally, I want to thank my friends and family without whose love and support I would not be able to undertake any of this work. For my friends, Steve Bonsey, Mike Morin, and Andy Stoessel, who keep me healthy and sane by running me around the squash court. For my family, Bill and Nan Harris, Gladys Douglas, Laurie, Kate, and Kim Douglas, and the memories of my father, Duncan, and brother, Craig, who keep me grounded as only family can. For my spouse, Kristin, whose constant love and encouragement make all things possible. And to our children, Johanna, Timothy, and Luke, whose childhood will always be marked by the events of September 11, 2001. I thank the three of you for sharing your lives with me and I dedicate this book to you with the hope and the prayer that you will continue to find your own place in God's mission of reconciliation.

ON WAGING RECONCILIATION

HOUSE OF BISHOPS OF THE EPISCOPAL CHURCH
SEPTEMBER 26, 2001

We, your bishops, have come together in the shadow of the shattering events of September 11. We in the United States now join that company of nations in which ideology disguised as true religion wreaks havoc and sudden death. Through this suffering, we have come into a new solidarity with those in other parts of the world for whom the evil forces of terrorism are a continuing fear and reality.

We grieve with those who have lost companions and loved ones, and pray for those who have so tragically died. We pray for the President of the United States, his advisors, and for the members of Congress that they may be given wisdom and prudence for their deliberations and measured patience in their actions. We pray for our military chaplains, and for those serving in the armed forces along with their families in these anxious and uncertain days. We also pray "for our enemies, and those who wish us harm; and for all whom we have injured or offended."*

At the same time we give thanks for the rescue workers and volunteers, and all those persons whose courageous efforts demonstrated a generosity and selflessness that bears witness to the spirit of our nation at its best. We give thanks

---

* The Book of Common Prayer, 391.

too for all those who are reaching out to our Muslim brothers and sisters and others who are rendered vulnerable in this time of fear and recrimination.

We come together also in the shadow of the cross: that unequivocal sign that suffering and death are never the end, but the way along which we pass into a future in which all things will be healed and reconciled. Through Christ "God was pleased to reconcile to himself all things whether on earth or in heaven, by making peace through the blood of his cross" (Col 1:20). This radical act of peace-making is nothing less than the right ordering of all things according to God's passionate desire for justness, for the full flourishing of humankind and all creation.

This peace has already been achieved in Christ, but it has yet to be realized in our relationships with one another and the world around us. As members of a global community and the worldwide Anglican Communion, we are called to bear one another's burdens across the divides of culture, religion, and differing views of the world. The affluence of nations such as our own stands in stark contrast to other parts of the world wracked by the crushing poverty, which causes the death of 6,000 children in the course of a morning.

We are called to self-examination and repentance: the willingness to change direction, to open our hearts and give room to God's compassion as it seeks to bind up, to heal, and to make all things new and whole. God's project, in which we participate by virtue of our baptism, is the ongoing work of reordering and transforming the patterns of our common life so they may reveal God's justness—not as an abstraction—but in bread for the hungry and clothing for the naked. The mission of the church is to participate in God's work in the world. We claim that mission.

"I have set before you life and death...choose life so that you and your descendants may live," declares Moses to the children of Israel. We choose life and immediately set our-selves to the task of developing clear steps that we will take personally and as a community of faith, to give substance to our resolve and embodiment to our hope. We do so not alone but trusting in your own faithfulness and your desire to be instruments of peace.

Let us therefore wage reconciliation. Let us offer our gifts for the carrying out of God's ongoing work of reconciliation, healing, and making all things new. To this we pledge ourselves and call our church.

We go forth sober in the knowledge of the magnitude of the task to which we have all been called, yet confident and grounded in hope. "And hope does not disappoint us, because God's love has been poured into our hearts through the Holy Spirit that has been given to us" (Rom 5:5).

"May the God of hope fill us with all joy and peace in believing through the power of the Holy Spirit" (Rom 15:13).

INTRODUCTION

IAN T. DOUGLAS

Hanging behind the altar in the banquet hall turned chapel at the Radisson Hotel in Burlington, Vermont, was a four-foot high cross, fashioned by an anonymous artist from Providence, Rhode Island.[1] The materials of the cross and corpus were constructed of discarded bits and pieces of wood the artist had collected in lower Manhattan, from a New York City construction site, just three days prior to the horrific events of September 11, 2001. In the belt of the Jesus figure hanging on the cross were five nails, from the five wounds of Christ, and in the figure's right hand was a hammer. Painted on the horizontal of the cross were the words *"Construire de nuevo mi mundo."* "Rebuild the world in me." Rebuild the world in Jesus from the debris and broken pieces of our lives.

The symbolism of the cross and its words was not lost on the bishops of the Episcopal Church and their spouses who had gathered in Burlington in the early autumn for their regularly scheduled meeting. "Rebuild the world in me." What would it take to rebuild the world following the tragic events of September 11 when terror struck New York City, Washington, D.C., and rural Pennsylvania with a force never before witnessed on United States soil? What would these religious leaders need to rebuild the world in Christ in this time of crisis?

The chosen topic for the fall 2001 meeting of the Community of Bishops—as the combined gathering of bishops and their spouses has come to call itself—was globalization. The subject could not have been more appropriate for the times. As the bishops and spouses were to discover during the week they were together in Vermont, the forces of economic globalization, the struggles and cries of the world's poor and sick, the sins of racism and xenophobia, and the ongoing legacy of Western colonialism, are all related, in strange and complicated ways, to the evil unleashed on the world on September 11.

Visibly shaken by the events of September 11, a mere nine days earlier, the participants came to the meeting with various feelings of shock, anger, confusion, exhaustion, and fear. In many ways these feelings were no different from the majority of United States citizens who simply could not believe that terrorists had struck so forcefully at the heart of America's symbols of wealth and military might. Perhaps only those few bishops and spouses who hailed from outside the United States, such as Haiti and parts of South America, had an inkling as to the connection between globalization and the crisis of terror raging across the United States. In plenary presentations and in small group discussions, in Bible study and in walks along Lake Champlain, being fed around the altar and in conversation over meals, the community of bishops would grow together over the week and come to a new place of understanding and commitment to God's mission in this time of globalization and crisis.

Credit for choosing the theme of globalization for the meeting goes to the presiding officer of the House of Bishops, the Most Rev. Frank T. Griswold. As Presiding Bishop of the Episcopal Church, USA, he takes most seriously his role as the chief shepherd of the gathered bishops. His episcopate has been characterized by a focused effort to bring the bishops together as a community of conversation and mutuality. Inviting outside speakers to resource the House of Bishops in their conversations on topics ranging from human sexuality to leadership in difficult times has been a hallmark of Bishop Griswold's presiding episcopate.

As a man of deep prayer and reflection, the Presiding Bishop waits on the leading of the Holy Spirit in his discernment of topics for the bishops' meetings. And the Burlington meeting was no different. The Presiding Bishop's interest in globalization had been peeked by his experiences with other leaders of Anglican churches from around the world at the 1998 Lambeth Conference and more recent meetings of the Primates of the Anglican Communion. In the spring of 2001, the Presiding Bishop and the Planning Committee for the House of Bishops began to consider how to engage the topic of globalization. In April of the same year Bishop Griswold approached me to ask if I could envision and resource the presentations and discussion on globalization. As honored as I was by the invitation, it struck me that the general theme of globalization was entirely too large to manage without some focus or particular take on globalization. Further, as a missiologist (a student of Christian mission) I believed that the bishops needed to engage the theological and ecclesial implications of the relationship between the forces of globalization and God's mission in the world. Only by talking about globalization within such an ecclesiological and missiological framework could the community of bishops and spouses gain a handle on such an immense topic.

While I was formulating my ideas about how to resource a missiological discussion of globalization for the bishops, I was also working with the Presiding Bishop and his staff to put together a June retreat of missiologists for Bishop Griswold. The Presiding Bishop is a person who values the intersection of contemplation and prayer, the indissoluble unity of the life of the mind and the life of the spirit. Pursuing a discipline of thought and prayer, the Presiding Bishop tries to spend three or four days on retreat with a handful of academic theologians each June. These gatherings, facilitated by the Presiding Bishop's Canon Theologian, the Rev. Dr. James Griffiss, provide Bishop Griswold with time and resources for theological conversation in the midst of prayer. When approached to resource the House of Bishops with their discussion of globalization, Dr. Griffiss and I had been working together for several months planning a June 2001 retreat for the Presiding Bishop of theologians and missiologists from around the Anglican Communion.

It was during the Presiding Bishops' retreat of missiologists in June, at the College of Preachers on the grounds of the Washington Cathedral, that the program for the September 2001 Community of Bishop's began to take shape. In the course of the retreat, Bishop Griswold was particularly moved by three informal presentations on: the Bible and mission by Professor Grant LeMarquand of Trinity Episcopal School for Ministry in Ambridge, Pennsylvania; mission in the midst of the HIV/AIDS pandemic by Professor Denise Ackermann of the University of Stellenbosch in South Africa; and mission and religious plurality by Professor Christopher Duraisingh of the Episcopal Divinity School in Cambridge, Massachusetts. It seemed as if these presentations could be important resources for the bishops' discussion of globalization. Before leaving the College of Preachers all three professors had agreed to participate in the September event.

It was clear, however, that there was one big piece missing in the developing program on mission and globalization, namely: the economics of globalization. Returning to the Episcopal Divinity School (EDS) in Cambridge, Massachusetts, where I teach, I began to draw upon informal contacts and colleagues at Harvard University who might help with this need. The Rev. Leng Lim, an Episcopal priest from Singapore by way of the Diocese of Los Angeles, was just completing a Master of Business Administration at the Harvard Business School and was loosely connected to EDS during the course of his studies. Similarly, Professor Richard Parker, an economist at the Harvard Kennedy School of Government and an active lay leader at Christ Church, Cambridge, was referred to me as a wonderful resource. When approached, both Leng Lim and Richard Parker immediately agreed to help the bishops to consider the economic dynamics of globalization.

The only piece left to engage in the initial planning for the gathering of bishops and spouses was their ongoing commitment to anti-racism work. By both General Convention mandate and by their own initiative, the bishops have been engaging the sin of racism in their life and work together for over a decade.[2] It seemed to me and the Planning Committee that any engagement of the dynamics of globalization and mission needed also to be grounded in the bishops' commitments to overcoming racism. Dr. Valerie Batts, a well-known and widely respected anti-racism theorist and facilitator, who is no stranger to the Episcopal Church, was asked to help with this important work. And so, within a week of the Presiding Bishop's June 2001 retreat, all of the presenters had been selected for the September gathering.

Crafting these excellent resource people with their proposed topics into a unified program that had both integrity and continuity with the chosen topic of mission and globalization was not difficult. Using the title "God's Mission in a Global Communion of Difference" the bishops and spouses would begin with a biblical study on the nature of God's mission in the world.[3] Next would come the bishops' and spouses' direct experience of difference through a session on anti-racism. Having engaged their own experience of difference in light of God's story of mission, the bishops and spouses would then examine globalization from three different perspectives: economic, socio-cultural, and religious. Following the discussion of globalization from these three macro-perspectives, the community of bishops would begin to reflect theologically on the nature of globalization by focusing on changes in mission thought within the context of the global Anglican Communion. The discussion of Anglicanism would hopefully lead the bishops, as a common community, and individually in their dioceses, to ask how they are called to engage globalization in light of God's mission. In doing so the discussion would have come full circle: beginning with God's mission as discovered in the Bible, examining their own experience of difference, moving through globalization writ large, and returning to their own commitment to mission in the context of the contemporary Anglican Communion. All seemed to be in place, then September 11 occurred.

After the initial shock and horror of the terrorist attacks, the immediate question was: should the Burlington meeting be cancelled given the national tragedy? If it was decided to go ahead with the meeting, how many bishops and spouses would be able to travel to Vermont, given the vagaries of air travel after the hijackings? And finally, the question needed to be asked as to how pertinent were the planned presentations in light of the events of September 11.

Having taken council with the Planning Committee and his staff, the Presiding Bishop claimed that "not only is there a need for the community of bishops to be together in this time of crisis, but the chosen topic of globalization could never be so pertinent and timely." The Presiding Bishop was absolutely correct. From the perspective of the presenters, we were all in agreement that little needed to be changed in our presentations. If anything, the events of September 11 only served to heighten and focus the life and death issues of globalization that we were planning to lay before the bishops and spouses.

Collected in this volume then are the seven papers presented to the bishops and spouses at their September 2001 gathering in Vermont. The papers are faithful to the material delivered in plenary sessions of the House of Bishops, although the authors have edited, and in some cases added to, them in light of the bishops' statement "On Waging Reconciliation."

Chapter One is Grant LeMarquand's biblical study of mission: "From Creation to New Creation: The Mission of God in the Biblical Story." Going beyond more commonly utilized biblical mission verses, be they passages from the Exodus story or the Great Commission in Matthew, Professor LeMarquand lifts up the creation story in Genesis and the full summation of all with God in Revelation as key missiological texts. In doing so he shows that all of Holy Scripture, from the opening to the closing books of the Bible, becomes coherent and finds its true meaning as an exposition of God's mission in the world.

In Chapter Two, Valerie Batts discusses the need to confront "modern racism" as a means for understanding and effecting reconciliation. The bulk of the paper had been previously published and was distributed to the bishops for study in advance of their September gathering.[4] Dr. Batts' presentation in Vermont built on the material in the original paper and, in keeping with her pedagogical commitments, was highly experiential and process oriented. Following her time with the bishops and spouses, Batts added new introductory and concluding material to her original paper. The full text is produced here as "Is Reconciliation Possible? Lessons from Combating 'Modern Racism'."

The next two chapters directly address the economics of globalization. Although well versed in the theoretical underpinnings of globalization, neither Richard Parker's nor Leng Lim's paper is simply an analytical overview of the science of global market forces or the mathematics of supply and demand equations. Each, in his own way, challenges the bishops to a new level of leadership, given today's global economic order. Professor Parker in Chapter Three, "Globalization: The Social Gospel, and Christian Leadership Today," calls the bishops to reclaim their engagement with the social ills of the world as their forebears did a century ago. Similarly in Chapter Four, "Globalization and the West: A Call for Moral Imagination," Leng Lim looks for a new kind of imaginative leadership from the bishops in these times of globalization.

Denise Ackermann's paper provides a radically different view of globalization than that of the economists who precede her. Writing out of the social and cultural context of South Africa, Professor Ackermann begins to ask what God's mission is in light of the unbelievable circumstances of the HIV/AIDS pandemic in her home country. She offers seven interrelated propositions for discussing the theological implications for a world and church in the midst of a global pandemic. Appropriately titled: "Mission in the Midst of Suffering: The 'Bleak Immensity' of HIV/AIDS, A South African Perspective," Ackermann's essay moves the discussion of globalization beyond economics and leadership needs to the social and theological implications of a world living with HIV/AIDS.

Chapter Six continues a theological examination of the global context in which we find ourselves, examining, in particular, cultural and religious pluralism. Christopher Duraisingh's "Encountering Difference in a Plural World: A Pentecost Paradigm for Mission" challenges the church to follow a practice of mission today that is built upon: "a de-centering of selves, a courageous border-crossing, and empowering of multiple, even contesting, voices within a shared communion." This is the first time that bishops and other readers have access to the full text of Professor Duraisingh's presentation. While flying out of out of Logan Airport in Boston, Massachusetts, to Burlington, Vermont, shortly after the September 11 attacks, Professor Duraisingh's computer, briefcase, and all papers were unexplainably confiscated by airport security. While other non-South Asian looking passengers on his plane retained their computers and hand baggage, Duraisingh had to fly without his papers and other materials. He was thus forced to stay up most of the night before his address to the bishops recreating his presentation from memory and notes he could scribble on hotel stationary. Although Duraisingh was too polite and retiring to say so publicly, it was not lost on the bishops and spouses that they were witnessing firsthand the effects of a new "racial profiling" in the United States.

The nature of God's mission is examined further, this time in the specific context of the Anglican Communion, in Chapter Seven, "Restoration, Reconciliation and Renewal in God's Mission and the Anglican Communion." In this paper, I review briefly the changes in mission thought of the last century alongside of the changes in demographics of both the Anglican Communion and world Christianity in the same time period. Having demonstrated that neither the world nor the philosophical and theological constructs by which we understand mission are the same as they were a mere four decades ago, I then ask where God is leading us in mission in these trying and turbulent times. Signs of hope and renewal in God's mission are suggested in order to encourage bishops and other church leaders to action.

Framing the seven presentations are the "Opening Remarks" and "Closing Reflections" offered by the Presiding Bishop. As the presiding officer of the House of Bishops it is Bishop Griswold's responsibility and authority to call the church leaders together as a common body of prayer, reflection, and action. In his opening remarks, the Presiding Bishop sensitively and pastorally acknowledges and honors the loss, pain, and suffering brought about by the evil of September 11. He calls the bishops and spouses gathered in Vermont to be vulnerable and open to each other so that together they might discover what God is wanting the church to be about in these trying times. Similarly, in his "Closing Reflections," the Presiding Bishop acknowledges the suffering unleashed on the world because of September 11 and recognizes that the "war on terrorism" must be fought. Drawing on the lessons, discussions, and presentations of the week, Bishop Griswold challenges the bishops to a new level of participation and commitment to "God's project, God's work, God's mission" of reconciliation. It is in this context of mutual learning, mutual support, and mutual challenge that the bishops enthusiastically and wholeheartedly embraced the statement "On Waging Reconciliation."

To think that the September 2001 meeting of the House of Bishops was exclusively and single-mindedly oriented to writing some kind of statement or pastoral letter to the Episcopal Church would sorely miss the point of the gathering. The bishops and spouses gathered not so much to transact business and make pronouncements to the world and the church, but rather they came together as a community of wisdom to wait on the power and leading of the Holy Spirit in these times of globalization and crisis. The many textures, tones, and thoughts of the bishops, spouses, and guests gathered in Vermont during those beautiful autumn days thus cannot be contained in a singular communiqué. To give a sense of the depth of prayer, reflection, and engagement of the community of bishops and spouses, the prayers used at the Eucharists (written by the Rt. Rev. Geralyn Wolf, Bishop of Rhode Island), and offerings from the Most Rev. David Gitari, Archbishop of the Anglican Church of Kenya who attended the whole meeting, and Mrs. Karlah Gibbs and Mrs. Cristina Daniels, writing on behalf of the "Spouses' Gathering" are included as appendices.

Appreciating that no single communication can adequately portray the realities of a meeting of the House of Bishops, "On Waging Reconciliation" does stand as the public statement from the bishops on their September 2001 gathering. In the weeks and months following the release of "On Waging Reconciliation" the United States would identify Osama bin Laden and his Al Quaeda terrorist network as the perpetrators of the violence and evil of September 11. Mobilizing its military might, the United Sates would move on the Taliban regime in Afghanistan who harbored bin Laden and his Al Quaeda terrorists. While United States bombs and attacks would rout out, in relatively short order, the Taliban and Al Quaeda in Afghanistan, terror and uncertainty would continue to plague United States citizens in the form of anthrax-contaminated letters and new threats of airline hijackings. It is in this context of extreme fear, death, and military action in the "war on terrorism" that "On Waging Reconciliation" has been received with both acclamation and opposition.[5]

"On Waging Reconciliation" has found its detractors in both the secular and religious press. Complaints about the statement accuse it of being morally relative and not denouncing forcefully enough the evil of September 11. In this time of fear and unknowing, the bishops' call for reconciliation, self-examination, and repentance seems to run contrary to those in the United States that are seeking easy answers (and swift military victories) in an either/or world of good versus evil.

The *U.S. News & World Report* commentator, John Leo, was particularly upset with the bishops' call to wage reconciliation. His commentary, "Turning a blind eye to evil" in the October 12, 2001 issue of *U.S. News*, accused the House of Bishops of producing "an unusually disgraceful statement on the terrorist attacks."[6] Leo saw the bishops' communication as representative of a form of moral relativism and multiculturalism in American society that espouses no standards of right and wrong. To bolster this point, he mistakenly concluded that the bishops' reference to the death through starvation of 6,000 children in the course of a morning was equated to the initial estimate of people killed in the World Trade Center. What Leo and others who share his view about the seeming "moral relativism" of the bishops do not know is that the reference to thousands of children dying in a two-hour time span was taken from Professor Richard Parker's paper on globalization written long in advance of the events of September 11.[7] Nevertheless Leo concludes that the "multicultural-therapeutic left is small but concentrated in businesses that do most of the preaching to America—universities, mainline churches, the press, the entertainment industry."[8] He argues that the voices and opinions of such leaders have no place in a United States society confronting the threat of terrorism.

What was lost on Leo and others who would accuse the bishops of moral relativism is that, far from preaching "sloppy multiculturalism and all-purpose relativism," the bishops were actually lifting up gospel values of forgiveness and reconciliation in the face of cultural pressures to vilify and annihilate those who have done us wrong. The bishops were unwilling to give into easy answers to those seeking vengeance and retribution for September 11. Rather they heralded another way of seeing the world, another way of being related, the way known and made real in the incarnation of Jesus Christ. In his letter to the editor of *U.S. News & World Report* as a response to John Leo, the Presiding Bishop witnessed to the way of Jesus:

> The Episcopal Church is part of the world-wide Anglican Communion and the bishops reflected during the week-long meeting about faith and the question posed by Jesus, "Who is my neighbor?" We observed that as Christians we are called to radical peacemaking, which is, as we said, "nothing less than the right ordering of all things according to God's passionate desire for justness, for the full flourishing of humankind and all creation."[9]

Picking up on the critique offered by John Leo were voices in the Episcopal Church who likewise wanted to portray "On Waging Reconciliation" as some weak-kneed, effusive statement of political correctness. Editorial comments in independent church periodicals have characterized the bishops' statement as incomprehensible or characteristic of anti-war political beliefs "frozen in the Vietnam era."[10] Like Leo, these dissenting voices see the Episcopal House of Bishops as seriously out of step with the popular cultural position of United States society calling for revenge and retribution for the events of September 11. Perhaps this is true. Perhaps the bishops are, in fact, swimming against the cultural tide in their efforts to follow the Prince of Peace. Few, however, can deny the fact that it has been a long time since anything said by the House of Bishops of the Episcopal Church was taken so seriously as to occasion a stinging editorial from a major news weekly magazine. The question thus needs to be asked: Are the bishops not offering in these difficult times a kind of leadership to the church and the world that is sorely needed, although countercultural and prophetic?

The essays, the reflections of the Presiding Bishop, and the voices in the appendices of this book are thus presented as an outgrowth of the leadership of the House of Bishops. The material offered here does not pretend to give simple answers and explanations to the complex and conflict-ridden circumstances of this time in world history. In these trying times the bishops of the Episcopal Church, as Christian leaders seeking to rebuild the world in light of the tragedy and triumph of the cross, have committed themselves to the work of reconciliation, individually in their personal experience, communally in the life of the church, and globally in the wider world. Such waging of reconciliation will not be easily effected with yet another activity or agenda of the Episcopal Church, but rather will be realized in the promise of Jesus Christ as the healer and redeemer of a broken and sinful world. "On Waging Reconciliation" is thus not a program but a pledge of the bishops and a call to the church. It challenges each and every one of us to a deeper engagement with, and a recommitment to, God's mission "to restore all people to unity with God and each other in Christ" in this time of globalization and crisis.[11]

NOTES

[1] At the time of the meeting, the artist who created the cross wished to remain anonymous. The artist has since been identified as the Rt. Rev. Geralyn Wolf, Bishop of Rhode Island. The cross was later purchased by the Diocese of Pennsylvania.

[2] Resolution B049 of the 2000 General Convention requires that there be ongoing anti-racism training for all lay and ordained leaders of the Episcopal Church. The bishops are committed to this work and try to include anti-racism initiatives in their regular gatherings.

[3] Because of scheduling difficulties, presentations had to be rearranged such that the bishops and spouses ended up hearing Dr. Batts' anti-racism paper first followed shortly thereafter by Professor LeMarquand's biblical study of mission.

[4] Valerie Batts, *Modern Racism: New Melody for the Same Old Tunes* (Cambridge, MA: Episcopal Divinity School Occasional Papers, 1998).

[5] For a positive review of the bishops' statement see: James Solheim and Jan Nunley, "Bishops call 'waging reconciliation' the answer to globalization, terrorism," *Episcopal News Service*, September 28 2001, #2001-277, www.dfms.org/ens/2001-277.html; and Scott Becker, "Responding to violence with wisdom and morality," *The Seattle Times*, 26 October 2001, www.archives.seattletimes.nwsource.com.

[6] John Leo, "Turning a blind eye to evil," *U.S. News & World Report*, October 12, 2001, 55.

[7] See Chapter 3 below: "Globalization: The Social Gospel, and Christian Leadership Today" for the original text and reference offered by Professor Parker.

[8] Ibid.

[9] From an unpublished "Letter to the Editor" by Frank T. Griswold, Presiding Bishop.

[10] See: David Kalvelage, "From the Editor: Waging Reconciliation," *The Living Church*, 28 October 2001, 11; David Apker, "Viewpoint: Frozen in Time," *The Living Church*, 2 December 2001, 16; and, David Roseberry, "Texas Rector Criticizes Griswold on 'Waging Reconciliation,'" available from: VIRTUOSITY@EPISCOPALIAN.ORG, VIRTUOSITY archives—January 2002, week 2 (#11).

[11] This statement affirms the *missio Dei* as the starting point for mission and echoes the Catechism's teaching on the Church's participation in this mission. See "An Outline of the Faith" in The Book of Common Prayer (New York: The Church Hymnal Corporation for the Episcopal Church, 1979), 855.

OPENING REMARKS BY THE PRESIDING BISHOP

COMMUNITY OF BISHOPS
September 20, 2001

FRANK T. GRISWOLD

It's wonderful to see you all and thank you for making, in some instances, awkward and difficult travel arrangements as well as making awkward and difficult decisions to be here. I think it's terribly important that we be gathered as a community at this time.

We come together in very unusual and difficult circumstances. The terrible events of last week in New York and Washington, with yet-to-be fully appreciated ramifications in terms of the dead and the presumed dead, reach across our country into a number of your own dioceses. It also reaches around the world and it transcends all religions: Christians, Jews, Muslims, Sikhs, and Buddhists were all represented by those who died or who are presumed missing. I think it's fair to say we have all personally and collectively suffered a trauma and in fact we are dealing with the effects of trauma now. I think it's very important to say that clearly. All of us have been wounded; neither the nation nor we are immune from this hurt. All of us have been deeply wounded and the effects of that wound simply have to be lived. And I think they're best lived in community.

What we've seen happen, among other things, is the death of our sense of immunity as a nation. We've had to face our vulnerability and our fragility writ large. And in that we find ourselves in solidarity with other parts of the world where terrorism and sudden death are daily realities, possibly not in as dramatic and well reported a form as what happened last week, but nonetheless, to those who live in those contexts, these things are just as real. And so many of the messages I've received from other parts of the Anglican Communion have contained something of that: "We are with you in solidarity because we know what it is to live with terrorism." So I think September 11 joins us in a new way to the world community.

We find ourselves in a liminal place: we're on the threshold of what? The President of the United States is going to speak tonight; that won't answer all the questions. There are so many voices; I'm weary of listening to CNN and the other news sources. Opinion upon opinion, opinion upon opinion, and then there are all these emotions within ourselves, within our clergy, within our congregations. It's a thin place in which we find ourselves.

I've been struck, as I know all of you have been as well, by how important sacred space has been to countless thousands of Americans across this country. They simply needed to be in sacred space. Often people who had long ago lost any contact with the formality of a religious tradition simply had to be with others and continue to feel that need. The chapel at the Episcopal Church Center, which always has had, at the mid-day Eucharist particularly, some people from the larger community, has been filled. On September 14 it was so overcrowded that communion had to be given out in the lobby as well as in the chapel itself. And I know you've had similar experiences in your own dioceses. So when people are in a thin place, having to face their own vulnerability and fragility, they're open in a deeper way to the mystery of God.

You as bishops have been engaged in what Clay Matthews [The Rt. Rev. Clayton Matthews, Bishop for Pastoral Development] likes to call "emotional labor." You've been creating a container in which to hold the pain, the fear, the anguish, and anger of your people and your clergy. And you've had to be noble and clear and centered and judicious and absorb any number of reactions and emotions, while your own emotions and feelings have had to be held somewhat in check; possibly let out at home, possibly let out in some curious ways. I know I've eaten a lot more in the last week than I normally eat. I thought, "Why have I finished an entire box of candy in three minutes?" I thought—something's going on and I'm not acknowledging it, but what I've just done tells me that I am in a place of disarray and disorientation.

I think this meeting, then, gives us a chance to lay down some of the emotional labor we've expended in this last week, and to share the burden of it with others. I hope that this week, even though it has a very clear program to it, will afford you plenty of space, because one thing that was very clear to me last week in New York—and I'm sure it was true in other places as well—people needed to talk. My normal pattern on a weekday is to go to the gym at the Harvard Club at 6:00 in the morning, where people might say good morning to one another but you never go any further than that. And last week, I found that I didn't have time to finish my usual routine because so many people wanted to talk and tell stories.

I think we need to give one another the gift and the grace of conversation. Tell one another how you're feeling because if you don't name your emotions, then you're the victim of your emotions. And naming them doesn't simply identify them, it also gives you a different kind of relationship to them. It doesn't mean that everything falls into order.

Last week at the meeting of the Episcopal Church Center community someone said, "What should we think? How do we get our minds together?" I said, "You can't. Because you've suffered a trauma and you're just going to have to allow a multiplicity of feelings, sometimes contradictory, bump into one another and over time, largely through relationships with others and talking with others, there can be a coalescence, a settling down. And in time there will be an integration and you'll be able to move forward."

So, be available to one another, porous and vulnerable, beyond the issues within the life of the church. I must say, last week our issues seemed small indeed compared to what had broken upon us. Some of you may be here with feelings of guilt: you should be home because you could do more, or tensions have tugged at you between being here and being there. And so I very much hope that our time together as a community of bishops and spouses will give you a renewed sense of the episcopé we share—our ministry of care and oversight on behalf of Christ the Good Shepherd—in such a way that we can return home refreshed, grounded, and renewed through our relationships and sharings with one another.

Part of dealing with trauma is restoring order and balance. One thing I've had to caution some of the staff members at the Church Center in New York about is their zeal in volunteering to the point where they feel almost driven. And I've said, "You know to be really helpful means that you balance some hours of volunteer assistance with some hours of life as usual, attending to your responsibilities here." And I think for us to stand back from some of our very intense involvements over the past week may reframe some things and allow us to return in a different way that will make us ultimately more useful and more helpful to our people and our clergy.

I would like to share two images, two experiences. On September 14, the day of national mourning and remembrance, I went to the Seaman's Church Institute, which was very much the distribution center for food, for dry socks, for clean underwear, for towels, for whatever the National

Guard, the police officers, the firefighters, the Con Edison technicians, the rescue workers needed. And from the Seaman's Church Institute, we would take things to various distribution sites around the cordoned off area. I was struck again and again by how grateful people were. "Thank you for dry socks. Thank you for a sandwich." I had a wonderful sense of our church, through that venerable institution, being incredibly active and present in the life of the city, particularly in that area.

I went past St. Paul's Chapel, close to Ground Zero, and the first thing I noticed was that the Episcopal Church flag and the American flag were flying. They were filthy with dust and debris, but still there they were and the gate to the church was half open. I could see that the church door was unlocked, so we went in, [my wife] Phoebe and I, and several others. And everything was exactly where it should be, everything was in order, there was no sense of any chaos. The only thing that was different was the thick layer of fine dust over everything.

I could see the sacristy door was open, so I went in; I had on my mask, my hardhat, and all kinds of things. I found a piece of paper and a pen and I wrote: "Just stopped by, my prayers and my love, Frank Griswold, Presiding Bishop." I left it there. As I turned to leave, the priest appeared and he said, "I'm just here for whomever and for whatever purpose the church can be useful." And I had this sense that St. Paul's was sort of contemplative center in the midst of the chaos that surrounded it. The churchyard was thick with debris and dust, trees had been knocked over, thousands of pieces of paper were scattered all over the graves, and here was a center of calm and quiet welcome. So I thought of the Seaman's Church Institute as the Martha function and St. Paul's Chapel as the Mary function.

As I left, there was a little brass crucifix on the altar that I paused to look at. And I saw that the tiny brass arms could contain it all—all the chaos, the violence, the hatred, the grief. All the emotions that are out there, everything that has happened can actually be contained by the One in whom we are reconciled.

That evening, at Mark's invitation [The Rt. Rev. Mark Sisk, Bishop of New York] I was at the Cathedral of St. John the Divine and we had a service. I think the estimate was that about 1,100 people were there and at the end of it—and I think this happened all over the country—people went out with lighted candles. Take your light out into the darkness. Well, Mark and I got out on the steps of the cathedral and stood there, other people came out and stood there, just stood there. I finally said to Mark, "I think maybe if we go down the steps and stand on the sidewalk, that will give people permission to go with their light into the darkness." I even said to some, "Disperse, go with your light." No one moved. In fact, the opposite occurred. People passing by joined the group and some even managed to find candles of their own. So instead of the crowd getting smaller, it got larger and then impromptu singing began, "The Battle Hymn of the Republic," "We Shall Overcome," "Amazing Grace." I will confess Mark and I left part way through but we were told by the archdeacon several days later that people were there until 10:00 at night and it was 6:30 or quarter to 7:00 P.M. when we left. Simply because they wanted to be together; they needed to be together. An incredible experience.

Which brings us to our topic. "God's Mission, God's Work in a Global Communion of Difference" and I think we could extend "Communion" to a "World" of difference. Such has certainly been underscored by the last week. I cannot think of any topic that could be more pertinent in the life of this community right now, particularly in the light of what has happened. A hard look at the dynamics and effects of globalization is exactly what we need, for our own souls' help and for the welfare of our people. Last week's violent and deadly attack upon the United States, as sort of the icon of the West, is an attack upon what is perceived to be an alien and threatening worldview, not just symbols of an economy but a whole way of seeing.

I think certainly there is an invitation in all of this when I hear the President and others talk about how "we must make sacrifices." I think they're talking mostly in terms of whatever may lie ahead in terms of security or military action. I think we also have to look at what we take for a good, namely our national interests, and look at some of them in terms of how they're perceived in other parts of the world. The two weeks before all this happened, I was in Italy and Ireland. In Ireland—and Ireland's a very friendly nation—the editorials in the *Irish Times* always referred to the "unilateralist point of view" of the United States, our "unilateralist policies." Even among our friends, there's some question about our deep commitment to the common good and the global community.

Here I think, as persons of faith, we have to be clear about God's project as one of reconciliation. At the General Convention, in talking about Jubilee, I used the Hebrew phrase *tikkun-olam*, "repair of the world." That's what our Jewish brothers and sisters see as the end of Jubilee, *tikkun-olam*, where all relationships are reordered according to God's justness. God's justness being profoundly relational and having to do with communion: communion between people, communion between people and the creation. And so in a way this cross of Christ holding a hammer* is about *tikkun-olam*, repair of the world. This repair of the world is our vocation as well, that is, the incarnation of *Shalom*. *Shalom* is the undoing of all patterns that bind, restrict, and break down the human community, that stand against the reality of communion and reconciliation. So the mission of the church is to participate in God's project. We need to be about that unambiguously. We can't proclaim it to others if

---

* The Presiding Bishop refers to a sculpture of found objects depicting the crucified Christ holding a hammer in his right hand, hanging behind him in the worship space for the House of Bishops meeting.

we are unwilling to live it ourselves. That's been part of my emphasis on a reconciled community. How can you authentically speak about reconciliation if you can't live a reconciled life yourself?

So, on the one hand we work within the community. On the other hand, the community opens out toward the world. We need to ask ourselves what it means to be reconcilers, as the Episcopal Church, and as a province of the Anglican Communion. I hope and pray that our time together will help us to inhabit the very *Shalom* we seek to impart to the world.

1

FROM CREATION TO NEW CREATION

THE MISSION OF GOD IN THE BIBLICAL STORY

GRANT LeMARQUAND

The topic of mission and the Bible is vast.[1] I want to begin by asking a rather obvious question: where does one start such a discussion?

ENCOUNTERING THE BIBLE IN MISSION

One possible place to begin talking about Bible and mission is with the intersection between the biblical text and the reader who encounters this text in new ways in the context of missionary activity. The German philosopher Hans-Georg Gadamer spoke of all interpretation as having two horizons —the horizon of the text and the horizon of the reader. Meaning and understanding, he said, takes place at the intersection of these two realities. This came home to me a few years ago with some force when I realized that the traditional date of the Feast of the Transfiguration and the date of the bombing of Hiroshima were the same—August 6. From then on I have not been able to separate the two in my mind. The contrast between the blinding death light of the atomic bomb and the light of the glory of God in the face of Jesus is too strong a contrast for me to be able ever to dissociate the two.

Likewise I recall my first Christmas in Africa. It was 1987. My wife, Wendy, and our baby boy David had been in Kenya, and I for about a year. Chara, our daughter, had been born in November. We were supposed to have gone to teach in a small theological College in Mundri Sudan, but the Anglican Church of Canada wisely discerned that the war in the Sudan was heating up and we were diverted to Kenya. A few months after we arrived in Kenya, four of our would-be colleagues in Sudan were kidnapped by the Sudanese Peoples' Liberation Army and disappeared for almost two months in the Sudanese bush. After his release, one of the hostages, the Rev. Marc Nikkel, a mission partner of the Episcopal Church serving in the Sudan, returned to Africa. Unable to return to Sudan, he taught with us in Kenya for almost a year. We had maintained a strong interest in things Sudanese, so it was a joy to have Marc living next door. A few days before Christmas he gave me a report prepared by some Mennonites who had surveyed the situation in a particular area of Sudan around the town of Rumbek, an area of the Southern Sudan which had recently been devastated by the war. The authors of the report detailed atrocities beyond description. One of the most striking details, however, was the fact that in a vast area of hundreds of square miles they had found no living children: they had been killed, succumbed to starvation, fled as refugees, or carried off as slaves. A few days after reading this report, I opened my Bible to read the lesson for the daily office: it was December 28 and this was the lesson:

> Now when they had departed, behold, an angel of the Lord appeared to Joseph in a dream and said, "Rise, take the child and his mother, and flee to Egypt, and remain there till I tell you; for Herod is about to search for the child, to destroy him." And he rose and took the child and his mother by night, and departed to Egypt, and remained there until the death of Herod. This was

> to fulfil what the Lord had spoken by the prophet, "Out of Egypt have I called my son." Then Herod, when he saw that he had been tricked by the wise men, was in a furious rage, and he sent and killed all the male children in Bethlehem and in all that region who were two years old or under, according to the time which he had ascertained from the wise men. Then was fulfilled what was spoken by the prophet Jeremiah: "A voice was heard in Ramah, wailing and loud lamentation, Rachel weeping for her children; she refused to be consoled, because they were no more." (Mt 2:13–18)

As with the Transfiguration and Hiroshima, the stories of Sudan and the massacre of the innocents under Herod are now somehow fused in my mind. Sometimes reading the Bible in a new situation, or with new eyes, reading the Bible in a "mission" context, will confront the reader, perhaps even assault the reader, with its message. To speak of the Bible and mission may lead us to reflect on Scripture in ways that we had not previously dreamed. I went to Africa ostensibly to teach the Bible to theological college students—I ended up being taught the Bible in remarkable ways.

The task here is less to open up stories of my own existential engagement with biblical texts than to reflect on what the Bible says *about* mission. And surely this is a difficult enough task. I realize that every attempt to interpret the Bible is done from a particular context. No doubt my experiences and beliefs will color my understanding of Scripture, either illuminating or distorting the message. Since the Bible is such a foundational text for Christians, however, we are not at liberty to shy away from a task simply because it may be difficult.

Every thoughtful Christian who thinks about mission has some desire to root their theology of mission in Scripture. However, there appear at present to be two quite different starting places of biblical reflection on the theme of mission. I would like to examine briefly two sets of biblical texts that frequently come up in "Bible and mission" discussion, and notice what at first appear to be divergent themes that emerge from these texts. I would like then to examine the biblical story a bit more comprehensively, looking at the beginning and the end of Scripture, to see if the biblical story as a whole can help us to put these two apparently diverging texts and themes into a more fruitful canonical context.

THE GREAT COMMISSION[2] (MT 28:16–20)

As a faculty member at a theological education institution that from time to time has spoken of its identity as "a great commission seminary" one might expect the Matthean version of Jesus' command to his disciples to go out into the world (Mt 28:16–20) to appear somewhere in this discussion. Of course the danger of beginning with this text is that such a starting point may tempt us to think of mission exclusively in terms of "evangelism" or "disciple making." I have no desire to downplay these crucial activities—far from it! Unfortunately, however, these words tend to be heard either individualistically (evangelism being popularly understood as being about "personal decision") or ecclesially (disciples being understood as being about "church growth" or "church planting"). Please do not misunderstand me: I believe that people everywhere should hear the message of God's love in Christ, should be invited to make him their Savior, and encouraged to join the fellowship of the church for mutual edification and service. To put these themes in the central place in our theology of mission, however, may (and sometimes does) imply that mission is primarily about "us": about our reaching out, about our growth, as individuals and as a church. But as we shall see, I hope, when the Bible talks about mission, it is first of all talking about God.

Of course the Matthean version of Jesus' mission command to his disciples is not the only text of its kind. Luke has two such commissions—one in the gospel and one in Acts. John also has a unique version of the great commission.[3] We will look at each in turn, beginning with the two Lukan passages:

> Then he said to them, "These are my words which I spoke to you, while I was still with you, that everything written about me in the Law of Moses and the prophets and the psalms must be fulfilled." Then he opened their minds to understand the scriptures, and said to them, "Thus it is written, that the Christ should suffer and on the third day rise from the dead, and that repentance and forgiveness of sins should be preached in his name to all nations, beginning from Jerusalem. You are witnesses of these things. And behold, I send the promise of my Father upon you; but stay in the city, until you are clothed with power from on high." (Lk 24:44–49)

> "But you shall receive power when the Holy Spirit has come upon you; and you shall be my witnesses in Jerusalem and in all Judea and Samaria and to the end of the earth." (Acts 1:8)

Notice the themes: the disciples are to proclaim forgiveness of sins to the nations; they are to do this in the name of Jesus and in the power of the Spirit. Although the message is given to them to proclaim, the foundation of the proclamation is the action of God—seen in the story of Israel and fulfilled in the life, death, and resurrection of Jesus. The mission proclamation, according to Luke, does not have its origins with the disciples but in the action of God. The gospel of John also has its own version of the "great commission":

> Jesus said to them again, "Peace be with you. As the Father has sent me, even so I send you." And when he had said this, he breathed on them, and said to them, "Receive the Holy Spirit. If you forgive the sins of any, they are forgiven; if you retain the sins of any, they are retained." (Jn 20:21–23)

Although John's witness is distinct (in so many ways), some similarities with other versions of the "great commission" are apparent: forgiveness of sins is central again; the power and presence of the Spirit is considered to be necessary for the mission to take place.

Most importantly, John tells us that mission does not begin with us, but with God: "As the Father has sent me, even so I send you." Mission is not a program of the church, or a great new idea thought up by Victorian Christians as the religious arm of colonialism (much as it is tempting to read nineteenth-century church history in this way). Neither is "mission" a way of getting new members into the "club" so that we can collect more "dues" (tithes) to maintain our building programs and salaries. Mission is not about our projects, but about God's. To put it somewhat anachronistically, mission has its source in the life of the Trinity. The Father sends the Son, the Son sends the church, equipped in the power of the Spirit.

Matthew's most oft-quoted version of the "great commission" shares some of these themes, but presents them to us in a rather different way:

> Then the eleven disciples went to Galilee, to the mountain where Jesus had told them to go. When they saw him, they worshiped him; but some doubted. Then Jesus came to them and said, "All authority in heaven and on earth has been given to me. Therefore go and make disciples of all nations, baptizing them in the name of the Father and of the Son and of the Holy Spirit, and teaching them to obey everything I have commanded you. And surely I am with you always, to the very end of the age." (Mt 28:16–20)

Once again themes familiar to the Lukan and Johannine commissions are also found here: the disciples of Jesus are commissioned to bring a message to the nations, to the gentiles. Although forgiveness is not mentioned explicitly, I believe that we can safely assume that the message of forgiveness is implicit in the mention of baptism in this passage.

It is crucial to focus our attention on God's part in this process. Certainly the Trinitarian theme, which we saw implicit in the Lukan and especially the Johannine texts, is made explicit here in the baptismal formula. Often missed in most explications of this text, however, is the end of the passage. I have often heard this passage read or quoted only up to the end of v.19 or sometimes only to the halfway point of v.20. The end of the passage, however, is crucial: here we find the promise of Jesus' continued presence with the church in the mission task. What is not often noticed is that this promise is the climax of a theme which Matthew began at the beginning of the gospel. In the first chapter of the gospel, Matthew tells us (and only Matthew mentions this) that Jesus is to be called "Emmanuel: which means God with us" (Mt 1:23). The mention of Jesus as God's presence in the world and the promise of Jesus' continued presence in the church-in-mission form an "inclusio" bracketing the whole gospel.

In the middle of the gospel we find another remarkable text:

> "Again, I tell you that if two of you on earth agree about anything you ask for, it will be done for you by my Father in heaven. For where two or three come together in my name, there am I with them." (Mt 18:19–20)

This text is remarkable not only because it echoes the beginning and the end of the gospel with the promise of Jesus' presence, but because of the interesting Jewish context of this verse. When Israel found itself in exile in Babylon and estranged from the presence of God in the temple, a system of worship was formulated which placed the Torah in the central position. According to the Mishnaic tractate *Pirke Abot* (3.2),

> R. Hananiah b. Teradion said: If two sit together and no words of the Law [are spoken] between them, there is the seat of the scornful, as it is written: *Nor sitteth in the seat of the scornful.* [see Psalm 1] But if two sit together and the words of the Law [are spoken] between them, the Divine Presence [Shekinah] rests between them....

Just as the Jews in Babylon, bereft of God's presence in the temple and its rituals, replaced the temple with the Torah, so the early Christian community is promised that the physical absence of Jesus does not leave them comfortless. Jesus, the very divine presence, according to this passage, will be with us. And according to the end of Matthew's gospel, he will be with us especially as we participate in God's mission to "all nations."

Mission, we see from these texts, is about God: about God's love and forgiveness proclaimed, about God sending Jesus, about the promise of the spirit's presence as the task is continued by the church. Mission is not first and foremost about a human program or about human technique. Mission has its origins, and its continuing, and its fulfillment, in the life of the Trinity. Evangelism, disciple making and church planting are necessary and vital aspects of our life, because they are a part of God's own reaching out to the nations.

LIBERATION FROM OPPRESSION (EXODUS 3)

A second possible starting point, and one with which I also have great sympathy, is the Exodus story. Much so-called Third World theology begins in Exodus because here we have a story about slavery and oppression and about political deliverance. The Exodus story has in fact become somewhat paradigmatic for many theologians seeking to understand the vocation of the Christian and of the church in situations of institutionalized racism, systemic oppression, state-sponsored violence, and unjust international structures. Theologians and biblical scholars from Latin America, from the African American community, from South Africa, from Korea, and from many other communities have turned to the book of Exodus and found a message that appears to stand against the evil realities of social injustice. Here are the people of Israel, who are suffering in slavery under the unfair yoke of an oppressive dictatorship, who find liberation, freedom from bondage, and deliverance into a new land and a new way of life. The similarity between Israel's suffering under the taskmasters of Egypt and the suffering of so many around the world today is too obvious a parallel for most Third World theologians to ignore.

Most striking for me, once again, is what this narrative says about God:

> Then the LORD said, "I have seen the affliction of my people who are in Egypt, and have heard their cry because of their taskmasters; I know their sufferings, and I have come down to deliver them...." (Ex 3:7–8)

In v. 10 God sends Moses to Pharaoh. God uses a human mediator in his work of liberation, but Moses is not the deliverer. It is God who is the missionary in this situation—"I have seen"; "I know"; "I have come down to deliver." God is the one who does the mission; God's servants simply share in the mission that belongs to God.

And notice that the goal of liberation is not the "self-determination" of the people of Israel. The destination of the Exodus is Mount Sinai. God tells Moses that when Israel is delivered from Pharaoh the result will be a doxological one:

> [God said to Moses], "But I will be with you; and this shall be the sign for you, that I have sent you: when you have brought forth the people out of Egypt, you shall serve God upon this mountain." (Ex 3:12)

The mission of the Exodus is God's idea; the deliverance is carried out by God, and the purpose is the right ordering of Israelite society around the worship of God and the life of the covenant expressed in the Torah.

In short both of these texts—the so-called "great commission" and the great text of liberation in the book of Exodus[4] are both about *God's mission* in the world. Certainly it is a mission into which human beings are recruited, but in the end it is not about us but about God, about God's reaching out to the world in love.

It is strange how the churches of the Western world are so often divided between "great commission" people and "liberation" people as if these visions of mission are mutually exclusive. Perhaps paying more attention to the growing and dynamic churches of other parts of the world may help us to learn to heal this dualistic disease that has infected our church life. More importantly, I believe that we need to put these "mission texts" within the context of the biblical narrative as a whole. We have not been well served in the past by approaches, both scholarly and popular, which divide the Bible into bits but then never put it back together. Both naive proof-texting and erudite form-critical scholarship have (ironically) been guilty of the same thing: refusing to allow the Bible to be read as a story. I have no desire to iron out difficulties uncritically or to minimize differences between biblical texts. Clearly the various books of the Bible were written by a multitude of different authors, over several millennia, in three different languages, in a variety of political, social, and religious situations. As Christians, however, we are not given leave to throw up our hands and say it is all a mess of traditions and contradictions with no coherence or inner consistency. The canon does have a particular shape, a plot line, if you will, which is somehow *our* story.

GENESIS 1–12

The first twelve chapters of Genesis set the stage for all that follows. In these short chapters we are presented with the first two and the beginning of the third act of what N.T. Wright has called a five-act play,[5] these acts being "creation," the "fall," and the beginning of the story of Israel.

The story begins, of course, with God making a "good" world. Here is where mission theology must begin—with a God who is not content (excuse the anthropomorphism) to remain alone in "godness," but who reaches out and extends the privilege of existence to the universe. Mission is a part of the nature of God. We might say (as God later says of Adam) that it is not good for God "to be alone." Within this good creation human beings are also given a task:

> Then God said, "Let us make humankind in our image, after our likeness; and let them have dominion over the fish of the sea, and over the birds of the air, and over the cattle, and over all the earth, and over every creeping thing that creeps upon the earth." So God created humankind in his own image, in the image of God he created them; male and female he created them. And God blessed them, and God said to them, "Be fruitful and multiply, and fill the earth and subdue it; and have dominion over the fish of the sea and over the birds of the air and over every living thing that moves upon the earth." (Gen 1:26–28)

Of great importance for our purposes is the designation of human beings as God's image. I take this to be not so much a statement about ontology, as if there was some dimension or aspect of human existence that could be designated as the *imago dei,* as it is a statement of our purpose, our task, our commission. I believe that the human side of mission theology begins here: it is not so much that we are "in" God's image as that we are "to be" God's image in the world.

I spent many years being confused about the first two commandments of the Decalogue. They appeared to me to be redundant. It seems to me now that they are not. The first commandment instructs us to have no other gods. The second commandment forbids graven images, or idols. The second commandment says this, it seems, because to have graven images robs human beings of the task, the mission which they were given at creation: you are to be God's image in the world; do not abandon this representative mission to God's creation. My assertion is that mission begins prior to the fall. The mission of God, the mission of humanity is not *primarily* about fixing things—it is first of all about representing the life of God in the world in all that we do.

But of course the world is in need of fixing. Genesis 3 is about a love story gone awry,[6] about the dreadful consequences of human sin. The world is broken. Chapters 4–11 of Genesis recount the progression of human sin after the fall and expose the network of broken relationships resulting from human sin and evil.

Not to be lost in these chapters is the remarkable story of the tower of Babel. This story is usually read as if humans had somehow progressed to the point where they could actually challenge God with their technological achievements. God comes down and confuses their language in order to spoil the fun because the power and greatness of humanity threaten him. I think that the story should actually be read as a story about human empire (it is no coincidence that "Babel" is etymologically related to "Babylon"). In Genesis 10 we read that there are already nations and languages and so in its canonical and literary context it is more likely that we should see the sin of Babel as the hubris of empire that represses differences and forces subjugated peoples to conform to the culture and language of the conqueror. This imperial task is in direct contradiction to the divine command at creation to "fill the earth" (Gen 1:28) and to the post-flood command to "spread abroad on the earth" (Gen 10:32). Read in this way, the story of Babel is a story of liberation, a story in which God "coming down" (Gen 11:5,7) to confuse the language of the peoples is an act of freeing the subjugated so that they can once again "spread abroad over the face of the whole earth" (Gen 11:9). An empire speaking one language comes under judgment so that those who are freed after the fall of Babel's tower can continue the God-given task of being fruitful, of multiplying, of creating the diversity of culture that God intended.[7]

The third act, after creation and the fall, is the story of Israel, which begins with the calling of Abraham and Sarah in Genesis 12.

> Now the LORD said to Abram, "Go from your country and your kindred and your father's house to the land that I will show you. And I will make of you a great nation, and I will bless you, and make your name great, so that you will be a blessing. I will bless those who bless you, and him who curses you I will curse; and by you all the families of the earth shall bless themselves." (Gen 12:1–3)

Interestingly, the patriarch and matriarch are promised things that they cannot achieve. For example, they are promised "a name" (in contrast to the people of Babel who had decided to make a name for themselves). Abraham and Sarah are promised a family—and this in spite of their great age. They are promised a land, although Adam and Eve and the family of Noah had been told to scatter over the face of the earth. In other words, the story of Abraham and Sarah is a story about grace. Things that had previously been commanded, or in the case of Babel "demanded," have now been promised. What Abraham and Sarah cannot do for themselves because of the pervasive nature of the fall are now given as gifts.

Most importantly for our purposes, God promises that Abraham and Sarah's family will be a blessing to the nations. The grace given is not given for them alone, but for the world. The story is not just the story of the beginning of the nation of Israel, it is the beginning of God doing a new thing for the whole world, the story of God creating a new people who would be a light to the nations (Isa 49:6). There is a Rabbinic saying in which God is made to say, "I will make Adam, and if that doesn't work I will make Abraham to set things right." The good news is this: "God so loved the world that he sent Abraham."

Starting our investigation of "mission" in Genesis has the advantage of reminding us that mission is more than fixing things that are broken, since God seems to have a purpose and a mission before there are any problems to fix. God even commissions (co-missions) those made in his image before there is sin and evil in the world. Genesis also reminds us that Israel is not chosen by God simply to be blessed, but also to be a blessing to all nations. God does not abandon the world now broken in the fall. God comes and calls a people to himself for the sake of the world.

REVELATION 4–5

I would like to focus now on the end of the story, on a text not usually considered a "mission" text: Revelation chapters 4 and 5.[8]

> After this I looked, and lo, in heaven an open door!
> And the first voice, which I had heard speaking to me
> like a trumpet, said, "Come up hither, and I will show
> you what must take place after this." (Rev 4:1)

The reference to an "open door" in heaven signals to those familiar with this genre of literature that this is a typical apocalypse. It is now fairly widely accepted that apocalyptic literature may have an eschatological emphasis and focus on questions about the future, but the primary purpose of an apocalypse is to open heaven, to give a glimpse at the unknowable, the unseeable. For a period the seer has a vision of the world and of history from a God's-eye view. Reading Revelation, therefore, is somewhat like reading the sign over the blacksmith's shop: "all kinds of fancy twistings and turnings done here." In order to unlock the Revelation the reader must have not just "the key" but a whole fist full of keys: a sensitivity and knowledge of the symbolic world of the Greco-Roman period, some hunch about the social, religious, and political contexts, and (most of all) a love for and appreciation of the Old Testament story.

> At once I was in the Spirit, and lo, a throne stood in
> heaven, with one seated on the throne! (Rev 4:2)

For those who know the Old Testament, the reference to the throne is perhaps the easiest hidden code to decipher— familiar texts like Isaiah 6 and Daniel 7 remind us that the throne is God's place. What may be less obvious is that throne imagery seems to be used when there is some question about who is really in charge. In Isaiah 6, Uzziah's long reign has just come to an end. Isaiah is confronted with a vision of the true king, the true Lord. In Daniel 7, the kings of the earth have defeated and oppressed God's people—but there is an ancient of Days, and he has a throne. The probable political context of the book of Revelation is the reign of the madman Domitian, a megalomaniac who demanded complete submission and worship of his subjects; a man so hated that his own Roman citizens attempted to destroy every statue and every coin which bore his image after his death. John is comforted in being shown a vision of the true king, that there is still one who is truly on the throne.

> And he who sat there appeared like an emerald. Round the throne were twenty-four thrones, and seated on the thrones were twenty-four elders, clad in white garments, with golden crowns upon their heads. From the throne issue flashes of lightning, and voices and peals of thunder, and before the throne burn seven torches of fire, which are the seven spirits of God; and before the throne there is as it were a sea of glass, like crystal. (Rev 4:3–6a)

This vision is probably meant to be seen as a collage, the stones reminding us of great value and great beauty; the stones, the lightning, the fire, the crystal, somehow reminding us of both power and the purity of light.

The crystal sea is an important image, since the sea was actually a very troubling symbol for the people of Israel. The only book of the Old Testament that has a sea setting is Jonah—and there the sea is far from safe. Israelites were landlubbers who kept away from sea travel unless absolutely necessary. God delivers Israel *from* the sea in Exodus. The ocean is a place of chaos and sea monsters. But here, before God's throne, the sea is ordered, tame, in control.[9]

The 24 elders are another fairly obvious image to Christian readers of the Old Testament: 24 appears to be a composite number, the 12 tribes of Israel and the community of the 12 disciples put together. All of God's people together reigning. This image of thrones and crowns for God's people was an image that was difficult for me to grasp for a long time,

23

but it is, I think, an important one. The picture of God's people presented here is one of humanity restored to God's original intention. As we have already seen, Genesis 1:28 speaks of humankind created in the image of God and commissioned to "rule" over the whole creation. I understand this concept of rule or "dominion" not as "domination" but as steward-ship, as "taking care of" God's world under God's own loving Lordship. To be in God's image is to "till the earth and to keep it" as the second creation account has it (Gen 2:15). Here in Revelation 4 we see humanity restored to a place of stewardship under the loving Lordship of the one on the throne.

> And round the throne, on each side of the throne, are four living creatures, full of eyes in front and behind: the first living creature like a lion, the second living creature like an ox, the third living creature with the face of a human being, and the fourth living creature like a flying eagle. And the four living creatures, each of them with six wings, are full of eyes all round and within, and day and night they never cease to sing.... (Rev 4: 6b–8a)

Lest we forget that God hates nothing that he has made, lest we forget that God has a purpose for all of creation, the vision places not only people, but also the representatives of all creatures around the throne of God. The zoology here is a bit Aristotelian: all living things are divided into four fam-ilies: domestic animals, wild animals, birds, and human beings. Interestingly the description of the living creatures is similar to the description of the angelic being of Isaiah 6 ("six wings"). And the creatures have a song: "Holy, holy, holy, is the Lord God Almighty, who was and is and is to come!" (Rev 4:8b).

In this first song on the hit parade of heaven, God is praised not for any action but simply because God "is": because God is holy, completely other, and separate. The three-fold "Holy" reflects the difficulty that the Hebrew lan-guage had in describing God in Isaiah 6. There is no Hebrew word for "very." The emphatic adjective is expressed by repeating the thing being emphasized: so if someone is "very good" the Hebrew speaker says she is "good good." God is beyond this: "good, good, good," "holy, holy, holy."

> And whenever the living creatures give glory and honor and thanks to him who is seated on the throne, who lives forever and ever, the twenty-four elders fall down before him who is seated on the throne and worship him who lives for ever and ever; they cast their crowns before the throne, singing, "Worthy art thou, our Lord and God, to receive glory and honor and power, for thou didst create all things, and by thy will they existed and were created." (Rev 4: 9–11)

The second song on heaven's pop charts praises God as the creator. Again we are asked to look back to the Genesis account of creation. Not only is God holy, but God has extended the privilege of being to others. I do not think that this implies any lack of self-sufficiency in God, or that God was somehow lonely, or needed us. Creation is an act of grace, of self-giving love. God's will was that the universe come into being. Here again we see God as a missionary God, extending beyond himself, calling the universe into being and therefore into a relationship with the One who made it. God, even if we conceive of God in Trinitarian terms, as being a community of love existing before the world was made (Jn 17:5), says in effect, "it is not good that I remain alone" (Gen 2:18). Just as Adam and Eve are given to one another in the second creation account, so God says "I will not be alone, I will reach beyond myself."

The word "whenever" adds a rather humorous touch to this verse. We are told that the four living creatures "never cease to sing...day and night" (Rev 4:8) and that "whenever" they do so the elders fall down and worship. We are to envision (somehow!) an eternal falling down, it seems, on the part of the elders, since they know their unworthiness. But on God's part we see an eternal bestowing of gifts of robes and thrones and crowns. "You take these gifts.... No, we're not worthy....You take these." It's all rather like a heavenly tennis match.

> And I saw in the right hand of him who was seated on the throne a scroll written within and on the back, sealed with seven seals; and I saw a strong angel proclaiming with a loud voice, "Who is worthy to open the scroll and break its seals?" And no one in heaven or on earth or under the earth was able to open the scroll or to look into it, and I wept much that no one was found worthy to open the scroll or to look into it. Then one of the elders said to me, "Weep not; lo, the Lion of the tribe of Judah, the Root of David, has conquered, so that he can open the scroll and its seven seals." And between the throne and the four living creatures and among the elders, I saw a Lamb standing, as though it had been slain, with seven horns and with seven eyes, which are the seven spirits of God sent out into all the earth; and he went and took the scroll from the right hand of him who was seated on the throne. And when he had taken the scroll, the four living creatures and the twenty-four elders fell down before the Lamb, each holding a harp, and with golden bowls full of incense, which are the prayers of the saints; and they sang a new song, saying, "Worthy art thou to take the scroll and to open its seals, for thou wast slain and by thy blood didst ransom saints for God from every tribe and tongue and people and nation, and hast made them a kingdom and priests to our God, and they shall reign on earth."
> (Rev 5:1–10)

The third song (and perhaps the fourth and fifth are simply stanzas of this third song) worships God because God is the redeemer, because "when we had fallen into sin and become subject to evil and death, you in your mercy, sent Jesus Christ" (The Book of Common Prayer, 362). Unlike the deistic view that God is creator, but aloof, distant and uncaring, the biblical perspective is that God's mercy compels God to act, to save, to redeem. Here we see that mission does include fixing what is broken, saving what is lost. This paragraph conceives of Jesus, the Lamb of God, as the missionary *par excellence*. It is hard to read this passage without remembering John 3:16: "God loved the world so much that he sent his

Son." That text is surprising enough in its Johannine context: throughout John's gospel the "world" is that place which is in rebellion against God, that place which hates God and rejects God's Son. The Son, on the other hand, is in a relationship of love with the Father before the creation. The Father loves the Son so much that he gives all things into his hands. One would expect, therefore, that John 3:16 would say: "God loved the Son so much that he gave him the world." But no, God loves the world and out of this undeserved love God gave, God sent.[10]

But there is more to this story, since John 1 has already told us that Jesus is the Word made flesh, the incarnation of the unknowable God. God so loved the world that he did not remain aloof, but God himself came in the person of Jesus. This is not God sending someone else to do an impossible mission "should you choose to accept it," God is the missionary, the one who crosses cultures, giving up all the privileges of Godhead and becoming a servant (Phil 2:5–11). Here in the Revelation it is not just the one who is seated on the throne who receives the worshiped of the creatures and the elders: the Lamb is worshiped.

Notice the scope of God's mission here. It is not merely that God has redeemed Israel, or some other worthy ethnic group. God's vision of the mission is universal: "every tribe and tongue and people and nation." The distinctions and particularities are not erased or homogenized. Our cultural and language differences remain. This is not gray colorless soup, a melting pot, but a mosaic, as a Canadian might say, or a rainbow people, as Desmond Tutu might say. At the end of the Revelation all the nations bring their distinctive treasures into the New Jerusalem (Rev 21:24). This is the fulfillment of God's promise to Abraham: that through him all the nations of the earth would be blessed.

> Then I looked, and I heard around the throne and the living creatures and the elders the voice of many angels, numbering myriads of myriads and thousands of thousands,

> saying with a loud voice, "Worthy is the Lamb who was slain, to receive power and wealth and wisdom and might and honor and glory and blessing!" (Rev 5:11–12)

The song continues, but joined now by an innumerable crowd. The word "myriad" is the largest number the Greek language has a word for (like googolplex in English, my son tells me). And it is not just one myriad (10,000) but myriads of myriads. The writer is quickly running out of language here.

> And I heard every creature in heaven and on earth and under the earth and in the sea, and all therein, saying, "To the one who sits upon the throne and to the Lamb be blessing and honor and glory and might for ever and ever!" And the four living creatures said, "Amen!" and the elders fell down and worshiped. (Rev 5:13–14)

The Revelation reminds us that mission is about God's purpose to unite all things in Christ (Eph 1:10). The church does not have an option about whether or not it wants to be interested in mission. God is already doing the mission. The question is whether we will join in with the myriads of myriads and thousands of thousands.

NOTES

[1] Useful works on the Bible and mission include:

Roland Allen, *Missionary Methods: St Paul's or Ours?* (Reprint; Grand Rapids: Eerdmans, 1962).

Peter Bolt and Mark Thompson, eds. *The Gospel to the Nations: Perspectives on Paul's Mission* (Leicester: IVP, 2000).

David Bosch, *Transforming Mission: Paradigm Shifts in Theology of Mission* (Maryknoll, NY: Orbis, 1991). See especially "Part 1: New Testament Models of Mission."

Paul W. Bowers, "Church and Mission in Paul," *Journal for the Study of the New Testament* 44 (1991): 89–111; idem. "Fulfilling the Gospel: The Scope of the Pauline Mission," *Journal of the Evangelical Theological Society* 30 (1987): 185–98; idem. "Paul and Religious Propaganda in the First Century," *Novum Testamentum* 22 (1980): 316–23.

David G. Burnett, *The Healing of the Nations: The Biblical Basis of the Mission of God* Revised ed. (Carlisle: Paternoster, 1996).

Kenneth W. Clark, "The Gentile Bias of Matthew," *Journal of Biblical Literature* 66 (1947): 165–72.

Scott Cunningham, *"Through Many Tribulations": The Theology of Persecution in Luke-Acts* (Sheffield: Sheffield Academic Press, 1997).

C.H. Dodd, *The Apostolic Preaching and Its Developments* (New York: Harper & Row, 1936).

Jacques Dupont, *The Salvation of the Gentiles: Essays on the Acts of the Apostles* (New York: Paulist, 1979).

Beverly Roberts Gaventa, "'You Will Be My Witnesses': Aspects of Mission in Acts of the Apostles," *Missiology* 10 (1982): 413–25.

Dean S. Gilliand, *Pauline Theology and Mission Practice* (Grand Rapids: Baker, 1983).

Martin Goodman, *Mission and Conversion: Proselytizing in the Religious History of the Roman Empire* (Oxford: Clarendon Press, 1994).

Michael Green, *Evangelism in the Early Church* (London: Hodder & Stoughton, 1970).

Ferdinand Hahn, *Mission in the New Testament.* (London: SCM, 1965).

Adolf von Harnack, *The Expansion of Christianity in the First Three Centuries* (London: Moffat, 1908 [1902]).

Roger E. Hedlund, *The Mission of the Church in the World: A Biblical Theology* (Grand Rapids: Baker, 1991).

Edmond D. Hiebert, "An Expository Study of Matthew 28:16–20," *Bibliotecha Sacra* 149 (1992): 338–54.

Richard A. Horsley, and Neil Asher Silberman. *The Message and the Kingdom: How Jesus and Paul Ignited a Revolution and Transformed the Ancient World* (New York: Grosset and Putnam, 1997).

Joachim Jeremias, *Jesus' Promise to the Nations* (Philadelphia: Fortress, 1982 [1956]).

Walter Kaiser, *Mission in the Old Testament* (Grand Rapids: Baker, 2000).

Herbert J. Kane, *Christian Missions in Biblical Perspective* (Grand Rapids: Baker, 1976).

Robert J. Karris, "Missionary Communities: A New Paradigm for the Study of Luke-Acts," *Catholic Biblical Quarterly* 41 (1979): 80–91.

Andreas J. Köstenberger, "The Challenge of a Systematized Biblical Theology of Mission: Missiological Insights from the Gospel of John," *Missiology* 23 (1995): 445–464.

Andreas J. Köstenberger, and Peter T. O'Brien. *Salvation to the Ends of the Earth: A Biblical Theology of Mission*. (Downers Grove: IVP, 2001).

William J. Larkin, Jr. & Joel F. Williams, eds. *Mission in the New Testament: An Evangelical Approach* (Maryknol, NY: Orbis, 1999).

James LaGrand, *The Earliest Christian Mission to "All Nations" in the Light of Matthew's Gospel* (Grand Rapids: Eerdmans, 1995).

Lucien Legrand, *Unity and Plurality: Mission in the Bible* (Maryknoll: Orbis, 1990 [1988]); idem. *The Bible on Culture: Belonging or Dissenting?* (Maryknoll, NY: Orbis, 2000).

Pedrito U. Maynard-Reid, *Complete Evangelism: The Luke-Acts Model* (Scottdale, PA/Waterloo, Ont.: Herald Press, 1997).

Ramsey MacMullen, *Christianizing the Roman Empire A.D. 100–400* (New Haven and London: Yale University Press, 1984).

Scot McNight, *A Light Among the Nations: Jewish Missionary Activity in the Second Temple Period* (Minneapolis: Fortress, 1991).

James McPolin, "Mission in the Fourth Gospel," *Irish Theological Quarterly* 46 (1969): 113–22.

Steve Mosher, *God's Power, Jesus' Faith and World Mission: A Study in Romans* (Scottdale, PA/Waterloo, Ont.: Herald Press, 1996).

A.D. Nock, *Conversion: The Old and the New in Religion from Alexander the Great to Augustine of Hippo* (London: Oxford, 1933).

Peter T. O'Brien, *Consumed by Passion: Paul and the Dynamic of the Gospel* (Homebush West, NSW: Lancer, 1993).

Teresa Okure, *The Johannine Approach to Mission: A Contextual Study of* John *4: 1–42* (Tübingen: J.C.B. Mohr [Paul Siebeck], 1988).

George W. Peters, *A Biblical Theology of Missions* (Chicago: Moody Press, 1972).

Titus Presler, *Horizons of Mission.* (Cambridge, MA: Cowley, 2001). See especially Chapter 2: "The Missionary God in Scripture."

David Rhoads, "Mission in the Gospel of Mark," *Currents in Theology and Mission 22* (1995): 340–55.

H.H. Rowley, *Israel's Mission to the World* (London: SCM, 1939); idem, *The Missionary Message of the Old Testament* (London: Carey Kingsgate, 1944).

Donald Senior and Carroll Stuhlmueller. *The Biblical Foundations for Mission* (London: SCM, 1983).

Wilbert R. Shenk ed., *The Transfiguration of Mission: Biblical, Theological & Historical Foundations* (Scottsdale, PA/ Waterloo, Ont. Herald Press, 1993).

David C. Sims, "The Gospel of Matthew and the Gentiles," *Journal for the Study of the New Testament 57* (1995): 19–48.

Rodney Stark, *The Rise of Christianity* (San Francisco: Harper SanFrancisco, 1996).

Dorothy Jean Weaver, *Matthew's Missionary Discourse: A Literary Critical Analysis.* (Sheffield: JSOT Press, 1990).

[2] The term "the great commission" is not found in Scripture. The earliest use of the expression that I can find is as the title of the first chapter of the three-volume *History of the Church Missionary Society* (London, 1844).

[3] It is possible that Mark may originally have had a word from the risen Jesus sending his disciples into the world in mission. The longer ending of Mark, which contains, among other things, the following words, is not original to the gospel:

> Afterward he appeared to the eleven themselves as they sat at table; and he upbraided them for their unbelief and hardness of heart, because they had not believed those who saw him after he had risen. And he said to them, "Go into all the world and preach the gospel to the whole creation. He who believes and is baptized will be saved; but he who does not believe will be condemned. And these signs will accompany those who believe: in my name they will cast out demons; they will speak in new tongues; they will pick up serpents, and if they drink any deadly thing, it will not hurt them; they will lay their hands on the sick, and they will recover." (16:14–18)

As it stands now, the gospel of Mark ends at 16:8. The original ending of Mark, if it ever extended past v.8, is now lost. See Bruce Metzger, et al, *A Textual Commentary on the Greek New Testament* (3rd ed.; London, New York: UBS, 1971), 122–128, for the evidence.

[4] In Holy Scripture we must not think that the Exodus story is the only text of liberation. Throughout the Bible God is seen as a God who is concerned about the widow and the orphan, who judges the arrogant, the proud, the rich, and lifts up the poor and the oppressed. See, for example, the book of Amos, the "Magnificat" (Lk 2:46–56); the first sermon of Jesus (Lk 4:14–30). Examples could easily be multiplied.

[5] N.T. Wright. *The New Testament and the People of God. Christian Origins and the Question of God, Volume One* (Minneapolis: Fortress, 1992), 141–42.

[6] The phrase is Phyllis Trible's. See *God and the Rhetoric of Sexuality* (Philadelphia: Fortress, 1978).

[7] Cf. José Miguez-Bonino, "Genesis 11:1–9: A Latin American Perspective," in *Return to Babel: Global Perspectives on the Bible* (ed. John R. Pope-Levison and Priscilla Pope-Levison; Louisville: Westminster/John Knox Press, 1999), 13–16.

[8] I am grateful to Professor Larry Hurtado of the University of Edinburgh for a number of helpful insights on these chapters in Revelation.

[9] As a Canadian, I must point out the obvious fact that the "sea of glass, like crystal" could be taken as an allusion to an ice rink which must mean that there is hockey in heaven, a great comfort!

[10] See Andrew Lincoln "God So Loved the World," 38–46 in *The True & Living Word: Sermons from the Community of Wycliffe College,* ed. Chris Barrigar and Grant LeMarquand, (Toronto: Anglican Book Centre, 1998).

2

IS RECONCILIATION POSSIBLE?

LESSONS FROM COMBATING "MODERN RACISM"
VALERIE BATTS

REFLECTIONS ON WAR AT THE DAWNING OF THE TWENTY-FIRST CENTURY

Transformation in the world context involves a multifaceted process of generating a different conceptualization of possibilities for how humans will live together in a global community where "war" no longer means the same thing as it meant historically. The "theater of war" concept, developed at least 500 years ago, when Europeans designated "battlefields" as the acceptable arena for conflict, was one thing. The "battlefield" in the twenty-first century, however, is quite another thing. We have seen, particularly in the wake of September 11, that the battlefield is now the *entire globe.* Today's global arena for war means that, at a fundamental level, each citizen of each country will need to come to view war in the twenty-first century in a new way. We can start this process in the United States. One way is to acknowledge and rethink the origins and current impacts of intra-group tensions within our own country.

As I witnessed the events of September 11, my own response as a citizen of the United States was complex. On the one hand, I was horrified and deeply saddened as I realized how many people were dying. Then I got scared as I thought about my brother-in-law and his family who live and work in Manhattan and my cousins who work in Washington, D.C., near the Pentagon.

Next came a vivid memory from October 1969. After what was called a "riot" in my newly desegregated public high school in eastern North Carolina, National Guard troops were called into my school and placed in each classroom. They remained there for many months. This fact seems especially ludicrous to me now in light of the violence our nation and the world have witnessed since 1969 and most recently in the months following September 11. Yet the posting of the National Guard in my school represented a "worst-case scenario" that most whites in our community had anticipated for years. Such folk believed that if blacks and whites did not stay in our respective places, with whites clearly on top, we would end up with racial violence. Blacks were feared as the aggressors yet, ironically, none of the National Guard—the only people who had guns—as I recall were black.

It was always clear to me that as an African American young adult who spoke out against injustice, I could be a target for the National Guard and other government officials if I was not careful. I also knew, at some level, that my brother, my friends, or I could be a random target because of the color of our skin, even if we were not speaking out against injustice. Such "racial profiling," as it is now called, was one of many "laws of the land" that we had to deal with growing up black in the 1950s United States South.

Looking back on my life in the segregated South, I realize that among the buffers from the intense racism and white supremacy of the time, was the tiny black Episcopal Church in which I was coming of age. In church I met the first white person I could trust, our priest, Father Jack

Spong, who was then and continues to be a challenger for justice in the faith community and beyond. My father was for many years a senior warden in the parish and took his job seriously. Even in the Christian tradition, commitment to justice and equality is often obscured by the politics of our economic and social history of oppression or liberalism, so much so that it is hard to see our call to humility in the modern day. As a result I also grew up knowing how oppressive Christianity can be.

As the '60s progressed, and I became increasingly politically conscious, it became clear to me that the United States government defined political activism that attempted to change governmental policy toward groups as: "a threat to national security" at least, and as "terrorism" at worst. Many of my friends and I lived with much pain and anger at being part of a country that professed "freedom of speech" yet was a country where we saw repeated injustice and *knew* that harm was inevitable if we "got out of line."

Interestingly when I recently talked with a divinity student colleague about conflicts after September 11, her response was very different. She grew up as a middle class, white, United States citizen in rural Maine. She was raised to believe that "America" was a free and open society and that anyone who worked hard could get ahead. As a teen, she participated in and led many social events for soldiers who came through her town on their way to and from military missions to protect our soil from the "evils of communism." She did not even fully know, for example, that segregation continued in the South of the United States until the late 1960s and had no understanding about its continuing impact. Becoming aware of injustices both within our society and across the world has been an often painful and wrenching process for this student as she tries to reconcile her earlier views with what she sees around her. A future religious leader, she is trying hard to find ways to contribute her on-going learning to her community in ways that can be heard and utilized for community transformation and reconciliation.

ASSUMPTIONS AND DEFINITIONS

Reconciliation is, at its core, a process of transformation for both sides in a conflict. The same transformation is also critical to an effective multicultural strategy of change. In our work on anti-racism and multiculturalism at VISIONS, Inc. we define multiculturalism as: the process of recognizing, understanding and appreciating one's own culture as well as the culture of others. Multiculturalism stresses learning to appreciate the impact of differences in social location based on such variables as race, gender, class, age, sexual orientation, religion, physical ability, and language. This learning process is dynamic as we begin to see the impact of differences, our sense of ourselves, of others, and of the world shifts. We impact others and others impact us differently. There is an interactive process occurring, potentially at four levels: the personal, interpersonal, institutional, and cultural.

MULTICULTURAL PROCESS OF CHANGE

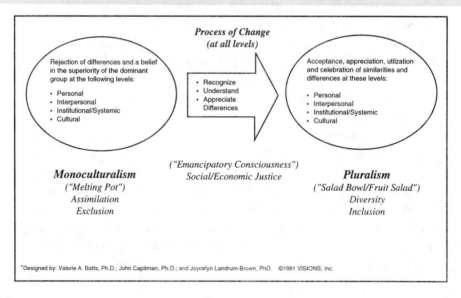

Process of Change
(at all levels)

Rejection of differences and a belief in the superiority of the dominant group at the following levels:

• Personal
• Interpersonal
• Institutional/Systemic
• Cultural

• Recognize
• Understand
• Appreciate
Differences

Acceptance, appreciation, utilzation and celebration of similarities and differences at these levels:

• Personal
• Interpersonal
• Institutional/Systemic
• Cultural

Monoculturalism
("Melting Pot")
Assimilation
Exclusion

("Emancipatory Consciousness")
Social/Economic Justice

Pluralism
("Salad Bowl/Fruit Salad")
Diversity
Inclusion

*Designed by: Valerie A. Batts, Ph.D.; John Capitman, Ph.D.; and Joycelyn Landrum-Brown, PhD. ©1991 VISIONS, Inc.

Figure 1

Several social activists in recent history have described how this multicultural reconciliation process plays out in oppressed/oppressor contexts. Diane J. Goodman, in *Promoting Diversity and Social Justice: Educating People from Privileged Groups*, refers to the dynamic as the "intertwined fate of the oppressor and the oppressed."[1] She quotes from the work and experience of several critical leaders in this field:

> According to Paulo Freire (1970), humanization is the vocation of human beings: "As oppressors dehumanize others and violate their [the oppressed's] rights, they themselves also become dehumanized." Freire further states, "Dehumanization, which marks not only those whose humanity has been stolen, but also [though in a different way] those who have stolen it, is a *distortion* of becoming more fully human."[2]

Nelson Mandela, in his book, *Long Walk to Freedom*, adds:

> I knew as well as I knew anything that the oppressor must be liberated just as surely as the oppressed. A man who takes away another man's freedom is a prisoner of hatred, locked behind the bars of prejudice and narrow-mindedness. I am not truly free if I am taking away someone else's freedom, just as surely as I am not free when my freedom is taken away from me. The oppressed and the oppressor alike are robbed of their humanity.[3]

Martin Luther King, Jr. also noted this connection: "I can never be what I ought to be until you are what you ought to be, and you can never be what you might be until I am what I ought to be."[4]

True reconciliation can happen, then, only when all parties understand each other in ways that lead to behaving differently. For those with historic and current social, economic, and political power, i.e., United States citizens of European ancestry, white Australians, white South Africans, and many others of European descent, reconciliation requires acknowledging the historic and continuing impact of racial privilege as well as working with the "targets" of this power imbalance in order to effect reconciliation at the personal, interpersonal, institutional, and cultural levels.

Racism, however, is not the only form of oppression in need of reconciliation. Since 1984, my colleagues and I at VISIONS, Inc. have used in our anti-oppression work a framework for understanding the multiplicity of ways in which dysfunctional power imbalances can occur in the United States and in the wider world (Figure 2).

Although forms of oppression vary, we have found the model and the process of change outlined in the remainder of this chapter to be useful in identifying and challenging power imbalances and thereby leading to a process of transformation and reconciliation. I invite you to "try on" our model of combating "modern racism" as one framework of strategies necessary for "waging reconciliation."

A MODEL FOR COMBATING "MODERN RACISM"[5]

The national debate continues regarding whether or not affirmative action is still a necessary and effective strategy for attempting to correct historic power imbalances between the races. This debate is another example of the complex and insidious ways in which racism and racial prejudice in this country continue to inhibit the effective creation of a society in which true equal access to opportunity exists for every citizen.[6] In my graduate school work at Duke University in Durham, North Carolina, in the late 1970s, I worked with researchers who were demonstrating that such debates are actually covert or "symbolic" ways of expressing deeply ingrained biases that are typically unrecognized as such.[7] In the remainder of this chapter, I will describe my process of coming to understand this subtle or "modern" form of racism. I will also offer a model for identifying and changing modern racist behaviors. This model has evolved from consultation and training services offered to individuals and groups from the public and private sector since 1984.

Types of Oppression	Variable	Non-Target Groups	Target Groups
Racism	Race/Color	White	People of Color (African, Asian, Native, Latino/a Americans)
Sexism	Gender	Men	Women
Classism	Socio-Economic Class	Middle, Upper Class	Poor, Working Class
Elitism	Education Level	Formally Educated	Informally Educated
	Place in Hierarchy	Managers, Exempt, Faculty	Clerical, Non-Exempt, Students
Religious Oppression	Religion	Christians, Protestant Christians	Muslims, Catholics, and Others
Anti-Semitism		Christians	Jews
Militarism	Military Status	WW I&II, Korean, Gulf War Veterans	Vietnam Veterans
Ageism	Age	Young Adults	Elders (40+ by law)
Adultism		Adults	Children
Heterosexism	Sexual Orientation	Heterosexuals	Gay, Lesbian, Bisexual, Transgender
Ableism	Physical or Mental Ability Bodied	Temporarily Able-Bodied	Physically or Mentally Challenged
Xenophobia	Immigrant Status	U.S. Born	Immigrant
Linguistic Oppression	Language	English	English as a Second Language Non-English

VISIONS, Inc., 2000

FIGURE 2

The model begins by describing *personal, interpersonal, institutional,* and *cultural* expressions of modern racism. Examples of white behavior will be given, followed by a discussion of the impact of modern racism on blacks and other target group populations.[8] A description of target group responses will be offered. Relationships between these expressions in blacks[9] and other people of color and whites are then analyzed. The model will conclude by reviewing the change process I have developed with many colleagues. Our interventions strive to eliminate guilt and blame and to encourage acceptance of responsibility and understanding of personal and systemic dysfunctional consequences of practicing modern racism and internalized oppression.

MY LEARNING CONTEXT

As briefly alluded to above, I was born in the segregated South of the United States in the early 1950s. My parents were educators and were involved in efforts to ensure quality education for black children. My father was the principal of the first black middle school in our community. This school was built under the doctrine of "separate but equal" in the mid-nineteen sixties. I remember numerous "battles" that he, my mother, their friends, and neighbors fought to keep bringing adequate resources into our community. I remember our struggles to integrate public facilities. I remember both the fear and the determination within our community to bring about equal access. I remember when the struggle began to change from economic and social parity to integration.

I completed my junior year of high school in the last year of the existence of the segregated Booker T. Washington High School. I completed my last year of high school at the forcibly desegregated Rocky Mount Senior High School. Upon reflection, I believe my interest in addressing the subtle forms of racism began then. As a student activist, I was

42

involved in several efforts to expose unstated assumptions and to encourage honest acknowledgment and dialogue about racial prejudice. Something kept telling me, "If we do not examine people's hearts, this desegregation process will not work."

Upon entering college in 1970, I became part of the largest class of black students to enter the University of North Carolina at Chapel Hill up to that time. There were approximately 200 of us. There were about 200 other black students already on campus. Given a student body of over 20,000, we were a small and largely invisible group. Part of how we survived this "foreign" experience was by forming a black support group, the Black Student Movement (BSM). Even when taking age into account, the "culture shock" I experienced during those first years at UNC was as great as any I have experienced while traveling across the U.S. and internationally as an adult.

Chapel Hill, North Carolina, was and still is a liberal Southern community. Howard Lee was mayor during those years, making him among the first black mayors since reconstruction. Hubert Humphrey won the presidential election in Orange County, North Carolina. It was the only county in the state that Ronald Reagan did not carry in his presidential campaign. The late Richard Epps was elected student body president and made national headlines as the "first black student body president" of a major Southern university.

At the same time, other black students and I were still battling assumptions of inferiority and continual pressures to assimilate to white cultural norms. Such efforts typically occurred as "off the mark" attempts to help us by whites or were expressed by them in the ways that indicated that we were unseen or our cultural expressions were misunderstood and/or minimized. The absence of role models or symbols of our worth and value also contributed to the perpetuation of assumptions of inferiority. As black students we developed many "survival strategies," (i.e., manipulating guilty whites, playing the clown, and working extra hard) some of which ultimately proved detrimental to us. The seeds were being sown for the life's work I was to move on to.

After leaving Chapel Hill, I decided to teach in a predominantly black Southern medical school. It was an important re-immersion experience.[10] I reconnected with the richness and security of black culture. I also began to see how the "survival strategies" that I had seen among us as students existed also among black people in predominantly and historically black environments. I began to ponder the impact of racism on blacks and how it can affect us even when we are the majority group in an educational system. I also began to notice how black students responded differently to black and white teachers.

I left this work in 1977 and went back to graduate school, this time at Duke University. The social psychology literature was beginning to assert that racism was all but gone in the United States. Public opinion polls were showing increased acceptance of blacks in all walks of life.[11] Three years later, the federal government took the position that we as a country had solved the racial problem and made efforts, for example, to dismantle the voting rights act. Some analysts suggest that social science as a discipline participated in this process of denial.[12] Current examples of such participation are still alive and well.[13]

The stance that racism had all but been eliminated in our country was quite problematic for me. It discounted both my experience as well as what I saw around me. In talking with others, I discovered that it was troubling to many blacks and whites who realized that it is not possible to change over three hundred years of history in a mere twenty to thirty years, even under the best of circumstances.[14] I was not alone in seeing continued resistance to integration of public institutions and facilities and to equal opportunity efforts to change the status quo and bring blacks and other people of color into positions of power and influence. This resistance became a symbol of a modern form of racism.

Fortunately, there were social psychologists at Duke working to challenge the notion that racism had declined significantly in the then-thirteen years since the passage of the Civil Rights Act of 1964. Their work provided a theoretical framework for conceptualizing the experience I had been having throughout my journey into "desegregated America." The differentiation of racism into "old-fashioned" and "modern" forms was very useful.

The view that blacks are inherently inferior to whites has been referred to as "old-fashioned" racism.[15] Its corollary, of course, is the myth of white superiority. Until 1954, racism was the law of the land. Old-fashioned racism involved behaviors, practices, and attitudes that overtly defined blacks as inferior and whites as superior. Blacks were thus entitled to fewer of society's benefits and resources. Behaviors, such as whites expecting blacks to defer to them in department stores, or practices such as having separate entrances to these stores, with blacks coming through small back entrances, are examples of the old forms. Laws prohibiting contact between blacks and whites, ranging from separate school systems to segregated seating on buses, are also examples. Lynchings, cross burnings, and Ku Klux Klan (KKK) activities are extreme forms. Even the paternalistic treatment by whites toward their black nannies is a kind of old-fashioned racism. The nanny is loved and valued as long as she understands her subservient role. She is expected to be seen and not heard around adults, to appreciate the family leftovers, to take her meals in the kitchen with the children, as well as to be called by her first name by them.

These forms of racism all have in common the overt acceptance of blacks as less than equal and whites as better than blacks. The civil rights movement that reached its zenith in 1965, with the passage of the Civil Rights Act, made many of these behaviors illegal for the first time. Although anti-lynching laws had been passed earlier, they were more stringently enforced as a consequence of public response to the new ruling. As overtly racist behavior in the public arena became illegal, it also became unpopular even in personal, private settings.[16] Although KKK activities did not stop entirely, legal sanctions were brought against many of its members.[17] Society supported student groups who protested white-supremacist activities on our nation's campuses, rather than the supremacists' rights to freedom of speech. It appeared that our country's three-hundred-year legacy of subjugation of brown peoples was beginning to abate.

At the same time this explicit resistance to old-fashioned expressions of negative racial attitudes grew, we still saw painful struggles across the country as black people attempted to attain parity in the public and private sector. We saw this more subtle type of resistance justified on non-racial grounds.

EMERGENCE OF MODERN RACISM

Modern racism has been defined as "the expression in terms of abstract ideological symbols and symbolic behaviors of the feeling that blacks are violating cherished values and making illegitimate demands for changes in the racial status quo."[18] It is, further, the attribution of non-race-related reasons for behaviors that continue to deny equal access to opportunity to blacks and other targets of systemic oppression.[19] It is still based on the assumptions, the underlying beliefs, that blacks are inferior and whites are superior. The negative affect that accompanies these beliefs does not change just because of changes in law and practice. Rather the affect has to be submerged given the changes in what is viewed as legal and acceptable in the society.

What happens, then, when whites are in a position of having negative affective responses to blacks or other people of color? Given the lack of appropriateness of old-fashioned racist behaviors, it is likely that the affect will be expressed in subtle and covert ways.[20] The impact of the expression of this subtle or modern racism is as detrimental to change in our society as old-fashioned racism. The expression of such behaviors continues to result in blacks and other people of color being targeted to receive fewer of the benefits of being a citizen of the United States. The impact also perpetuates the "invisible knapsack of privilege" that whites are more likely to experience and take for granted.[21] Illustrations include: explanations of white flight in response to school desegregation such as, "It's not the blacks, it's the buses"; beliefs that affirmative action is "reverse discrimination"; acceptance of "the doctrine of color blindness"; or minimization by whites of the systemic causes and impacts of continued disparate treatment that whites and people of color receive in the United States.

Behavioral strategies used in the struggles to change old-fashioned racism typically included cultural exchange activities as well as confrontational training seminars or workshops. The cultural exchanges often heightened awareness of differences, but without continued contact did not create substantive change in attitudes or behavior. Confrontational-change workshops often left participants feeling blamed or attacked. Other participants came away having a sense of what it feels like to be oppressed, but feeling guilty and powerless.

When I left Duke University and started working as a professional psychologist, I began to conduct workshops to challenge modern racism.[22] Participants have come from across the United States and from a variety of settings: public and private schools, universities and community colleges, mental health agencies, psychotherapy practices, hospitals, religious groups, community groups, arts groups, affirmative action organizations, legal services, corporations, state and local governments, and long-term care settings. On-going consultation relationships with several organizations from the public and private sector have also provided information on how modern racism occurs and on strategies for change.[23]

Modern racism can be expressed at the *personal, interpersonal, institutional,* or *cultural* level. In its typical expression these levels interact.[24] Following is an example drawn from one of our workshops that illustrates how each level operates and a definition of each level.

AN EXAMPLE OF THE MULTIPLE LEVELS

A female workshop participant who grew up in Louisville, Kentucky, was a teacher in a northern public school system. She was trying to understand why the black and Latino students in her classes perceived her as a racist when she felt she treated everybody the same. If anything, she admitted, she tried harder to make things fair and equitable for them. In her tone of voice was the message, "After all, I feel sorry for all the injustices these children face and for the poor conditions surrounding their lives. I'm trying to help them. Why don't they value my efforts?"

The school teacher was genuine in her desire to help, yet exploration of her behavior led her to realize that outside of her awareness, she was operating on a personal assumption that black and Latino students are inferior due to their upbringing in non-mainstream (i.e., less adequate) communities. She behaved toward them in interpersonal situations as if they were helpless and less capable. This form of racism is different from old-fashioned racism in that the woman's genuine desire was to correct for past inequities, not to perpetuate them. The consequence, however, was the same. The students were still being treated like second-class citizens and thus were being set up to either accept the inferior helpless point of view or to reject the white person or the educational system she represented.

An exploration of this woman's racial learning was revealing. She was born in a northern city in the late '40s. As a young child, she liked to ride at the back of the bus when she and her family members went downtown on Saturdays.

Her family moved to Louisville when she was nine. This was before buses had been desegregated in that town. The woman remembered vividly the first Saturday that she and her mother took the bus in her new hometown. She got on the bus and eagerly started to walk toward the back as she had always done. Her mother called out to her to stop and sit at a seat near the front. As nine years olds are prone to do, she resisted, saying, "No, come on, let's go to the back." Her mom grabbed her arm nervously saying, "Sit down." She pulled her down. The woman remembers feeling confused and puzzled. She noticed with interest her mother's discomfort, but said no more.

They reached their destination, went shopping, and then returned to the bus for the ride back home. The young girl again got on first and decided to try to go to the back. She was hoping her mother's previous behavior was just a fluke. Just as she said, "Look, Mom, there are seats at the very back, let's hurry," her mother grabbed her and shook her, saying, "If I ever catch you going to the back of the bus again, I'll spank you." Her mother was shaking with apparent fear and rage. The woman remembers being shocked, then scared. She looked around the bus and noticed for the first time that all the people at the front of the bus were white and that all of the people at the back were black.

The woman immediately flashed on other things she had heard from her family about colored people and said to herself, "Oh, I am supposed to stay away from these people." She remembers feeling sad and scared on the ride home. She was finally learning her place as a white person. She remembers that all through public school she stayed in her place and kept to her own kind although she never quite believed it was right. She went to college during the '60s and became an active supporter of the Civil Rights movement. She decided to go into teaching partly as a result of taking a sociology course in which she learned about the problems facing disadvantaged minorities. She remembers being filled with guilt during college about the ways blacks had been treated. She was ashamed of her family and angry with them. She genuinely wanted to make things better for black people.

This woman tried hard from the time of her college years "not to see color." As she started teaching black and Latino students, she dismissed subtle nagging sensations of guilt, disgust, or fear. She convinced herself that "people are just people" and turned any remaining negative affect into pity for the "victims" of systemic oppression. She stayed away from whites who expressed overtly negative racial attitudes and tried hard to be fair and honest and to get her students of color to perform just like white students.

As will be outlined in detail later, this woman's personal and interpersonal responses actually set up the perpetuation of dysfunctional interracial behavior even though that was not her intention. Further, she was employed by a school system that had a majority of black and Latino students, while 80% of the school personnel were white. Few of these white staff members had contact with people of color in their personal or professional lives, except for students. The school system saw its role as helping to prepare students to succeed in the United States of America, as defined by white, male, Protestant, middle-class, middle-aged, heterosexual, and physically able norms.

The school's culture reflected the values of this "normative" group as well. Most black and Latino students felt isolated and alienated in the environment. In addition to experiencing interpersonal racism from school personnel like the workshop participant, they also were experiencing racism in its institutional and cultural expressions. There were no bilingual education programs. The administration could not see the usefulness of such activities, as their job was to teach these children standard English. When Latino students spoke to each other in Spanish, they were often reprimanded. Black English was viewed as substandard even though many of the black children communicated clearly that they were, in fact, bilingual as well. They spoke black English at breaks and at home, yet knew how to speak and write the way they were being trained to do at school. In both cases, the students were comfortable with their two cultures; school personnel were not.

Similarly, most of the textbooks stressed "American" (i.e., United States) and European culture. Except on special occasions, typically because of student or parent interest, little attention was focused on African, African-American, or the variety of Latino cultures. Faculty and administrators felt the students would not be adequately prepared for the "real world" if they spent a lot of time focusing on such "frills" as jazz, salsa, life in Brazil or Cuba, or issues in South Africa. For the students of color, these were very important issues. No attempts to use these interests to teach basic skills were being considered. Again, the assumption of those in charge about how learning should occur, both in terms of process and content, did not allow for inclusion of cultural differences.

In summary, a definition of each level of racism is offered below:

Personal:

At this level, racism is prejudice or bias. It is the maintenance of conscious or unconscious attitudes and feelings that whites are superior and that blacks or other people of color are inferior or that these groups' differences are not acceptable in some way. Personal level racism includes cognitive or affective misinformation or both.[25] The misinformation may be learned directly, as through overt messages, or indirectly, as through observation.

Interpersonal:

Behaviors based on conscious or unconscious biased assumptions about self and other are interpersonal manifestations of racism. It is often through uncomfortable or tense cross-cultural interactions that individuals discover subtle racist behaviors within themselves or others.[26]

51

Institutional:

An examination of power relationships reveals institutional racism. The question to be asked is, to what extent do the intended and unintended consequences of policies, practices, laws, styles, rules, and procedures function to the advantage of the dominant group and to the disadvantage of people of color? To the extent that whites in this society have the political, economic, educational, social, and historical power and access to institutionalize prejudices (i.e., the myths of white superiority and black inferiority) against blacks and other people of color, whites are in a position to practice or maintain institutional racism.[27]

Cultural:

The ability to define European-American and Western cultural preferences as "right and beautiful" is the consequence of having institutional power and access in this country. When the standards of appropriate action, thought, and expression of a particular group are perceived either overtly or subtly as negative or less than, cultural racism has occurred. Conformity to the dominant culture is then viewed as "normal" when, in fact, the myth of the inherent superiority of the group setting the standards is operating. If such is the case, it is likely that a given individual will need to change her behavior to fit those of the dominant group just to be accepted as competent, attractive, or talented.[28]

Maniifestations of Modern Racism

As illustrated in the example of the schoolteacher, modern racism is often not malicious by intent. Understanding the expressions or levels outlined in the previous section helps in clarifying how the consequence of particular behaviors can result in racism, regardless of motivation. The schoolteacher, for instance, was very supportive of institutional changes that would bring in more black and Latino teachers. Yet, her personal and cultural biases and preferences made it hard for her to accept a prospective Latino language teacher who, in English classes, taught Spanish to English speakers and English to Spanish speakers, and then had them spend some time dialoguing in the non-native and then the native languages in each class. The white teacher found herself agreeing with the administration that while this idea perhaps had some merit, it was not efficient and it was redundant with what the students learned in Spanish language classes.

Following is a description of suggested ways that modern racism occurs. It is useful to consider that the behaviors outlined can manifest themselves at each of the four levels defined above. It is also the case that currently racism is likely to manifest itself in subtle forms. This is not to discount, of course, the increase in overt old-fashioned racist behavior that has continued to escalate across the United States since 1985.[29] These reactions might be thought of as the backlash from a decade or so of denial in our country that racial problems do continue to exist.[30] Modern racism theory attempts to explain the impact of the growing silence on racial issues in society from approximately 1975 to 1985 as well as the current controversy or tendency to explain racism away or to be reluctant to see it.

Institutional gains made between 1954 and 1965 were clear and obvious. As civil rights issues became more substantive, however, and therefore more of a challenge to the power brokers, the character of racism began to change. Derrick Bell notes:

> Rather than eliminate racial discrimination, civil rights laws have only driven it underground, where it flourishes even more effectively. While employers, landlords, and other merchants can no longer rely on rules that blatantly discriminate against minorities, they can erect barriers that although they make no mention of race, have the same exclusionary effect. The discrimination that was out in the open during the Jim Crow era could at least be seen, condemned, and fought as a moral issue. Today, statistics, complaints, even secretly filmed instances of discrimination that are televised nationwide... upset few people because, evidently, no amount

of hard evidence will shake the nation's conviction that
the system is fair for all.[31]

Let us take the issue of education, for example. The first
battle for equality was to allow blacks entry into previously
all white schools. The struggle for this civil right was arduous
but resulted in a clearly definable outcome: blacks going to
schools with whites. Once this goal was accomplished, whites
quickly wanted to move to the position that the issue was
resolved.[32] But insuring equity requires more than having
blacks in schools with whites.[33] The larger questions, such as,
how many blacks and other people of color help control the
curriculum that all children receive; what relevant materials
will be used that reflect and affirm diverse cultures as equal
or important and that expose the myth of white and Western
superiority; where schools will be located; and how much
money will be spent on children's education, were not yet
addressed.[34]

The other reality is that whites, as a group, never really
accepted open enrollment. Instead, white flight was clearly
the option taken by the majority, while blacks and other
target groups remained in schools that they no longer controlled. This phenomenon became more entrenched as
bankers, realtors, and developers engaged in housing and
lending discrimination while the federal government fails to
enforce housing discrimination law. It was a much more
silent strategy than the anti-integration mobs of the late
1950s and early 1960s. Yet its power to negatively impact the
educational experience of much of the country's youth has
yet to be fully realized.

Stated differently, our society's actions, by its shift toward
a belief that racism has ended, discounted the unavoidable
impact of more than three hundred and fifty years of history.
It did not allow individuals and institutions to alter structures, materials, attitudes, and, in many cases, behavior to
fully create equity in a multicultural sense. Rather, it forced
whites and people of color to struggle in new ways to

attempt to handle the remains of these centuries of oppression. Legislative changes were made but the hearts and minds of people remained the same.[35] John Dovidio and Samuel Gaertner assert that this difficulty in acknowledging racism was made even more difficult in such a climate because of a deeply held U.S. value on "doing the right thing."[36] If racism is now "wrong," how can we admit that we still struggle with it?

The following list of behaviors or manifestations of modern racism for the dominant or non-target groups are offered from my colleagues' and my experiences to help explain this struggle.[37] The accompanying examples come from our work in educational settings.

1. Dysfunctional rescuing:

This form of modern racism is characterized by helping people of color, operating on an assumption that they cannot help themselves; setting them up to fail; being patronizing or condescending; helping people of color in such a way that it limits their ability to help themselves. This "help that does not help" is often motivated by guilt or shame. It may be conscious or unconscious and is often embedded in the "culture of niceness or politeness," thus making its limiting aspects hard to discern.

Examples of dysfunctional rescuing are:

A white teacher "gives" a black student who is making a "B+" an "A" instead of challenging her. The student is active in the black student association and is obviously quite bright. The teacher feels vaguely guilty about societal injustices and worries that the student might see him as racist. The teacher is not active in campus efforts to change institutional racism and believes that if he just "does right by blacks" everything will be okay.

A white department head brings a 30-year-old black female into a previously all white male biology department. He feels good about insisting that she be chosen and denies the importance of the reluctance of his colleagues. The entire faculty has been at the institution for at least ten years and has failed to support the hiring of any target group members. The department chair fails to recognize the potential set-up for failure involved in bringing target groups into a hostile environment without a plan for impacting the culture. "Tokenism" is another name for this process of "doing what's right" without preparing the existing organization for this change.

2. Blaming the victim:

In this form, modern racism is expressed by attributing the results of systemic oppression to the target group; ignoring the real impact of racism on the lives of blacks or other people of color; blaming people of color for their current economic situation; or setting target group members up to fail and then blaming them.[38] To provide structural and status changes but to give inadequate support, i.e., time, training, or mentoring, for the development of positive and constructive outcomes, is one illustration. The non-target accepts little or no responsibility for current inequities and puts all the responsibility on target group members for negative outcomes.

Examples of blaming the victim include:

A black student is labeled as having misplaced priorities because of her work on black issues on her campus; she is considered bright but too busy being angry to study. She was not accepted into a student leaders campus honorary society because her concerns were viewed as "too narrow."

A Latina female becomes depressed and exhibits paranoid symptoms in a faculty meeting after being the lone Latina and female faculty person for a year in a previously all-white-male department where she is largely avoided or patronized. The chairman recommends she get psychiatric treatment.

3. Avoidance of contact:

Modern racism may also be manifested by not having social or professional contact with people of color; making no effort to learn about life in communities of color; living in all white communities; or exercising the choice that whites most often have of not being involved in the lives of people of color.

Examples of the avoidance of contact are:

A white university administrator who lives in an all white neighborhood says, "I just don't have the opportunity to meet black people."

A white supervisor is a very pleasant person but does not confront a situation when two black male employees engage in conflict. The supervisor, however, would confront the situation if the employees were white.

4. Denial of cultural differences:

In this expression, modern racism means minimizing obvious physical or behavioral differences between people as well as differences in preferences that may be rooted in culture; discounting the influence of African culture and of the African American or Asian American experience; or being color-blind in a way that masks discomfort with differences.

Examples of the denial of cultural differences include:

A white faculty member describing the only black faculty member he works with, and trying hard to avoid saying that the faculty member is black.

A white administrator says with much exasperation, when being given information about racial differences in retention of blacks in his university, "What does race have to do with it? Aren't people just people? Skin color doesn't matter, we are all just people."

5. Denial of the political significance of differences:

Finally, modern racism may be manifested by not understanding or denying the differential impacts of social, political, economic, historical, and psychological realities on the lives of people of color and whites, minimizing the influence of such variables on all our lives and institutions. This modern racism may be accompanied by an attitude that cultural differences are just interesting or fun. Such a stance results in an unwillingness to acknowledge the multiplicity of ways in which the impacts of the myth of white superiority continue. The stance also minimizes white privilege as well as the insidious nature of the prevalence of the mentality and practice of "West is Best" by those in positions of power and control in key aspects of life in the United States and most of the world at the beginning of the twenty-first century. This type of modern racism is firmly entrenched and is perhaps the most binding. Unraveling the hold of a dominant Western perspective will take a massive rethinking of many of our ways of being and doing in the United States, especially in light of September 11.

Examples of the denial of the political significance of differences are:

A white middle level manager came to a workshop very upset about the affirmative action plan his company has implemented. He was convinced that affirmative action was reverse discrimination and said, "We don't need affirmative action here. We hire blacks." Blacks comprised 10% of the management positions (up 8% in two years because of the plan) and 90% of the custodial positions.

A white faculty member dismissed Jesse Jackson's campaign for President of the United States as minimally important at best, for after all, Jackson had no governmental experience. When students pointed out the number of voters Jackson had registered and the large number of popular votes he had obtained, the faculty member said, "That's not really important; what's important is that he is not a qualified applicant."

INTERNALIZED OPPRESSION

As discussed in the definition of institutional racism above, African Americans and other targets of racism are in a reactive posture. This is not to minimize in any way the personal, economic, and political power that target group members have available to them. It is intended to challenge targets and non-targets to think seriously about the extremely detrimental impact of maintaining a society where institutional power is distributed predominantly to one group.

It is difficult for those who suffer at the hands of oppression not to buy into, at some level, the misinformation that society has perpetuated about victim status.[39] Internalized oppression is the incorporation of negative or limiting messages regarding our way of being and responding in the world as targets of systemic oppression. We define our uniqueness as inferior or different in an unhealthy manner that is not useful. As the character of racism changes, so does the reaction of people of color to it. Most forms of internalized oppression had their origins in situations when their manifestation was necessary for physical or psychological survival.[40] Such behaviors are most likely to occur initially as survival responses in institutions or in situations where the target person perceives a threat. Five expressions of internalized oppression have been identified.[41]

1. System beating:

This expression of internalized oppression involves attempting to get over, on, or around the system; manipulating others or the system through guilt, psychological games, or illicit activities; acting out anger; or playing dumb, clowning, being invisible. The strategy involves an awareness that one is an outsider; the belief that the target group member cannot succeed by being direct and/or by being herself or himself. The target group person feels a need to "take care" of whites' feelings or to hide parts of oneself for fear of being misunderstood or viewed unfavorably because of his or her "difference." It may also take the form of using anger or hostility to manipulate whites.

Examples of system beating are:

A black student manages to go through four years of college with a reading deficit. He is a star basketball player and learns through the grapevine how to take courses where he can "get over" and receive a passing grade.

A Latino teacher in an "upscale" independent school does not speak out, for fear of being disliked, when faculty and staff condemn Latino yard workers for speaking Spanish and using English poorly.

A black hospital employee intimidates all of her white superiors such that she just comes and goes to work as she pleases, and does as little work as possible. Any negative feedback is defined by this employee as racism on the part of her bosses.

2. *Blaming the system:*

This manifestation is characterized by deflecting responsibility for one's actions; putting all the blame on the other or the system for one's problems; or refusing to learn about and acknowledge mental, emotional, and stress-related issues as real. This expression results in an externalizing and blaming of others that in effect gives away the target group members' ability to effect change. It sometimes masks a sense of hopelessness in the target group's ability to visualize and/or implement a more desirable system.

Examples of blaming the system include:

A black student, who is not studying, blames his teacher and the "system" for his bad grades. He is unwilling to accept what role his lack of preparation may have in his failure to succeed.

A Latina employee applies for a job for which she is not qualified, and says it is the system's fault when she does not get hired. She is unwilling to take advantage of opportunities to get the appropriate training and "blames" it on the fact that her English is poor.

3. *Anti-white avoidance of contact:*

This form of internalized oppression includes avoiding contact with whites; distrusting all whites (obsessive concern and suspicion); being overly sensitive to rejection; rejecting people of color who are perceived as "not black enough" or "not Chinese enough," etc.; escaping (through fantasy, dreams, drugs, alcohol, sex, food, withdrawal). Such a stance is fueled by a rage that can be self-destructive to the person who carries it. The utility of anger is to stop injustice and to insist on and create equity; when it becomes internalized it can hamper the autonomy of the target group person.

Examples of anti-white avoidance of contact are:

A Chinese employee refuses to talk to a white supervisor about a job-related problem because he says the supervisor will not understand. He does not admit that he is really uncomfortable talking to whites. He therefore limits his own chances for a positive change in his situation.

A black calls another black an "Uncle Tom" because the latter is working hard to get a promotion and because he is light-skinned. This perpetuation of "colorism" and of a denial of the impressive "profound work ethic" among black people is self-limiting.

4. Denial of cultural heritage:

In this expression, internalized oppression means distrusting one's own group; accepting that one's group is inferior; giving deference to whites; ejecting or devaluing one's cultural heritage; valuing and overemphasizing white standards of beauty; valuing and accepting whites as the highest authority and white standards as superior. Such a stance colludes with the myths of "white superiority and inferiority of people of color."

Examples of denial of cultural heritage include:

A Latino patient does not want a Latino nurse or doctor because the patient thinks they are not as well qualified as a white nurse or doctor.

A black employee, who does not associate much with blacks, is uncomfortable considering her African heritage, and, when with whites, aggressively expresses negative opinions of blacks as a group.

5. Lack of understanding or minimization of the political significance of racial oppression:

Internalized oppression can also be manifested by being passive and unassertive; feeling powerless (learned helplessness); misdirecting anger to persons with less power; having difficulty expressing anger; avoiding conflicts at all costs; turning anger inward, resulting in high blood pressure, strokes, ulcers; buying copiously (symbolic status striving, resulting in conspicuous consumption of goods such as clothes and cars); in-group fighting; displaying sexist or other "ism" behaviors, e.g. heterosexism or classism; taking advantage of the lack of information or feelings of powerlessness of other people of color. This stance involves failure to examine the pervasive nature of racism and the multiplicity of ways in which target group members are set up to collude with its perpetuation. It can also result in an unwillingness to accept that the historical legacy of racial oppression has not been corrected systematically and its effects continue to impact most aspects of life.

Examples of a lack of understanding or minimization of the political significance of racial oppression are:

A black first level manager is unwilling to apply for a promotion because he does not think he will get it. He is sure that the organization will not promote a person of color simply because there are none presently. He has the necessary skills, but does not believe he can be successful. He does not understand how to seek out and organize support to promote systemic change.

An Asian supervisor always does what the white manager wants and is harder on the employees of color whom he supervises. He believes that the white supervisor cannot be, and should not be, successfully confronted, but feels powerful as he "pushes" his supervisees of color.

How Modern Racism and Internalized Oppression Interact

It is important to point out that the five modern racisms have their corollary, or parallel in the five internalized oppressions. Figure 3 shows their relationship to each other:

Behavioral Manifestations of Modern Racism and Internalized Oppression

Modern Racism	Internalized Oppression
1. Dysfunctional rescuing	1. System beating
2. Blaming the victim	2. Blaming the system
3. Avoidance of contact	3. Anti-white avoidance of contact
4. Denial of differences	4. Denial of cultural heritage
5. Denial of the political significance of differences	5. Lack of understanding of the political significance of differences

FIGURE 3

Challenging modern racism and internalized oppression begins as individuals give up the need to deny that "isms" still exist. Rather, they start to look for manifestations of oppression in the personal, interpersonal, institutional, and cultural contexts. Modern racism and internalized oppression are often played out in a complementary fashion. Given a white who practices dysfunctional rescuing, for example, many people of color will resort to system beating rather than confront the behavior, if they perceive it to be the safest choice or if they have no permission to be assertive with whites. Such actions reinforce the dysfunctional behavior on both parts and keep the system intact.

People of color, who, for a variety of reasons, have adopted a "Don't trust whites" stance, will often be misunderstood by whites who practice avoidance of contact. The white person will take the person of color's avoidance-of-contact stance personally, and will often use it as justification of further avoidance. Such whites discount the realities of racism for blacks or other people of color and do not seek information about their experiences. They are also likely to perceive blacks or Latinos, for instance, who are in a pro-black or pro-Latino posture as anti-white when the individuals are not.

At the institutional level, most welfare laws of the late 1960s were written from a dysfunctional rescuing position. Recipients, typically children and their mothers, were set up to fail and are now being blamed for their plight. Monetary benefits were inadequate, the process for attaining help was dehumanizing, and the incentives for getting training or for working were not available.[42] Those welfare recipients who attempted to beat the system used blame to justify their actions while avoiding any responsibility for changing their conditions.

Using the system when there are no other feasible options is "survival behavior" and not reactive internalized oppression. Indeed, a critical question to be asked as individuals are teasing out "the dance" between modern racism and internalized oppression is: when is a given target group members' "difficult behavior" reflective of a survival strategy? In the face of overt or covert racism, internalized oppression behaviors can be the key to psychological or physical survival. It is very important that such behaviors, which are reactive to racism, not be used to blame people of color or other target group members for their adaptations to oppression.

PROCESS OF CHANGE

As has been illustrated, many examples of modern racism have been generated from our training and consultation efforts since 1984. Participants in these efforts typically share a common goal: learning how to incorporate an appreciation of cultural diversity and multicultural strategies in their work or organizational settings. They want to be able to create or enhance this appreciation both interpersonally and structurally. There is an apparent debate among change agents in this field regarding the focus or outcome of such strategies. There is considerable discussion regarding the questions: Are we providing diversity work, anti-racism work, or are we promoting multiculturalism? Where does anti-bias work fit into this discussion?

Such a debate can become distracting to the effort. It is our assumption that we are essentially looking at all of these issues in any successful change effort.[43] Diversity speaks to the need to change numbers and, in many cases, perspective. It addresses who is in a given organization and what ideas, images, processes, etc. are included in the group's work. Cultural diversity speaks specifically to the inclusion of such aspects from a cultural instead of, or in addition to, an individual perspective. Anti-bias efforts are also aimed at ensuring that multicultural work looks at all forms of bias or discrimination. We believe that successful anti-racist, multicultural work has to include this focus.

Anti-racism efforts speak to the need to explicitly address historic and current power imbalances. Addressing these imbalances successfully will include paying attention to how they play out with respect to all power discrepancies. Women of color, for example, are targets of racism and sexism. To address sexism successfully, one must address racism. To address heterosexism successfully, as another case in point, racism must be addressed as well since there is differential access for lesbians and gay men of color. In both instances, non-targets experience costs, in addition to privileges, as men and as heterosexuals. And the list goes on. It is not possible to successfully address racism in any lasting manner without raising these other aspects. The issue for change agents will be: where do we begin, not, will we consider all of these parameters?

We see multiculturalism as the process through which change occurs. Multicultural strategies are designed to increase the ability of individuals and groups to recognize, understand, and appreciate differences as well as similarities. This three-step process occurs most often in stages and involves first recognizing and unlearning one's biases. For most of us in the United States, our worldview incorporated negative perceptions or other dysfunctional adaptations to people who were different from the accepted norm. This norm, unfortunately, for most United States citizens from both non-target and target groups, involved an evaluation of how close one fits to being white, male, young to middle-aged (i.e., 25 to 45), heterosexual, United States born and American English-speaking, Protestant, middle-class and physically able.

The second step of a multicultural change process involves seeing, thinking about, and understanding the content of cultural group differences. Reclaiming one's ethnic background is part of this process, as well as giving up dysfunctional ethnocentrism. The goal is coming to experience that being equal does not mean being the same and that valuing diversity means being willing to accept the validity of ways of being other than one's own.

As a third step this belief begins to be applied personally and systemically. It includes explicit attention to power sharing, redistribution of resources, and redefinition of "what is right and beautiful" at all levels. As the implementation of this worldview starts to occur, appreciation becomes the process. Participants start to embrace the value, philosophy, and practice that any system, institution, program, or curriculum is enhanced by the acknowledgment and usage of cultural differences as a critical factor.

Personal and interpersonal change involves, then, acknowledging and valuing one's own cultural background and recognizing the particular dynamics found within different cultural groups. This process includes working through cognitive and affective misinformation about other cultural groups as well as about one's own group. It is facilitated by regular contact with persons from and information about different groups, as well as with on-going contact with members of one's own group as mentors. Willingness to try on new behaviors, to make mistakes, and to disagree are necessary parts of the process.

It is important to stress that unlearning modern racism and internalized oppression in all of its expressions is a *process*. Part of the reason that the character of racism shifted for most people in the United States rather than changed is because there was such an urgent need to fix the problem.[44] The goal in changing racism is to stay open when behaviors or practices arise which are, in their consequences, regardless of their intent, discriminatory. It also means examining fully the multitude of ways in which our society currently still functions economically, socially, politically, and culturally to the advantage of whites and to the disadvantage of people of color. As long as such institutional and cultural racism continues to exist, modern racism behaviors or practices will continue to emerge even among well-intentioned people.

Changing institutional and cultural racism involves a commitment by all members of an organization to examine norms, values, and policies. Overt power discrepancies must be changed. More subtle reward systems that reinforce status quo behaviors must give way to systems that include diversity and multiculturalism at every point. Institutions typically have to start by acknowledging the fear among those who control the current structure of either losing that control or of doing the wrong thing (i.e., being called a racist or making things worse by focusing on differences). These fears often manifest as anger, backlash, a need to control how change occurs, and/or as guilt, shame or the experiencing of target group authority figures as not experienced or competent enough. There is a need to acknowledge and work through those fears at all levels of the organization.[45]

Training in racism awareness and multiculturalism is crucial to removing fear and other barriers. Such training helps members of organizations appreciate what they will gain as individuals and as an organization by fully embracing multiculturalism. Training should occur both within and across different levels of the organizational hierarchy, and within and between different cultural groups.[46] It is crucial to a long-term successful intervention that all individuals come to see that some of the work in dismantling oppression entails working within one's own group; that is, whites need to learn to challenge and support other whites, and people of color need space for continual self definition, and within-group problem solving and agenda setting. Successful group coalitions at this point in our history entail the ability to coalesce and to separate.

Review of organizational structures, processes, norms, and values by multicultural teams is a crucial next step. Individuals working within a structure to create change will need to develop allies. Involvement of team members as facilitators, trainers, and institutional change agents with high visibility helps employees see that the organization's commitment is real and on going. The team should set up methods of communicating their process and important outcomes. Problem spots within the organization need to be highlighted and changed. Areas that are acknowledging differences and working well should be celebrated.[47]

Unlearning racism in all its expressions is offered as a model for understanding how oppression works in any target/non-target relationship.[48] It is crucial that individuals realize how each person is sometimes in both positions. Multiculturalism, then, involves committing to the process of altering the variety of ways in which individuals and groups establish one-up/one-down dynamics. To paraphrase James Baldwin's comments in an open letter to Angela Davis, "If they come for you tonight, they will be back for me in the morning."

A FINAL WORD AND A CALL

I believe the Episcopal Church's House of Bishops, as well as religious and spiritual leaders from around the world and in all traditions, have a critical role to play in developing an effective psychology and spirituality necessary to create a peaceful world discourse. The above model for combating modern racism and its many manifestations is offered as one way that religious leaders can become effective change agents for a reconciled human community. Many within the world's religious traditions have boldly or quietly done such in the past. Now is our time to do the same. If not now, when? If not us, who?

Another of the prophetic words of Martin Luther King, Jr., written about the United States in the 1960s, are bringing me both comfort as well as fear about what will happen if we do not provide such leadership at this time.

> I refuse to accept the cynical notion that nation after nation must spiral down a militaristic stairway into the hell of thermonuclear destruction. I believe that unarmed truth and unconditional love will have the final word in reality.[49]

Although Dr. King no longer lives with us to inspire us, his message lives on. As bishops and religious leaders dedicated to "waging reconciliation" we must "keep on keeping on" following King's prophetic words:

> Darkness cannot drive out darkness; only light can do that. Hate cannot drive out hate; only love can do that. Hate multiplies hate, violence multiplies violence, and toughness multiplies toughness in a descending spiral of destruction...The chain reaction of evil—hate begetting hate, wars producing more wars—must be broken, or we shall be plunged into the darkness of annihilation.[50]

NOTES

[1] Diane J. Goodman, *Promoting Diversity and Social Justice: Educating People from Privileged Groups* (Thousand Oaks, CA: Sage Publishing, 2001), 122.

[2] Ibid.

[3] Nelson Mandela, *Long Walk to Freedom: The Autobiography of Nelson Mandela* (New York: Little & Brown, 1994), 544.

[4] Martin Luther King, Jr., *Strength to Love* (Philadelphia: Fortress Press, 1981), 7.

[5] This model was originally published as: Valerie Batts, *Modern Racism: New Melody for the Same Old Tunes* (Cambridge: Episcopal Divinity School Occasional Papers, 1998). A form of the paper was distributed to the bishops as background reading in preparation for their meeting of September 2001.

[6] Cardell K. Jacobson, "Resistance to Affirmative Action: Self-interest or Racism?," *Journal of Conflict Resolution* 29 (1985): 306–29; Thomas F. Pettigrew, "Modern Racism in the United States," *Revue Internationale de Psychologie Sociale* 2:3 (1989): 291–303; "Affirmative Action," *Black Scholar* 25 (Summer 1995): 2–47.

[7] John F. Dovidio and Samuel L. Gaertner, eds., *Prejudice, Discrimination, and Racism* (Orlando: Academic Press, 1986).

[8] Target group is a term used to describe blacks (that is, Africans from across the Diaspora) and other people of color as well as other groups who have been historically and currently "targeted" within U.S. society as "less than" or different in an inferior way from the dominant population. The statistical odds for successful outcomes are less for members of a target group. Non-target groups, by contrast, are more likely to operate from a view that their "way" is better and to receive unearned privilege and increased life chances such as longer mortality, employment, access to credit, and higher incomes. See Figure 2, page 41.

[9] I assume in this paper, as has been my experience, that the dynamic of how racism manifests in black-white relationships in the United States South is the paradigm for understanding the myth of superiority based on color. I see that the dynamic played out among Africans across the Diaspora as well as among indigenous people worldwide, people of color from Spanish-speaking countries, and Asians from all parts of Asia and the Pacific Rim. When I use the term "black" I encourage readers to think inclusively and to note how the example I am sharing or the theoretical point I am making fits or does not fit for their target group experience.

[10] Janet E. Helms, *Black and White Racial Identity: Theory, Research, and Practice* (New York: Greenwood Press, 1990); William E. Cross, *Shades of Black* (Philadelphia: Temple University Press, 1991).

[11] John McConahay, Beatrice Hardee, and Valerie Batts, "Has Racism Declined in America?," *Journal of Conflict Resolution* 2:4 (1981): 563–79.

[12] Phyllis A. Katz and Dalmas A. Taylor, "Introduction," in *Eliminating Racism: Profiles in Controversy* (New York: Plenum Press, 1988).

[13] Jared Taylor, *Paved with Good Intentions: The Failure of Race Relations in Contemporary America* (New York: Carroll and Graf Publishers, 1992).

[14] Joe R. Feagin and Hernan Vera, *White Racism: The Basics* (New York: Routledge, 1995); Richard B. Ropers and Dan J. Pence, *American Prejudice* (New York: Insight Books, 1995).

[15] John McConahay and James Hough, "Symbolic Racism," *Journal of Social Issues* 32:2 (1976): 23–45.

[16] Dovidio and Gaertner, *Prejudice.*

[17] Anne Braden, "Lessons from a History of Struggle," *Southern Exposure* 8:2 (1980): 56–61.

[18] McConahay and Hough, "Symbolic Racism," 38.

[19] Valerie Batts, "Modern Racism: A T.A. Perspective," *Transactional Analysis Journal* 12:3 (1983): 207–9; John Hope Franklin, "A Continuing Climate of Racism" *Duke University: A Magazine for Alumni and Friends* 71:2 (1984): 12–16; Pettigrew, "Modern Racism."

[20] John Capitman, "Symbolic Racism Theory Criteria for Individual Differences: Measures of Prejudice and the Validity of the Feeling Thermometer" (Ph.D. dissertation, Duke University, 1980); Dovidio and Gaertner, *Prejudice*; Janel K. Swim, Kathryn J. Aikin, Wayne S. Hall, and Barbara A. Hunter, "Sexism and Racism: Old-fashioned and Modern Prejudices," *Journal of Personality and Social Psychology* 68:2 (1995): 199–214.

[21] Peggy McIntosh, "White Privilege and Male Privilege: A Personal Account of Coming to See Correspondences through Work in Women Studies," Stone Center, Wellesley College, Working Paper no. 189 (1988).

[22] Valerie Batts, "An Experiential Workshop: Introduction to Multiculturalism," in *Toward Ethnic Diversification in Psychology Education and Training*, ed. George Stricker, et al. (Washington, D.C.: American Psychological Association, 1990), 9–16.

[23] Valerie Batts, "An Overview of Strategies for Creating a Multicultural Workforce," *Consulting Psychology Bulletin* (Winter 1990): 3–6.

[24] James M. Jones, *Prejudice and Racism* (Reading, MA: Addison-Wesley Publishing Co., 1972).

[25] Pierre L. van den Berghe, *Race and Racism: A Comparative Perspective* (New York: John Wiley & Sons, 1967); Batts, "Modern Racism."

[26] Ropers and Pence, *American Prejudice*.

[27] Martha Minow, *Making All the Difference: Inclusion, Exclusion, and American Law* (Ithaca: Cornell University Press, 1990);

Claud Anderson, *Black Labor, White Wealth* (Edgewood: Duncan & Duncan, 1994); Melvin L. Oliver and Thomas M. Shapiro, *Black Wealth/White Wealth* (New York: Routledge, 1995).

[28] James Jones, "Racism in Black and White," in Katz and Taylor, *Eliminating Racism,* 117–135; Asa G. Hilliard, *The Maroon Within Us* (Baltimore: Black Classic Press, 1995).

[29] Katz and Taylor, "Introduction" in *Eliminating Racism*; Pettigrew, "Modern Racism"; Swim, "Sexism and Racism"; Jean T. Griffin, "Racism and Humiliation in the African American Community," *Journal of Primary Prevention* 12:2 (1991): 149–67.

[30] Andrew Hacker, *Two Nations: Black and White, Separate, Hostile, Unequal* (New York: Oxford University Press, 1992).

[31] Derrick Bell, "Risks, Rewards, and Reaffirmation," in: *Confronting Authority: Reflections of an Ardent Protester* (Boston: Beacon Press, 1994), 149–50.

[32] Joseph Katz, "White Faculty Struggling with the Effects of Racism," in: *Teaching Minority Students,* ed. James H. Cone, et al. (San Francisco: Jossey-Bass, 1983).

[33] Joyce E. King, "Dysconscious Racism: Ideology, Identity, and the Miseducation of Teachers," *Journal of Negro Education* 60:2 (1991): 133–45.

[34] Norman Miller and Marilynn Brewer, "Categorizing Effect on In Group and Out Group Perception," in Davido and Gaertner, *Prejudice, Discrimination, and Racism,* 209–29; Mwalimu J. Shujaa, ed., *Too Much Schooling, Too Little Education: A Paradox of Black Life in White Societies* (Trenton, NJ: Africa World Press, 1994).

[35] Patricia J. Williams, *The Rooster's Egg* (Cambridge, MA: Harvard University Press, 1995).

[36] Dovidio and Gaertner, *Prejudice.*

[37] Mary Sonn and Valerie Batts, "Strategies for Changing Personal Attitudes of White Racism" (Paper delivered at the

Annual Convention of the American Psychological Association, Los Angles, 1985).

[38] William Ryan, *Blaming the Victim* (New York: Vintage Books, 1976).

[39] Hilliard, *The Maroon Within Us.*

[40] Bell, "Risks"; Na'im Akbar, *Chains and Images of Psychological Slavery* (Jersey City: New Mind Productions, 1984); Suzanne Lipsky, *Internalized Racism* (Seattle: Rational Island Publishers, 1978); Fahkry Davids, "Frantz Fanon: The Struggle for Inner Freedom, Part 2," *Free Associations* 6:18 (1996): 205–34.

[41] Joyce Brown and Valerie Batts, "Helping Blacks Cope with and Overcome the Personal Effects of Racism" (Paper delivered at the Annual Convention of the American Psychological Association, Los Angeles, 1985).

[42] Ryan, *Blaming the Victim*; William Ryan, *Equality* (New York: Pantheon Books, 1981); Anderson, *Black Labor*; Oliver and Shapiro, *Black Wealth.*

[43] Mark A. Chester and James Crowfoot, "Racism in Higher Education I: An Organizational Analysis." Center for Research on Social Organization, University of Michigan, Ann Arbor, Working Paper no. 412 (1989); "Racism in Higher Education II: Challenging Racism and Promoting Multiculturalism in Higher Education Organizations." Working Paper no. 558 (1997).

[44] Pettigrew, "Modern Racism"; Minow, *Making All the Difference.*

[45] James H. Cone, Denise Janha, and John F. Noonan, "Exploring Racial Assumptions with Faculty," in *Teaching Minority Students*, 73–79; Mark Silver, "Reflections on Diversity: A White Man's Perspective," *The Diversity Factor* (Summer 1995): 34–39; J. E. Helms, *Affirmative Action: Who Benefits?* (Washington, DC: American Psychological Association, 1996).

[46] Margaret D. Pusch, ed., *Multicultural Education* (Chicago: Intercultural Network, 1981); Gerald Jackson, "The Implementation of an Interracial Awareness Coaching Program," *Corporate Headquarters* (Winter 1987): 9–30; King, "Dysconscious Racism"; Natalie Porter, "Empowering Supervisees to Empower Others: A Culturally Responsive Supervision Model," *Hispanic Journal of Behavioral Sciences* 16:1 (1994): 43–56.

[47] David Thomas and Robin Ely, "Making Differences Matter: A New Paradigm for Managing Diversity," *Harvard Business Review* (September–October 1996): 79–90.

[48] Ricky Sherover-Marcuse, "Towards a Perspective on Unlearning Racism: Twelve Working Assumptions," *Issues in Cooperation and Power* no. 7 (Fall 1981): 14–15; Batts, "An Experiential Workshop"; Linda A. Camino, "Confronting Intolerance and Promoting Multiculturalism: Frameworks and Strategies for Adults, Youth, and Communities" (Paper prepared for the Sun Prairie Research Project, University of Wisconsin, 1994).

[49] Martin Luther King Jr., *The Words of Martin Luther King Jr.* (New York: Newmarket Press, 1983) 91.

[50] King, *Strength to Love*, 51.

3

GLOBALIZATION, THE SOCIAL GOSPEL AND CHRISTIAN LEADERSHIP TODAY

RICHARD PARKER

If we are to talk about "globalization" today, we must first talk about death. I do not say that to shock you or because it pleases me to speak this way. Yet in the wake of what happened at the World Trade Center and Pentagon on September 11, 2001, death is much on our minds these days as America prepares for war. Whether the war will success- fully root out a relative handful of terrorists—or mark the beginnings of what my Harvard colleague, Samuel Hunting- ton, calls "the clash of civilizations" cannot be known. But I do know that what happened in New York and Washington has now squarely put before us the true scale of the moral and human issues this process called "globalization" entails.

Since September 11, 2001, we have been made pained witnesses to the harsher side of that process—and as a con- sequence now mourn the loss of more than 5,000 American lives.[1] But let me share with you some simple facts: Over the course of this coming year, more than 50 million— 50,000,000—people will die, most of them from preventable disease or malnutrition.[2] And the overwhelming majority of those, who live in the Third World, will be human beings the World Health Organization estimates need not have died had someone been willing to spend just a few dollars per person for food or medicine. To give some perspective, 50 million dead is greater than the total casualties of World War II—itself the most horrendously murderous war in modern history. It is eight times greater than the Holocaust, about which we all rightly insist "Never Again." It amounts each year to 10,000 World Trade Centers, which must also never be forgotten. And yet—year after year—this loss of life goes on not merely forgotten, but unknown to all but a tiny fraction of Americans.

There is an even more painful fact here: of those 50 million who will die *more than 12 million will be children under the age of five.* That is one million children needlessly dying every month, a quarter million every week, nearly 40,000 children every day. Put slightly differently, by the time I finish speaking to you this morning, more than 5,000 children will be dead—and you and I could have saved almost every one.[3] But we will not.

America today is preparing to go to war over 5,000 dead in the United States, and yet the cruel and nonnegotiable fact is that an equal number of the world's children die at the same catastrophic levels every two hours—and America is silent. And I believe we need to talk about why.

The word "globalization" is a perfectly "modern" term, unpoetic, efficiently neutral and technical, a description of what many even now believe is a "natural," and therefore "inescapable," process going on around the planet—a "golden straightjacket," as *New York Times* columnist Thomas Friedman calls it, that only the foolish and malign refuse to accept.[4] "Globalization" is also often described as "new," the consequence of amazing technological, informational, and market advances unknown even a quarter-century ago. But let me tell you a few things about this process called "globalization" that run contrary to that conventional wisdom.

Globalization is not a new phenomenon; quite to the contrary, it is at least half a million years old, and began when our prehistoric ancestors walked out of Africa, into the Middle East, Europe, and Asia—and eventually Australia and the Americas. Long after that first-stage globalization, human beings gradually settled down in fixed communities and territories, and began exchanging hunting and gathering for farming.

Now a new sort of "globalization" started. It was the exchange of culturally specific knowledge and things, of cultivatable plants and domesticated animals, of weapons and jewelry, of tools and toys, of techniques for casting pots and weaving cloth and shaping metals, and of stories—crucial stories about who we are, why we are here, who we worship and obey, and why. This second stage of globalization, of course, is hardly new either—it had been underway for at least 15,000 to 20,000 years, even before Christ's birth.[5]

The current period, 2001, that we vainly imagine to be so new and revolutionary is only the latest chapter in a fourth or fifth stage of globalization, a wave that began in Western Europe 500 years ago. There are of course undeniably "new" things about the world we live in today. Yet what so many briskly talk of as characteristically modern—as signs of our "new global era"—in fact rest on long-established patterns and achievements. Even those larger features we think are most distinct about our own "global" era today—the immense trade flows, or the instant information of the worldwide Internet, or the electronic financial markets that send billions of dollars coursing around the globe—all have a longer and deeper heritage than most of us understand.

Take global trade, for example, about which I know something. This may surprise you but America's international trade, measured as a percentage of gross national product, is basically no greater today under George W. Bush than it was under Theodore Roosevelt a century ago. The total volume of trade has grown—but so has the economy.

The same is true with international finance. We are so accustomed to being told breathlessly—and more recently anxiously—about the latest in the "new" world of global capital markets that we forget such markets were well developed by the time of the American Civil War. The mid-nineteenth century, after all, was a time when English investors poured money into Canadian railroad bonds, Rhodesian cattle ranches, and Ceylonese tea plantations; when Americans bought German chemical firms and sold sophisticated textile looms to Egyptians, and opened hotels in Shanghai and telegraph companies in Mexico City; when the French invested in Russian and Chinese manufacturers, Senegalese farms, Caribbean plantations, and New Caledonian mines. In other words, there is a reason why highly regarded economic historians like David Landes and Jeffrey Williamson have long tried to remind this ever-amnesiac culture of ours that the late-nineteenth century—not the late-twentieth century— was the great "Golden Age of Global Trade and Investment."[6]

Like that great golden age of trade and investment, the great global "Information Age" we are told started only yesterday, was already 150 years old when Bill Gates launched Microsoft. It was not the personal computer that created the Information Age—it was the steam-driven rotary printing press, an invention from the days of Napoleon that brought not just to the West, but also to the world, mass-circulation newspapers, magazines, and books. Consider this simple illustration of that steam press's impact: at the start of the nineteenth century, the world's biggest newspaper—the *Times* of London—sold barely 9,000 copies and averaged just 12–16 pages in length; 90 years later, the world's biggest newspaper sold well over one million copies a day, and ran 60 pages in length.

That is not all. Thanks to the steam press, the total number of newspapers and magazines exploded, from fewer than 1,300—almost all in Western Europe and North America—to more than 30,000 across the planet. Meanwhile, the average price of a book plummeted 90%, creating thereby not only an immense new world of voracious adult readers, but the ability to provide textbooks to millions of new students—a revolution that began spreading literacy across the planet at an unprecedented rate.[7]

There is more. When someone starts bubbling on to you about "The Internet Revolution," and about its amazing abilities to move information and ideas around the globe almost instantly, gently stop that person and simply repeat this name: "Samuel Morse." Because it was Morse, again in the early nineteenth century, who was the true "global-networking" revolutionary—long before Cisco or Yahoo or dot coms. Before Morse, information traveled little more quickly than it had for thousands of years—by land, at the speed of a horse; by sea, at the speed of a sailing ship. Before Morse, for example, the fastest a message could travel from New Delhi to New York was four to five months—God, a fast ship, and the weather willing. By the time he died, copper telegraph lines spanned the continents and the oceans—and that same message now went from Delhi to New York not in four to five months, but four to five seconds.[8]

Having shown you briefly why "globalization" is *not* new, let me say *why* it's important that you understand it is not new. Comprehending our present era as another stage in a process that is 500 years old in one way (and more deeply 500,000 years old in another) means that you and I can look backward for patterns and connections, for trends and similarities—and, most important, draw on the richness of our traditions, our ancestors, our values, and our faith to shape this world as those before have tried to do, living in that same faith.

For you, as Episcopal bishops particularly—as I will discuss shortly—this means the ability to draw on the church's own important responses to earlier stages in this *ongoing* globalization, and to see the significant leadership it provided that you are capable of providing to us.

Before turning to that history of Episcopal Church leadership, however, I want you to think back to what happened 500 years ago that gave birth to the present era of "globalization." Of course that era has largely been about the expansion of West European power across the globe—and *not* some vaguely mutual and equal process of all peoples. After Columbus, African fleets did not sail off to conquer India. Incan traders did not land in France, and carry back slaves and gold to Peru (let alone wine and cheese). The Chinese did not begin exporting opium to England (as England once did to China), and Indonesia did not colonize Holland for its spices. In short, we would all be more honest if we talked about our present era as part of the 500-year-long chapter involving the global "Europeanization," not the "globalization" of all. The values, logic, technology, and the social, political, and economic forms that are today remaking the world originated in Western Europe (or its North American child), not somewhere else.

Second, beyond renaming the process of globalization as "Europeanization" (with due attention to its North American offspring in the past 200 years), we need to see how the legacy of specific changes in European-born political, economic, and value structures—not some "natural" process—continues to define the current global era. A hundred years ago, just half a dozen European states—Britain, France, Germany, Belgium, Holland, and Portugal—ruled empires that directly or indirectly controlled 60% of the world's populations and territories. Today those political empires are gone, and there are more than 200 nation-states in their place. Yet let me share with you what at first might seem a conundrum, especially if you believe in the inexorability of "Progress." Since those empires ended, global economic inequality has gotten worse—not better. Since 1960 alone, the income gap between rich and poor states has doubled, leaving the richest states controlling more global income than they ever did back when they directly ran colonial empires—while more than a billion people today survive on less than $1 a day, and two billion more live on less than $2 a day.[9]

Let me dwell on this point a bit longer. For most of us, the reality that the end of these colonial empires has not allowed for greatly improving the lives of billions of people should be profoundly troubling. After all, as Americans, not only do we worship the ineffable majesty of "progress," we deeply believe that our own early escape from colonial domination was central to our success and affluence as a people. So why has it not been so for others?

That leads inexorably to a point I want to drive home— our need to see how the *systemic global connection of politics, economics, and ideology born in that earlier age of Europe's global empires is still shaping the world's overall development even today.* We know, of course, that much of the world over the past 500 years paid a terrible price for its subjugation by European empires—the enslavement of millions of Africans and the decimation by disease of millions of Native Americans being merely two of the more familiar examples for Americans.

Now the great economic take-off of the West in the nineteenth and twentieth centuries owed much to technological innovation and enormous effort and industry, to be sure— but it owed much as well to that exploitation and consequently uneven patterns of development imposed by the West that unfairly used the economic wealth of others for our own ends. Thus in the seventeenth, eighteenth, and even nineteenth century, the immense capital accumulation that funded the new technologies that gave birth to the Industrial Era in the West relied on surpluses transferred from the poor throughout the world. Fortunes that were invested in the new factories were made first in tobacco, coffee, tea, sugar, minerals, and land that relied on slavery, indentured labor, and—frankly—outright theft on an unimaginable scale. In the United States alone, for example, by 1860 slaves were the second-largest form of wealth after land itself—that is, human slaves were greater in value than all United States manufacturing plants or all the railroads combined.

Many thought that this would all change with the end of these great Western empires. But less has changed than one might have hoped—and the reasons why go back directly to the enduring systemic connections between politics, economics, and ideology; a connection that underscores just how "unnatural" and "un-inevitable" the evolution of the current world really has been and is.

After World War II, as more and more colonies won their freedom, they entered our "Europeanized" world unprepared by their old colonial masters. The Congo, for example, on the day Belgium set it free had exactly 12 college graduates among a population of more than 14 million. Moreover, these new nations were born amidst a global struggle between the United States and the Soviet Union (and later China) in which each superpower valued the loyalty of its allies over the greater good of national democracy and just economic development. In the Congo, the immediate effect of this was the murder of Patrice Lumumba, the country's first (and so far only) democratically elected president, and his replacement by a corrupt colonel named Moise Tshombe, whose 35-year murderous and kleptomaniacal reign was still being blessed by the West even after apartheid South Africa had become a pariah state.[10]

The Soviets and Chinese had their own horrible client states—the Albanias, the Rumanias, the Cambodias—but the United States was certainly not innocent in this world. The Shah in Iran, or the Marcoses in the Philippines, or the endless list of Mobutus and Pinochets and Somozas or Korean generals and Greek colonels were free to steal and torture and abuse because, as Lyndon Johnson once so colorfully said of one of our client leaders, "Well, he may be a son-of-a-bitch, but at least he's *our* son-of-a-bitch."[11]

The price of this "our son-of-bitch" policy—and its corruption of the fragile tendrils of both democracy and egalitarian economic development in newly liberated colonies— had led by the 1970s to a vast system of military and oligarchic regimes across the developing world that was not only condoned, but actively supported by the United States. Our intelligence services trained and equipped their torturers, our military schooled their death squads, and our bankers happily deposited and hid the immense wealth they freely plundered.

If today we still look back on the 1970s as an era of shame because of Watergate and Vietnam, a truer global appraisal would rank both these American failings as child's play compared to the immense perpetration of evil we permitted and even encouraged; an evil that filled shallow mass graves in Guatemala with highland Indians and the torture chambers of SAVAK with students in Iran, that sustained pestilential civil wars in Angola and Mozambique, wars whose machetes and land mines killed forty civilians for every combatant, and that led Argentine and Chilean soldiers to push the broken—but still conscious—bodies of their opponents out of helicopters at 10,000 feet.[12]

Today the old "evil empire" of Soviet Communism is gone—and there has been an important flowering of at least modestly democratic regimes in the developing world. In this, there is reason for hope and celebration. But, lest we forget, the political cost of blocking and overthrowing democracy in the name of anti-Communism was not the only price billions of Third World poor were made to pay. There was—and is—an economic price as well, that took a brutal new rise with the explosion of global oil prices in the 1970s.

Here in America, we remember the gas lines and the stagflation of those days as frustrating and inconvenient; but overseas among developing nations, entire economies without their own oil supplies ground to a halt—or began borrowing heavily from New York banks and Washington's multilaterals to maintain energy imports in a desperate race to outgrow poverty faster than their debts came due. But as we know, with all but a handful of exceptions, those countries lost the race, creating in the process a global debt crisis that the West resolved by forcing harsh new lending conditions on the developing world. These conditions, which famously came attached to "structural adjustment programs," meant to generate "export-led growth"—required poor countries to make massive cuts in education and health care, in road and hospital construction, and simultaneously raised heavy new taxes on their poor and middle classes, while cutting taxes on their rich. "Structural adjustment" also meant opening domestic markets to Western goods and reorienting domestic production away from local markets toward exports designed to earn hard currency that would pay down the old debts incurred by the energy crisis.

Given the intoxication, leaders like Margaret Thatcher and Ronald Reagan encouraged radical deregulation and worship of "the market" in its most primitive form. What no one bothered to notice at the time was that while such "structural adjustment" policies followed a certain kind of microeconomic textbook logic to the letter, it was a logic on paper that had never worked in practice.

As a vocal minority of economists warned, the successful rapid growth of the world's first capitalist economies such as Britain, Germany, and the United States, in fact had never relied on such "structural adjustment" models—nor had Europe's recovery after World War II, nor Japan's explosive growth in the 1960s and 1970s, nor the phenomenal rise of the so-called Asian Tigers in the 1970s and 1980s—and certainly not the monumental growth of China in the 1980s and 1990s. In fact, the truth was that *every developmentally successful economy in the last 200 years* protected its domestic markets from "free trade," limited currency convertibility, used tax and labor policies to lessen inequality, poured billions into education and physical infrastructure, and used the size and power of its government to favor industries, technologies, and regions considered important to national development, and in dozens of ways limited the unadulterated power of private markets and private wealth that, like the golden calf, has been worshiped so freely in this past quarter-century. In short, the fashionable microeconomic textbook models—with their evangelical celebrations of a modern-day social Darwinism—had *never* gotten the real world "right"; in fact, only the Keynesian macroeconomists and institutionalists had any claim to useful accuracy. But for 25 years, as the United States and Britain especially turned ever rightward, the Keynesians who said such things had been as welcome.as Paul Tillich at a Pat Robertson rally.

Today, of course, the World Bank and others freely acknowledge the failure of these "structural adjustment programs" they were promoting just a decade ago—and have even, in limited ways, apologized for the damage their punitive and pious economic fundamentalism caused.[13] But in some ways the apologies have come too late. All across the Third World, schools have closed, rural medical workers have been dispersed. Cheap food imported from the West has driven millions of farmers into cities, and the cities—lacking consumers—have failed to create the jobs needed to feed the hungry mouths that cry out. As a result, 100 countries have undergone economic decline since the 1970s, with sub-Saharan Africans alone living on 20% less than they did 25 years ago. Worldwide, of 4.4 billion in the developing world, 3 billion people live on less than $2 a day, 1.3 billion on less than $1, and 840 million go hungry. Three-fifths lack basic sanitation, a quarter lack adequate housing, and a third will die before reaching the age of 40.

Meanwhile, wealth and income has become so much more concentrated both in rich countries and among the rich in poor countries that the *United Nations now estimates that the 15 richest individuals are worth more than the combined gross domestic products of all of sub-Saharan Africa.* Globally, as a consequence of these profoundly misguided policies, the numbers of very poor during the 1990s alone *grew* by nearly 500 million—a number that would be vastly higher had China not completely ignored "structural adjustment." Because of China's refusal to accept "structural adjustment," it had the highest growth rate of a large economy in the past century, and in turn reduced its poverty rate by more than half.[14]

I have emphasized this brief history to underscore for you how we got to our current "new era" of globalization, and why it is neither new nor simply global. Rather it is the ongoing march of a 500-year-old advance by a handful of countries bordering the North Atlantic—along with certain belief systems embedded in them—that have extended their influence over the rest of the peoples of the world. Having said that, I now want to say something about the Episcopal Church and the Anglican Communion, and the responsibility, the challenge, and, most importantly, the opportunity they share.

As you all know, the Anglican tradition was born in the unique circumstances of the past 500 years, and has ever since participated—for good and ill—in that very North Atlantic expansion across the planet I have just described. In the past few years, a good deal of time has been spent discussing and repenting for the church's part in the inequities—and iniquities—of that past. To do so has been important, but today I will instead dwell on prouder legacies we have inherited—and why that legacy is the foundation for engaging the world today.

More than a century ago, here in the United States, as an earlier "Golden Age of Global Trade and Investment" flowered, it may have been a "golden age" for some, but in truth was an ongoing nightmare for many more. As millions of impoverished immigrants poured into the country, cities grew up overnight, swollen with slums and hunger and disease. Factory work was 12 hours a day, six days a week, with no pension, no disability, no unemployment or health insurance—and most certainly no unions. In the countryside, farmers watched as shipping rates, inflated by railroad monopolies, destroyed them. In the South, living conditions for millions of ex-slaves and poor whites rivaled Third World misery today. Politics was so endlessly corrupt that one observer said, "the very wealthy bought and sold leaders like trading cards."

Yet, as most of you remember, in the midst of this nineteenth-century American world, what remarkably emerged was a powerful new wave of reform that radically reordered power and wealth, and reshaped the balance between public and private as well as the weak and the strong. Beginning in the 1880s, and then accelerating right up to World War I, an amazing campaign of renewal swept the nation. Democratic and justice-driven to its core, it reasserted the values of the Founding Fathers and took Lincoln as its patron saint—and sought nothing less than the "deconsecrating" of its leaders and America's uniquely covenantal history.

At first, the struggles occurred at the state and local levels. Anti-trust legislation appeared, minimum hours and wages were set, new laws dictated food and drug standards, occupational health and safety standards were promulgated, new regulations limited the powers of Wall Street and railroads, and government reforms constrained the money and power of the wealthy in politics. Electoral primaries and new citizen referenda—and eventually passage of women's suffrage—deepened and renewed the voting base of democracy.

But the movement never rested until it reached Washington, and began electing new leaders there, leaders who then passed new legislation meant to secure a monumental and gigantic range of reforms. Muckraking journalists provided the information to congressmen and courts, who eventually broke up trusts like Standard Oil, and passed constitutional amendments permitting an income and wealth tax on the richest. Now food and drug standards became national, the banking system was reformed, and—in a budding awareness of the environment—a vast network of federal parks and forests protected nearly a quarter of all land west of the Mississippi.

Historians today call that period "the progressive era"—but in its own time, millions more called it, this glorious covenantal renewal, simply "the social gospel era." And in truth it was—explicitly and unapologetically—a determined, systematic, and detailed application of mainline Protestant values to a new urban, industrial *and—I hasten to add—globalizing* world. Moreover, the achievements of that social gospel movement has ever since defined American life.[15] Most of you know of theologians of this era such as Walter Rauschenbusch—but the reality is that the hard work of building and realizing the social gospel movement was done not by the theologians but by inspired bishops and priests, committed, Christian social scientists and philanthropists, reformers, journalists, and politicians whose mostly Episcopal, Methodist, Presbyterian, Congregational, Baptist, and Lutheran faiths led and sustained them.

It was a remarkable period—one in which the confidence of America's mainline Protestant leaders led them to associate Christian moral teachings with scientific advance and social and political reform. It was an era of leaders who saw in the achievement of justice on earth manifest signs of the heavenly kingdom in which they believed as Christians— leaders who passionately believed *they had not only the right, but also the obligation, not merely to witness, but to alter the course of human history.*

In this, of course, these leaders knew they stood in a long and proud tradition of mainline religious activism in American history. They knew the fabled role of the colonial ministers in the 1760s and 1770s—men much better known then than the Tom Paines we honor today—who had preached the gospel of independence and equality that had formed a new nation. They knew how in the 1840s and 1850s the same Protestant churches had been willing to divide, if need be, over the pressing matter of abolition—and knew that the words of "The Battle Hymn of the Republic" could have served as an anthem only to a people who judged what truly was at stake in ending slavery.

They knew also that it was first through the denominational women's auxiliaries of the nineteenth century that the movement for women's suffrage had been born. And that it was the American invention of Sunday schools for children that had helped inspire the movement for free public education. They knew that after the Civil War the thousands of young men and women who had gone South to feed and clothe and teach millions of newly freed African Americans had been drawn almost entirely from mainline Protestant ranks. And now in the late nineteenth century, these leaders knew that the legions of settlement-house workers and labor union organizers, as well as the drawing rooms of reformist heiresses and the college classrooms of brilliant new social scientists, were filled with dedicated men and women whose Christian faith had taken them there.

Episcopalians, I want to emphasize here, were among the vanguards of that social gospel movement. Back in the mid-1880s, the Episcopal Church pioneered among mainline denominations by creating an American branch of the Christian Social Union, and the Church Association for the Advancement of the Interests of Labor, a church body that famously advanced research, public education, and legislative reform for millions of working Americans—even at a time when figures like J.P. Morgan were vastly more likely to serve as senior wardens than were ethnic blue-collar factory workers. The Episcopal Church, likewise, was among the founders of the Federal Council of Churches, that "social gospel" predecessor of the National Council of Churches that embodied the collective power of mainline Protestants willing to work for dramatic social change. When evangelical conservatives like Pat Robertson and Jerry Falwell brag about the influence the moral majority and Christian coalition have had on America, they would do well to look back on the work of the Federal Council to see what religion's power and influence over public life really means.

By 1913, the Episcopal Church's commitment to the social gospel was well enough established that its General Convention easily adopted the following resolution:

> Resolved, that we the members of General Convention of the Protestant Episcopal Church do hereby affirm that the Church stands for the ideal of social justice, and that it demands the achievement of a social order in which the social cause of poverty and the gross human waste of the present order shall be eliminated, and in which every worker shall have a just return for that which he produces, a free opportunity for self-development, and a fair share in all the gains of progress.... The Church calls upon every communicant, clerical and lay, so to act that the present prejudice and injustice may be supplanted by mutual understanding, sympathy, and just dealings, and the ideal of thorough-going democracy may be finally realized in our land.[16]

There were individual clergy as well, men such as William Dwight Perkins Bliss, author of the *Encyclopedia of Social Reform*, and Phillips Brooks, the great rector of Trinity Church, Boston, whose commitment to social reform and justice is still carried on by hundreds of students at my university today through Harvard's social service and social justice center, the Phillips Brooks House.[17]

And then there were figures like legendary economist Richard Ely, who founded the American Economic Association, and who for years was the most influential economist in America, his textbook outselling all others.[18] Ely was a devout Episcopalian, who refused to conceive of economics as a kind of social physics, considering it rather as "the rational organization of human and physical resources in pursuit of social justice"—a definition of economics I still find powerful today.

And of course there were the great public figures like Theodore Roosevelt, who used to teach Sunday school at the Episcopal church I now attend. President Roosevelt's brand of reforming Republicanism might have difficulty finding a home in the Republican Party today—but he represents a glorious past for that party that had been born with Lincoln, a party that saw social justice and political democracy as essential for the market economy it so admired. More than a few historians, it should be added, have traced the seeds of his Democratic cousin FDR's New Deal to Teddy's GOP administration 30 years earlier.

Let me hasten to mention also the importance of women—hundreds of thousands of them—to this social gospel era. Then as now, it is so often true that men do most of the talking while women do most of the lifting—and in this, the social gospel period was no exception. I could spend the next hour reviewing for you the vital role that women played in this proud history of national renewal, but let me mention just one, my favorite.

Just before World War I, Frances Perkins was a young Mt. Holyoke graduate, a middle-class Episcopalian inspired by the social gospel—but like many young people uncertain where or how to put her energy and commitment to use. Then, on a fateful morning in Manhattan, just blocks from where one day the World Trade Center would rise, she personally witnessed a tragedy that in its time and its own way profoundly reshaped America.[19] What she saw was the famous Triangle Shirtwaist fire, a disaster in which a high-rise garment factory suddenly exploded in flames, trapping its young seamstresses high above the street, thanks to doors illegally locked by the factory's owners. Hundreds of those women died, most from smoke and flames, but many others as they desperately jumped from open windows while helpless onlookers watched. In the wake of the Triangle Shirtwaist fire, a horrified and angry nation passed new worker- and workplace-safety laws, but, as importantly, in that moment Frances Perkins found her life's calling.

Out of the ashes and misery of that horrible moment, she was—I can think of no other word—reborn, and threw herself into the cause of social reform, worker's rights, and industrial safety with unquenchable passion. Over the next two decades, she became one of the most respected and admired reformers in the nation, a tireless woman who worked in New York with rising reform figures (and, I might immodestly mention, fellow Episcopalians) such as Franklin and Eleanor Roosevelt and Fiorello LaGuardia. Frances Perkins would ultimately become President Roosevelt's Secretary of Labor—the first woman ever appointed to a presidential cabinet. There she would preside over the passage of landmark legislation that included not only the first national minimum wage and the first federal guarantee of workers' right to organize, but the first national welfare safety net for women and children—and, not least in its importance, America's modern Social Security system itself.

Why have I dwelt at such length on the past for you, when the subject is the present and the future? Today, here in Burlington, you have gathered as the leaders of a proud and powerful church—a church that has given this country nearly a third of its Presidents and nearly half the Chief Justices of its Supreme Court.[20] Your agenda is to weigh, in this new millennium, what this church owes not only the nation, but the world.

To many of you, the task must seem daunting in its very scale—especially when the challenges within your own dioceses consume so much of your time and effort. But what I hope I have shown you today is that the issues you face are old, not new—and that, in its own past, the Episcopal Church has shown itself capable of leading reforms that have remade human history. And you yourselves, in supporting the Jubilee program for debt relief of the world's poorest countries, have already shown you are willing to take the first steps toward that new era of leadership.[21]

But Jubilee is in fact *only* a first step. As an economist, I know there are many like me who would gladly help you craft further steps, and identify for you the wealth of practical programs and proposals that now languish, ignored by all but development professionals. In those works, you would find models for a new kind of global development such as the United Nations Development Program's quite unutopian plan which, if implemented, could reduce the number of global poor by half in little more than a decade, and everywhere increase the opportunities for justice. But it is you who first must choose to make such steps a priority of this church, to declare in effect your commitment to making the coming decade for all Episcopalians what I would call "The Decade of Global Reconciliation."

Let me close on a personal note. I've come here today as an economist, to help you as religious leaders better understand and deliberate over this issue of "globalization." But my choice to be here has much deeper roots, and comes from the fact that my father served this church as a rector and priest for 52 years until his death from cancer a decade ago. Now, preachers' kids are notorious for knowing intimately the weaknesses and failings of the church, but we are also equally capable of seeing most intimately its capacity for greatness and majesty, and the beauty of the faith it seeks to uphold. Going through my father's papers after his death, I found the following quote of Reinhold Niebuhr's, copied out in my father's hand from what text I know not:

> Nothing worth doing is completed in our lifetime; therefore, we must be saved by hope. Nothing true or beautiful or good makes sense in any immediate context of history; therefore, we must be saved by faith. Nothing we do, however virtuous, can be accomplished alone; therefore we must be saved by love.

As I explained to you at the beginning of this talk, 5,000 children would die of needless malnutrition or disease by the time I stopped speaking. Those children are dead now. I hope that as bishops of a great church, you will take a moment now to let your hearts acknowledge their deaths. You cannot save those children, but you can save millions of others whose deaths are—without your choice not to lament, but act—already at this moment foretold. That power to save not a child, but literally millions of them, is, I assure you, within your hands.

NOTES

[1] This figure has been revised steadily downward. According to *The New York Times,* January 15, 2002, the death toll stood at 2,716.

[2] The World Health Organization, *World Health Reports* (Geneva, WHO: 1996, 1998) are the sources on overall death rates. As the reports note, nearly 50,000 men, women, and children are dying daily from infectious diseases alone, most of them preventable or curable for as little as a dollar per person—while half the world's population (nearly 3 billion people) suffer from diseases caused by contaminated water.

For more detailed study on multiple causes for death, and their distribution by age, sex, and region—and poverty's overwhelming central role—see C.J.L. Murray and A.D. Lopez, eds. *The Global Burden of Disease: A Comprehensive Assessment of Mortality and Disability from Diseases, Injuries, and Risk Factors in 1990 and Projected to 2020* (Cambridge: Harvard University Press, 1996). The study notes in passing that 90% of global health spending goes to the 10% of global population in advanced Western nations.

[3] UNICEF, *The State of the World's Children, 2001* (New York: UNICEF).

[4] Thomas Friedman, *The Lexus and the Olive Tree: Understanding Globalization* (New York: Farrar, Straus, Giroux: 1999), Chapter 6.

[5] Jared Diamond, *Guns, Germs, and Steel: The Fate of Human Societies* (New York: Random House, 1997). This Pulitzer-Prize-winning book provides a sweeping introduction to the long view of globalization.

[6] See David Landes, *The Wealth and Poverty of Nations* (New York: W.W. Norton, 1998) and Jeffrey Williamson, *Globalization and History: The Evolution of a Nineteenth-Century Atlantic Economy* (Cambridge: MIT Press, 1999).

[7] For the nineteenth-century press, see Michael Schudson, *Discovering the News* (New York: Basic Books, 1978); also Allan R. Pred, *Urban Growth and the Circulation of Information: The United States System of Cities, 1790–1840* (Cambridge: Harvard University Press, 1973).

[8] Tom Standage, *The Victorian Internet* (New York: Walker & Co., 1998).

[9] Data and their sources, in Jim Yong Kim et al., *Dying for Growth: Global Inequality and the Health of the Poor* (Cambridge: Institute for Health and Justice, 2000), 13.

[10] On Lumumba, see William Blum, *Killing Hope* (Monroe, ME: Common Courage Press, 1996); for a condensed introduction to Mobutu, see Kate Whiteman, "The Single-Minded Pursuit of Wealth," *Johannesburg Mail & Guardian*, 9/9/97, 1997, at www.mg.co.za/mg/news/97sep1/9sep-mobutu2.html.

[11] President Johnson allegedly made the remark about Rafael Trujillo of the Dominican Republic in 1965, during the United States invasion of that country.

[12] The literature on the subject is vast. For a comprehensive (but dated) analysis, see *The Church Committee report on CIA and related intelligence activities* (U.S. Congress. *Senate Select Committee to Study Governmental Operations with Respect to Intelligence Activities.* Final Report. 94th Cong., 2d sess. S. Report No. 94–755, 6 vols., Washington, DC: GPO, 1976). For an introduction to the sheer range of materials, see the website maintained by Loyola College on national intelligence, at www.loyola.edu/dept/politics/intel.html#USIC.

[13] Joseph Stiglitz, the World Bank's former chief economist, who also was chairman of President Clinton's Council of Economic Advisors, and who won the 2001 Nobel Prize in Economics, is among the most vocal critics of the "structural adjustment" legacy. Cf. Stiglitz, "More Instruments and Broader Goals: Moving Toward the Post-Washington Consensus," The 1998 WIDER lecture, Helsinki, Finland, 1/7/98, on the

Web at worldbank.org. (His term, "Washington consensus," is the same here as "structural adjustment programs.")

[14] These data, from various official sources, can be found in Kim, op. cit., Chapter 2.

[15] For a broad overview, sources are many:

A.I. Abell, *The Urban Impact on American Protestantism* (Hamden, CT: Archon, 1943).

Paul Carter, *Spiritual Crises of the Gilded Age.* (Dekalb: Northern Illinois University Press, 1971).

Kenneth Cauthen, *Impact of American Religious Liberalism* (New York: Harper & Row, 1962).

Robert Handy, *Social Gospel in America* (New York: Oxford University Press, 1966).

Charles Hopkins, *Rise of the Social Gospel in American Protestantism* (New Haven: Yale University Press, 1940).

William Hutchison, *Modernist Impulse in American Protestantism* (Cambridge: Harvard University Press, 1976).

Martin Marty, *Modern American Religion, v.1: the Irony of it All 1893–1919* (Chicago: Chicago University Press, 1986).

Henry May, *Protestant Churches and Industrial America,* rev. ed. (New York: Harper & Row, 1977).

Ronald White, and Charles Hopkins, *Social Gospel: Religion and Reform in a Changing America* (Philadelphia: Temple University Press, 1976). A short introduction is "Social Gospel" in the *Encyclopedia of American Religious Beliefs.*

[16] *Journal of the General Convention of the Protestant Episcopal Church in the United States of America, 1913* (New York: The Sherwood Press for the General Convention: 1988), 122. Also the website of St. Peter's, Charlotte, NC (www.st-petersweb.org/lesson26.html) offers a brief introduction.

[17] To rediscover Bishop Brooks, remembered today mainly for writing the verses for "O Little Town of Bethlehem," see John Wolverton, *The Education of Phillips Brooks* (Carbondale, IL: Univ. Of Illinois Press, 1995). For the texts of many of Brooks' sermons, see "The Unofficial Episcopal Preaching Resource Page," at www.edola.org/clergy/pbarchive.html.

[18] See Richard Ely's autobiography, *Ground Under Our Feet* (1938, reprinted Ayer Publishing, 1977), and, for an overview, J.R. Everett, *Religion in Economics* (1946; reprinted, Porcupine Press, 1982).

[19] Cf. Naomi Pasachoff, *Frances Perkins: Champion of the New Deal* (New York: Oxford University Press, 1999).

[20] For the religious affiliations of US Presidents and Supreme Court justices, see www.adherents.com/adh_presidents.html (for Presidents), and www.adherents.com/adh_sc.html (for justices). Note that the presidential site, however, incorrectly identifies Theodore Roosevelt's faith as Dutch Reformed; he was in fact a lifelong member of Christ Church, Oyster Bay, New York.

[21] On the Episcopal Church and Jubilee Year 2000, see www.episcopalchurch.org/ens/99-185D.html. On the larger ecumenical campaign of Jubilee Year 2000 and its work on debt relief for the world's poorest nations, see www.j2000usa.org.

4

GLOBALIZATION AND THE LEAGACY OF THE WEST

A CALL FOR MORAL IMAGINATION

LENG LIM

INTRODUCTION

L et me begin by thanking Professor Richard Parker for his presentation (See Chapter 3). It is so rare to hear an economist speak with a historical sensibility and a care for the human condition. It is a pity these days that specialization of disciplines leads to a divided view of the world, such that economists seem more interested in numbers than in the care of the human household (which is *oikonomia,* the Greek root for both *economics* and *ecumenical*). Long gone is the age of the moral philosopher *and* economist, Adam Smith, when the disciplines were intertwined. Well, if the economists are not capable of dealing with the existential, it's time for bishops to cross disciplines and become schooled in economics.

My presentation will be multidisciplinary. Although ostensibly about economics, it is about leadership and the singular importance of moral imagination.

At the beginning of this meeting, eighty-five bishops and thirty-eight spouses answered a survey I had prepared, and I shall be sharing some of the results here (See page 122 for survey). These results will act as a kind of mirror by giving you a sense of your own resources and limits, your capacities and shortcomings—but mostly, I hope, of leadership opportunities.

WHAT IS GLOBALIZATION?

Globalization has led to more than 1.5 trillion United States dollars being exchanged each day in the world's currency markets. It has led to the world trading about a fifth of the goods produced.[1] Globalization has enabled the countries of East Asia to grow, as the goods and services they produce find eager consumers in the U.S. market, whose consumption is the engine of growth in the world. Globalization is about the increase of trade, and hence of the gross national product (GNP) of the countries that export; it is about countries or regions specializing in sectors in which they have a competitive advantage, thus becoming capable of competing in a global market place. In my own native Singapore, export-led trade *and* globalization has brought about spectacular growth with a GNP per capita matching the First World. (On the flip side, Singapore has gone into a severe recession this year following the downturn in the United States economy.) Globalization is about the breakdown of national barriers, and the formation of one worldwide market for the trading of goods and services, a market with an increasingly seamless flow of capital, knowledge, people, and information.

At the same time, there is great disquiet about globalization, as shown in the protests in Seattle mounted against the World Trade Organization (WTO). While multinational corporations (MNCs) have contributed to the development of several countries, many fear their domination. Consider, for example, that General Electric (GE) had revenues in the year 2000 of $129.8 billion, which is equivalent to the GNP of Finland. GE's net income (i.e. profits) of $12.7 billion in 2000 was equivalent to the entire economic output of El Salvador.

Corporations thus rival nation-states in wealth. This in itself is not of concern, as the wealth generated by corporations becomes part of that nation's gross domestic product (GDP). Nor is there concern about the fact that corporations are responsible to their shareholders, who after all put their equity at risk and should be rewarded. Moreover, these shareholders eventually reinvest or spend in the community. We must not believe that shareholder, consumer, and community interests are inevitably in conflict. Well-performing companies are often able to serve all three.

What is of concern regarding multinational corporations is that the major shareholders—many of whom are large institutions or rich individuals—live primarily in First World countries, while workers of MNCs are spread throughout the globe, often in Third World countries. Human behavior being what it is, First World equity owners will inevitably act in their own, and consequently, First World interests. In the Asian financial crisis of 1997, we saw a herd-like mentality among First World investors (which included the Japanese), whose previous indiscriminate inflows (motivated by hopes of high returns, sometimes called greed) had funded some risky firms, and whose capital outflows (motivated by fear) imperiled some worthwhile firms.

The *Human Development Report 1999*, published by the United Nations Development Program,[2] captures the effects of globalization and lists the following areas of concern.

1. Social fragmentation and reversals in progress and threats to human security.

Driving this is the widening disparity in income. For example, the assets of the three richest people in the world are more than the combined GNP of the forty-eight least-developed countries. Furthermore, job and income insecurity due to technological change, financial volatility (illustrated by the Asian Financial crisis of 1997), and civil and global unrest exacerbated by corporate support of mercenary military groups, and environmental degradation threaten human communities.

2. The race for knowledge and technology widens the gap between the haves and have-nots.

While technology has led to higher productivity and connectivity between people and nations, its use and access is skewed towards the rich. The new rules of globalization—privatization, liberalization, and tighter intellectual property rights—marginalize the weak and more vulnerable communities.

3. The threats to the quality of care.

Care of the young and of families is essential to stability and economic progress. Yet the wage system of globalization has jeopardized such care: women leave their traditional roles to join the work force; governments cut back on welfare; the market rewards formal participation in the wage economy but not unpaid care. Yet, the economy (and businesses) depends on the unpaid care human beings render to other human beings. The modern economy, however, neither invests in, nor encourages such care. A threat to human communities results from a squeeze between the conflicting incentives to make money and time needed to care for loved ones.

4. The challenges of capturing global opportunities for nations.

Investments, and access to capital, generate economic growth. Yet in 1999, the richest 20% of nations captured 82% of foreign direct investment (FDI), while the poorest 20% captured only 1% of FDI.[3] But even when capital can be captured in portfolio investments, its volatility in the markets needs to be managed. The financial crisis of the 1990s hit the most vulnerable through loss of savings and jobs. But poorer nations who hope to capture the opportunities provided by globalization need expertise and leadership, which they often lack.

How, then, did the world economic system develop such that these negative effects of globalization now threaten the global human community?

How the West Succeeded in Getting it "Right"

In trying to come to grips with globalization, we are really coming to terms with the legacy of modern capitalistic Western (sometimes called Northern) nations, and how they have succeeded in generating such immense wealth and dominating power. This leads us to consider some important questions: *Do the West's economic and political principles form a model to be followed? If so, must its values and cultures be imitated as well? Can other nations and economies compete and win in the same way, or can they compete and win in a different way? Shall countries even compete?*

These questions occupy the imaginations and nightmares of people from Chiapas, Mexico, to Jakarta, Indonesia; they are encapsulated in incidents from the Boxer Rebellion to the Meiji Restoration in China; and they vex people from Gandhi (who once tried eating meat in order to discover if that was the secret to British strength) to, yes, Osama bin Laden. By other names, this legacy of the West has been known as colonization, Christian proselytization, modernization, secularization, capitalism, and now, globalization. (To be honest, the West itself struggles with these issues too.)

In the survey you participated in at the opening of the meeting, you were given a choice of possible causes for the success of Western cultures and economies, and asked to select all that apply.

Your responses were revealing. In close contention at the top of the list were: science and technology (75%); colonization (73%); and capital and free markets (70%). Almost 68% checked government and law. These were followed by slavery (56%); luck (46%); and Christianity (42%).

Clearly there is a wide range of opinion. We shall now explore some of these "causes."

Jared Diamond, in his Pulitzer Prize winning book *Guns, Germs, and Steel: The Fate of Human Societies*, painstakingly shows how, relative to the African and American continents, the Eurasian landmass was much more advantageous.[4] Eurasia started with a larger potential pool of domesticable large animals and cultivatable plants. Because it was the only continental landmass with an East-West axis, domesticated food sources spread much more quickly across the same temperate zone. In contrast, the continents of North and South America, and Africa, were oriented North-South. They thus spanned latitudinal zones with large climatic changes. For a plant or animal domesticated in the Northern hemisphere to spread to a similar climate in the Southern hemisphere, it had to make the impossible trek southward across the equator. Eurasia's earlier development of surplus food sources, due to its larger potential pool of domesticable large animals and cultivatable plants, had several consequences. Populations increased in Eurasia and with the population increase came the evolution of more complex societies with their steel weapons, technology, and writing, all of which formed the basis for effective domination.

Diamond asks us to imagine what would have happened if the rhinoceros of Africa could have been bred, tamed and trained, or that kangaroos in Australia could have been mounted like horses and used as cavalry. These would have formed the vanguard of an African or Aboriginal army that would have laid siege to Europe. But the wild beasts of Africa and Aboriginal Australia were not domesticable, and advancement did not take place. Diamond shows us clearly that different environments have endowed different people with different assets.

The early domestication of animals in Eurasia meant that Eurasian peoples succumbed to, became naturally resistant to, and eventually became carriers of fatal animal-borne diseases. When Europeans in 1492 encountered the indigenous people of the Americas, European diseases, like smallpox, led to the wholesale elimination of entire groups of New World people. The Hispaniola Indians went from 10 million people to zero in a period of 43 years, eliminated, as Diamond notes, not on the battlefield by swords, but in bed by European germs. Of course, while much of this was initially unintentional, there were occasions where native susceptibility to diseases was exploited as a matter of policy.

Now, the interesting question for me as an ethnic Chinese is why wasn't it *my* ancestors who came to colonize the world but yours? We too shared the Eurasian continent. After all, a full half-century *before* Columbus sailed to the New World in his leaky ships, the Chinese Admiral Cheng Ho (1405–1433) had sailed all the way to Africa with 27, 000 men in convoys of three-masted galleons. And the Chinese had even been able to bring back a giraffe (which they thought was a unicorn) to the Emperor. But a few decades after Cheng Ho, China was to completely lose all knowledge of maritime technology. The faction that had supported maritime exploration lost out at the imperial court, and the emperor outlawed all maritime technology. With that one fateful decision, China went backwards technologically, closing its doors to the world, until the West forced it to open up in the 1800s. By that time China no longer had the military or technological edge.

China had peered out into the world, found it barbaric and wanting, and withdrew into its own. As Chinese emperors have always proclaimed, "What China wants, it already has. Why trade?" In contrast, the European powers had had a taste of the world (literally, through the spice trade), and desired more.

In Columbus's Europe, the political situation was in a state of flux as competing princes and fiefs vied for power. This allowed for the contestation and retention of conflicting ideas. So when Columbus was turned down for his voyage by a potential patron, he simply went to the next possible, repeating this five times. Once Columbus proved that he was successful, everyone else followed his lead. Without diminishing the holocaust that ensued for our native brothers and sisters of the New World, the point here is that Europe had a capacity to generate ideas, and to *prove the winning one through contestation, competition, and results.*

Western expansion was of course greatly abetted by military technology. This summer I visited Shimoda, Japan, to enjoy its famous hot springs. As Shimoda was also the site of Admiral Perry's forcible opening of Japan, I went to see the local museum. In the museum were exhibited Perry's guns and pictures of the steamship that carried him to the East.

The point I want to make here is not so much that the West is a military aggressor, this had been true of almost every human group, but rather the West has the history of being a successful *technological innovator.* The Renaissance and its fruit, the Enlightenment, brought about the Industrial Revolution, followed by the electronic, nuclear, digital, and genomic revolutions. In fact, it is this scientific superiority upon which the West's economy, military, and society so deeply depend.

What then of this encounter with the West? What shall we make of it? Allow me to tell a story. As a teenager, I was always fascinated with the coat-of-arms in the center of the stained glass windows in the Nave of St. Andrew's Cathedral in my native Singapore. (The same St. Andrew's that has been the site of much mischief for the Episcopal Church in recent history.)[5] The crest is that of my high school, Raffles Institution. It is in the cathedral window *not* because my high school is a diocesan institution. Rather, the crest shines forth because it is the family emblem of Sir Stamford Raffles, the founder of modern Singapore, as well as of my high school. Raffles, apart from obviously being a colonialist, was first and foremost an employee of the British East India Company, having started as a lowly clerk and then rising through the ranks.

The East India Company founded many of the major cities and ports of the developing world, including Bombay, Calcutta, Hong Kong, and Singapore; it established factories from Sulawesi to Vietnam. It traded in everything: tea, coffee, spice, jewels, silk, porcelain, human labor, opium, furniture, and arms. The Company, which was no better than a motley crew of pirates in its early years, originated modern world trade, including bringing tea to England (thus giving the English their most cherished therapeutic tool). The Company contributed to the American Revolution with that same tea.

Colonization was first and foremost then an economic enterprise, though it was not always profitable as armies are expensive to maintain. British colonization of the world thus took place by means of a chartered trading company that had shareholders who raised funds for exploration and armies for domination. Only when the British East India Company's holdings became too big to be managed was it nationalized, so to speak, setting the groundwork for the British Empire. It is important to see the organizational, political, and entrepreneurial skills Europeans, particularly the British, employed in pursuit of domination. This should not excuse a certain rapaciousness in European colonization—my Indian friends remind me that the largest diamond in the world, the Koh-i-nor in the British crown, is stolen.

Economic enterprises like the British East India Company thus yielded sophisticated legal, financial, and organizational knowledge that continues to benefit the West. Because of their complexity and longevity, these economic enterprises also needed something other than pure greed to succeed. The refrain God, glory, and gain summarizes that curious mix of virtues (honor, vision, sacrifice, courage, and tenacity) and vices (greed, prejudice, cruelty, condescension, and arrogance) necessary for the business of colonization. While Cecil Rhodes, after whom a scholarship and a country were named, might have been a winner at business, there were also losers. For every two Englishmen who ventured into employment with the Company, only one survived to return. Raffles himself died penniless, and his widow was forced by the Company to pay for expenses he had incurred while on Company business.

As Episcopalians and Anglicans, our connection with the British East India Company, and therefore with this colonial legacy, comes together in the one person who gave us our church tradition, and who also gave the Company its charter: Elizabeth I, the Virgin Queen. Under the Elizabethan peace, the English spirit flourished, contributing to both the development of the Church of England, and Anglo-Saxon economics. Anthony Wild, in his readable book, *The East India Company*, says, "England had played a minor part in Catholic Europe. Now, a new English pride linked to the Protestant faith gave the country a sense of destiny to fuel its expansionist ventures."[6]

So here we have it: economics, religion, politics, and the history of the world for the last 400 years—my high school, the Prayer Book, our tea—all linked together. I have told you this multi-layered historical, global, and personal story to illustrate one point. Human beings derive morals out of the stories they tell. These morals, and the passions they stir, direct much of our group interactions.

What are the implicit morals in the story of the West? If one believes that the story of the West is all about the exploitation, destruction, and humiliation of non-Western, and/or non-Christian people, then a moral imperative might be the payment of reparations, or some pending comeuppance. (The *schadenfreude* implicit in post-September 11 comes from this hope for just deserts.) If one believes that the story of the West is about the pioneering discovery of reason and rights (or science, capital, and democracy) then the moral is that Western civilization is to be defended —*for the sake of the rest of the world.* And if one believes Jared Diamond's story, that the West got it "right" because of sheer chance through the good fortune of being geographically advantaged, then the moral of the story is luck. And if it was pure luck, what is the correct lesson? Winner keeps all, or winner shares some?

As people of faith, moreover, if we believe that God was involved in the history of the West, then what? Here, let us be cautious. Enough embarrassment has been made about God being on the side of the Christian West. But the question remains: What might God be calling us to recognize as we consider the legacy of the West: the past colonization, the present challenge of globalization (which some want to call neo-colonialism) and the future repercussions of the actions and counter-actions inevitably emanating from September 11?

I raise these questions about the kind of stories we as American Episcopalians tell ourselves, and what underlying morals we draw from these stories. As we seek to deal with globalization (and now the added weight of September 11) we are dealing with the continuing legacy of the West. And, like it or not, the Episcopal Church in the United States epitomizes the West, for we are Americans by nationality, English by temperament, Christian by belief, modern in sentiments, and wealthy (all of which does not elicit equanimity from others).

Inevitably, different people both inside and outside the Episcopal Church will want to emphasize different aspects of these stories. Those identified with the West will feel either triumph or regret, with its underlying pride or guilt, neither of which are terribly good for clear-headed action. Those identified with the non-West will have a sense of injury or envy, with their underlying anger or shame, neither of which is good for clear-headed development. And there are those from both sides who say they feel nothing because the past is the past. But their equanimity evaporates in bad times. Then, there are those like myself, identified with both worlds, who feel all these emotions at the same time.

It is impossible to make any of these stories *the* true story. From the perspective of a common humanity—perhaps that is God's point of view—all these stories about the West are true. We must embrace a "both/and," instead of an "either/ or" spirit. As such, we are to see the laudable and damnable as inseparable, and so our choice is to commit ourselves to a spiritual practice of continual thanksgiving and repentance.

As leaders of this church, we must continually develop the capacity for holding together the complexity of deep truths. We already do this in our religion. For is not the Cross of Jesus both defeat and victory? Is not the Eucharist both brutal sacrifice and welcoming banquet? Is not the encounter with the Holy both an experience of being damned and being embraced? Is not baptism both a dying and a resurrection? So, in embracing our legacy as Americans and as Anglicans, we are compelled to acknowledge the laudable and the damnable in ourselves. If we can prevent ourselves from either browbeating others or chest-thumping ourselves, but look unflinchingly at the mirror, we might gain some humility, clarity, and strength. In so doing we will give the world much needed hope *that the mighty and wealthy can be transformed by grace and wisdom.*

WHAT WE HAVE TODAY

What the West has developed is a wealth-creating market economy. The market economy is a system of exchange, where individuals or groups work to maximize self-interest and create a dynamic of demand and supply. This dynamic in turn efficiently allocates resources where they are put to the best use. Adam Smith, on recognizing how self-interest was transformed by the market to serve the common good, almost deified this mechanism by calling it the Invisible Hand. (There are some real shortcomings to this system, which I shall discuss later, mainly having to do with the "hand" being powerful but indiscriminate, rational but not conscious.) We are perhaps too distant from the Old World to recognize the historical achievement of the market economy: it broke the back of feudalism and clericalism, with their entitlements based on birth and breeding. In this historical, rather than ideological, context, I think of the market economy as promoting freedom and opportunity.

One remarkable feature of this Western market economy is the technology that is created by firms (together with universities, research institutions, and their funding sources). An outcome of these technological breakthroughs is *economies of scale*, that is, large-scale production of goods at ever-lower (marginal) costs. Firms that do such push out high-cost firms. At the same time, firms who have achieved scale go beyond their domestic markets to seek newer and bigger markets for their goods, thus spurring greater import and export activities.

One of the remarkable achievements of this technological drive is that the one persistent problem of humanity through the ages has been solved, namely, the shortage of food. That people still starve is not because there is not enough food to go around, but that *access* to food is uneven, an occasion where the market is blind and unconscious.

The market economy is positivistic, in that it is not deontological. (So, when bishops make the moral argument that workers *ought* to be paid a living wage, you get a wry smile from those who know you are not as level headed as they are.) Yet, what the positivists will not readily allow is that the market economy rests upon, indeed requires, a normative base in order to do business. The normative base is made up of concepts (e.g., rule of law, contracts, private property), institutions (e.g., government, regulatory bodies, schools, church), and core beliefs/values (e.g., nature as a resource to be exploited, personal hard work, individual freedom and effort) that are grounded on a deontological (i.e. what is morally good), and ontological (i.e. who we are as human beings) foundation.

Our society therefore requires two paradoxical processes to be at work. The market economy quantifies resources and people, whose only value is the monetary wealth they can create. A business that is altruistic, therefore, cannot survive in the economic jungle of competition. Yet, for all of its impersonal and amoral nature, the market economy requires a human society with values—mutual good will, self-sacrifice, cooperation, and love—in order to exist. Indeed,

113

outside of the market place, human beings build communities so that they are not in the jungle of brutish *quid pro quo* exchanges. To the extent that the market economy imposes its positivistic way of life onto the normative base, the market will undermine itself by tearing apart the human fabric of society. To the extent that the normative base tries to make the market economy operate on some preferred value, say by legislating equality in market outcomes, it distorts market signals, and eventually threatens prosperity.

Put another way: there are two causes of poverty. The first is that there is not enough wealth creation, i.e. the market economy is not functioning well. The second cause of poverty is that whatever wealth is created is not distributed, i.e. the normative base is not working well. A distributive system that does not allow for the generation of wealth by individuals, or groups of individuals, consigns the entire nation to poverty, as in Mao's China. On the other hand, when wealth is concentrated only in the hands of the few (as in Duvalier's Haiti, and increasingly in the U.S. and the world), we have widespread poverty. The subject of debate is the choice of a system that strikes a balance between wealth creation and wealth distribution. It is important that religious leaders like us recognize the need for both.

WHAT IS WRONG?

What then is wrong with this market economy we have created in the West, and which the rest of the world feels compelled either to imitate or repudiate? Allow me to name six difficulties:

1. Externalities

Externalities are costs not captured or incurred by the market, or by the actors who created the costs. For example, people living downstream from a polluting firm suffer the cost of contamination, but the firm does not directly pay for those costs. Externalities and benefits of technology are distributed differently. Thus, an automated car factory produces cheaper cars, to the benefit of a large group of consumers, but the externality of that technological change is borne by a select group of retrenched workers. A system may externalize people by defining them as outside the system, as with slaves and illegal immigrants. Moreover, as Margaret Meade, the eminent anthropologist who was also an Episcopalian, has pointed out about our high-technology driven economy, "The unadorned truth is that we do not need now, and will not need later, much of the marginal labor—the very young, the very old, the very uneducated, and the very stupid."[7] However, externalities can translate into painful political and social costs.

2. Boom and bust cycles

A boom cycle occurs when the price of a good is inflated over its fundamental value. When a correction takes place, we get a bust. Over the history of capitalism, we have had several of these. There was the Dutch Tulip Bulb Mania of the seventeenth century that made the tulip bulb surpass the price of gold. There was Japan's real estate boom of the 1980s, followed by a bust from which they are still trying to recover. Most recently for us in the United States we have had a dot com boom, followed by a "dot bomb" bust. In any boom or bust cycle, there are big winners and big losers, with concomitant social and political consequences.

3. Schumpeter's technology wave

Joseph Schumpeter, a prominent economist, coined the termed "creative destruction" to show that technology destroyed but also created new value. He showed that technological change comes in cycles, but that over time, the cycles get shorter and shorter. The implication of shorter cycles is that the dislocation to human communities now takes place more frequently, creating great stress to the social fabric. Those who can *constantly* adapt, whether they are individuals, communities, or nation-states, and who can *continually* learn the new technology will get ahead, but those who cannot fall behind, sometimes terribly so.

The world community is beginning to recognize that some countries are going to be failed states for a long time to come—Cambodia, Haiti, Afghanistan, Sierra Leone. These states will find it a challenge to have any semblance of civil society, let alone one that can continually learn and adapt. As such, the promise of globalization becomes weaker for them.

4. Technological overreach

Our technological breakthroughs have outdistanced our ability to manage them, whether we are speaking of nuclear and biological weapons or genetic engineering. At the psychological level, human beings now deal with the threat of annihilation by our own hands. Even the positive products of technology pose a challenge. Our human ability to modify the very fabric of DNA calls into question our ontological and epistemological underpinnings. Is God really dead and are we now a self-authoring species? So while technological science races ahead, we lag in our ontology, epistemology, ethics, institutional processes, and psychological ability to comprehend.

5. The powerful write the rules of the game

The global marketplace contains a system of rules about how the game is to be played, but not everyone gets to write the rules. Most recently the Organization for Economic Cooperation and Development (OECD), made up of rich countries, gathered in secret to create the Multilateral Agreement on Investments (MAI). The OECD was about to foist the MAI on the world as a *fait accompli*. It would have limited the ability of governments to set rules controlling foreign corporations. Instead, foreign corporations would have had the ability to sue national governments. This would have undermined the ability of governments to set domestic policies, and for citizen groups to hold foreign corporations accountable. The MAI was eventually shelved when Public Citizen exposed the plan of the OECD.

6. *Stalin's observation*

Stalin said that one dead person is a tragedy, but a million dead people is a statistic. His observation that human beings become callous to huge tragedies is accurate—and the biggest challenge we face. Take, for example, the global HIV/AIDS pandemic. In the 1990s I found myself spurred to action because I had friends who were dying from AIDS. But today I am numb to the reality of the millions who are dying from AIDS in Africa. Why? First, I do not know these sufferers. While I am aware that Jesus in Matthew 25 asks us to seek him in the faces of the hungry, thirsty, and naked (i.e. the totally disenfranchised), I find this vision fleeting. I have what the Buddhist tradition describes as an ignorant dualistic mind that falsely separates me from you, us from them. Secondly, I also find that the human mind naturally protects against trauma. It is impossible to consider the existential horror that several thousand children will have died from hunger by the time this presentation is over. Every minute of my overeating, some child is dying of hunger. Therefore Stalin was right, we are rendered inactive by huge tragedies because we find ourselves reducing them to statistical data points. If the church is to be effective in "waging reconciliation," we must find a way to put a human, dare I say incarnate, face on global tragedies.

WHAT CAN BE DONE? THE ROLE OF LEADERSHIP AND MORAL IMAGINATION

The most important need in this historical moment is leadership and moral imagination. Imagination is everything. The economy that we have been discussing is an imagined structure. The constituent parts that make it up were created by folk who had new ideas and who imagined new ways to organize the world.

Consider how banks evolved, those seemingly stodgy places. A handful of people gives you several bars of gold for safekeeping for which you issue a receipt. Soon people start exchanging those paper receipts instead of gold, and paper money has been imagined. Later, someone comes to borrow some gold from you, which you lend out using a piece of paper. Soon you realize that the gold deposits are hardly ever redeemed all at the same time. Because of this, you start lending out more notes than you actually have gold to back up. So long as everyone believes you will pay back their deposits when they want it, they will not all withdraw at the same time. You get to make a lot more loans (and profitable interest) from your much smaller pool of assets. Now and then, however, a crisis takes place in the economy, and people, imagining the worst, demand their deposits all at once. You then go bankrupt. But, after having been bankrupt a few times (over several hundred years, to be exact), you get the government to guarantee the deposits by acting as the lender of last resort, and thus is born insurance. This is a very short history of banking, a process that is still developing, mainly by the creative force of imagination.

Imagination is the driving force. The move from feudalism to the market economy was imagined. The move from monarchies to democracies, with constitutions and independent judiciaries, was imagined. The Christian church has participated in creating this imagined world. It abetted slavery, imagining Africans to be less than human. When Christians believed differently, the church imagined the abolition of slavery. Likewise, the church initially stood idly by, and then participated wholeheartedly and imaginatively in the civil rights movement in the United States.

"The lamb shall lie down with the wolf and a little boy will lead them." Imagined.

"We believe that all men are created equal...." Imagined.

"I have a dream, that one day, little white children and little black children will walk hand in hand..." Imagined.

Everything is imagined, even the physical world, even us. We are the creation of God's imagination. When we imagine, we share in the creative life of God. Creation is a choice God makes.

We know that moral imagination dies when we say we have no choice. Because of past insult or injury, or the fear of some future indignation or injustice, we say to ourselves that we have no choice but to_____. And here we can fill in the blank with our favorite way to retaliate, or be victimized. Moses said to the ancient Israelites: "Thus says the LORD: I set before you life and death. Choose life that you might live."

In a culture and economy like ours that touts freedom of choice, we end up not really choosing anything that might matter. Shall it be Gap or Banana Republic? Republican or Democrat? Sushi or egg roll? The moment of true choice, when it comes, is stillborn, drowned out by our distracted fears and passions.

This past year I have struggled with forgiveness; forgiveness of my parents, of my intimate relationships, of this church. In the instances in which I was convinced that I was in the right and had every reason to walk away, I came to the realization that walking away was a choice. And I could choose to stay. Life, therefore, must be chosen. Moral imagination is a choice, a fork on the road to be consciously chosen.

The United Nations Development Program (UNDP) report says that the world's 200 richest people doubled their assets to $1 trillion between 1994 and 1998. Can you imagine yourselves getting to know 1% of those 200 people and asking them to give away 1% of their income? That would be $100 million per year. Now, such folk might not give it to the Episcopal Church—we are too small to merit such a huge infusion of cash. But they might give it to something larger —something beyond denominationalism or the institutional church, something worthy of $100 million. Perhaps our fundraising efforts are not imaginative enough because we dream small private dreams?

So what else dare we imagine?

Can we imagine answering Stalin? Can this church imagine putting a stop to the sentimentalizing, sacralizing, and sterilizing of pain and suffering, and instead help develop some practical spiritual tools to enlarge our capacity for bearing pain? Consider how hard it is to speak honestly about the pain we bear as individuals, let alone as leaders. Pain—from loneliness, sadness, betrayal, death, fear, cowardice, and failure—is a taboo subject, especially in the culture of the United States. A person in pain reeks of vulnerability, a state sorely to be avoided, especially by men. But rather than shutting down, shutting out, and shutting up, it is incumbent upon our spiritual practice to enlarge our own capacities for bearing pain with consciousness and awareness. It is time we started being honest and courageous enough to share with each other how we bear pain. Our gatherings, on Sundays and in meetings like these, might become a little more real and fruitful if we could share real techniques for living with pain. (Those same techniques would also allow us to live with greater joy.) Sometimes I wish we as professionals in the church would care less about orthodoxy (i.e. arguing about right beliefs) and care more about orthopraxy (i.e. delivering a workable method that we have genuinely tried ourselves, for helping people along the path).

Can we imagine a response to economic man, to the dreary acquisition of more things? St. Francis, our Amish brothers and sisters, and Gandhi imagined and demonstrated another way to be human, another way to organize communities—the path of renunciation. How can we support those who hear this call? (Francis after all, did have patrons.)

Or if renunciation is not our path, can we imagine a way to engage the economic structures? The Episcopal Church has impacted the market economy by working on shareholder-firm relationships, through proxy resolutions calling for socially responsible investments. This church was a leader in movement for divestment in South Africa during that country's apartheid era, and was responsible for starting the Interfaith Center for Corporate Responsibility. We already impact firm-household relationships (through livable wage initiatives) and household-financial institution relationships (through establishing credit unions). The Anglican Communion's participation in the movement for global debt relief, particularly the work of the Washington office of the Episcopal Church, was also a fabulous piece of imaginative leadership.

Likewise, the church has also had an effect, for good and for ill, on the normative base of the economy. It has provided the theological premise that the environment is a force to be subdued, thereby paving the way for the earth to be reduced to a set of commodified and commercialized resources. But as humanity faces up to the reality of species extinction and climate change, we in the Christian tradition are slowly beginning to imagine ourselves not as lords of the earth, but as its stewards. In so doing we are beginning to change the underlying paradigm and core values surrounding ecology and economy. Imagination at work again.

To impact the underlying structures of the economy, we will have to imagine partnering with non-governmental organizations (NGOs) and citizen groups. The United Nations *Human Development Report* says that there is a need for the reinventing of governance (particularly protecting people during periods of transition), imposing rules of conduct on corporations, redefining what is meant by human development, and reducing global crime and protecting cultural diversity. Furthermore, the bargaining position of poor countries needs to be strengthened vis-à-vis international institutions to enable them to take advantage of globalization through the establishment of an ombudsman mechanism in the World Trade Organization (WTO).[8]

Can you imagine such an engagement with these salient global issues? Four years ago, I was in China with the Peace and Justice Commission and the Social Responsibility in

Investment Committee of the Episcopal Church to meet with the China Christian Council (which represents all Protestant churches in China). The leaders of the China Christian Council requested that the Episcopal Church sponsor a visit of Chinese politicians to the United States in order that these leaders might better understand the role of religion in civic society. I do not think we responded. This was a pity, particularly in light of the fact that Pat Robertson was recently in China holding meetings with Chinese Premier Zhu Rongji to discuss religion in China. We get invited but do not take up the offer while it seems that others imagine big things and accomplish much.

In earlier decades in the industrial West, corporations, government, and labor unions, supported by leaders of civic society (pre-eminently the Christian church) agreed to the creation of welfare systems with safety nets to reduce income inequality (invariably bad for labor) and labor strife (invariably bad for business). Today, the globalizing world economy is at a threshold where it must create global institutions and processes that will decrease extreme poverty and deprivation, thus minimizing strife and desperation while increasing participation in the system. But the question is: who will step forward to be leaders in making the global economic order more just and fair? Can we imagine ourselves doing this?

The church must therefore actively seek a voice in the setting of economic rules. (Indeed, the first accounting rules were created/imagined by a monk in the sixteenth century.) It is incumbent that the Episcopal Church, together with other religious organizations and NGOs, pressure the rule-making institutions (like the WTO) to actively incorporate new rules that address the issues in which churches have an interest: the environment, women and children, and the preservation of indigenous cultures. Can the Episcopal Church, long a symbol of the establishment, imagine working with Roman Catholic prelates to gain a formal voice in the deliberations of the economic councils of the world? The United Nations allows for an Anglican Observer; the WTO, World Bank, and International Monetary Fund can surely have one too. Self-interest alone necessitates that those who seek to gain from globalization incorporate the views of the potential losers. The churches (and mosques and temples too) can represent the voices of those who are most at risk in the face of globalization.

Can you imagine the friends you will need to do this work? Returning to the survey you completed at the opening of this meeting, I asked you to list other religious leaders (except Jewish and Christian leaders) whom you count as your friends.

Once again, your answers were revealing. The largest group of respondents (forty percent) indicated no friendships with other religious leaders outside the Jewish or Christian religions. Thirty-three percent are friends with Muslim leaders. Buddhist, B'hai, and Hindu friendships represented five, three, and two percent respectively. A few responses noted Wiccans, Native American, Jain, and Mormon leaders.

While the survey indicates that you have gone out of your way to befriend Muslim leaders, I wonder if the numbers would be the same if it were not for the crisis of September 11. Can you imagine continuing to move out of the Christian-Jewish milieu to befriend other religious leaders?

When I was about twenty-two years of age, I went hitchhiking around Malaysia with a friend. One evening, we were picked up by a Malay-Muslim guy, who had a penchant for driving too fast while chanting the Koran. This man insisted that we visit his family. And so we were welcomed into a one-room hut with a hole in the ground for drainage. Ten members of his family crowded into this hut. I sat nervously, a Chinese Christian in a Malay-Muslim home, and remembered the race riots that had broken out twenty years before between our communities. Suddenly the man's father asked,

"What is your religion?"

"Christian," I said hesitantly.

Then he loudly proclaimed, "It doesn't matter what your religion is, there is one God."

Meanwhile, someone went out to buy us a dinner of curried meats. Shortly after dinner, we were sent on our way. Such unconditional generosity and grace! I believed that I had seen in the face of the "other" one of those angels whom Abraham had hosted. That encounter has stayed with me as a powerful experience of the unity of religions and the unity of humankind.

Can you imagine the kind of exposure to the wider world that you will need in order to lead in this time of globalization? Can you imagine requiring this kind of leadership exposure to the world of new candidates for the priesthood? Can we require that postulants spend six months in Africa or Asia on mission work? If the Mormons can do it, why cannot we? (What is the point of requiring fidelity to our left/liberal, or right/conservative positions if these positions are in turn too narrow to be of use in the coming century?) What would it be like for bishops to imagine traveling and working in other parts of the non-Western world in order to be a better episcopal presence here at home?

The survey you completed asked you to list countries outside of North America and Europe in which you have vacationed. At the top of the list were Israel (26), followed by Honduras, Japan, and Mexico (11 each).[9] Among those at the bottom of the list, with one each, were Afghanistan, Chile, Iran, and Zimbabwe. Most countries in Asia, Africa, and Latin America, however, did not even appear on the list. In addition, eleven of the respondents, said they have never vacationed outside of North America or Europe. Finally, 64% of those who answered the survey said they had never worked overseas.

I invite you to discuss the implication of this data. What countries are you paying attention to? How comfortable are you in traveling outside of a Western milieu? What are you curious about? In review of your patterns of travel I do want to turn your attention to four things.

First, only one person responding to the survey has visited my native Singapore. Now for the Archbishop of Singapore to have done so much mischief in the Episcopal Church, USA these past two years with the illegal consecration of missionary bishops, I am surprised you were not more interested, or curious about what Singapore is really like. What lies at the heart of your non-curiosity?[10]

Second, no one has been to Indonesia, a wonderful tourist destination, and also the world's largest Muslim nation. Malaysia too is missing from the list, which by many accounts may be considered the most successful Muslim nation.

Third, China is going to be a major player this coming century, and apart from our old historical ties through Bishop Ting and the China Christian Council, we have very little contact or investment in that country's religious awakening.

Fourth, more than twice as many have been to Israel as have crossed the border into neighboring Mexico. I suppose Israel is familiar because it is biblical and Mexico is not because it is Latin American.

You and I know that much of ministry is about being present. For those of us who pride ourselves on being well-spoken, it comes as a mild insult that, short of a terrible sermon, individuals care less what we say and more what we do. Parishioners care that deacons, priests, and bishops show up and are present—by the hospital bedside, returning phone calls, and writing notes. On your parish visitation, it is less your eloquence that matters (though that helps keep folks engaged), but your episcopal presence. Can you imagine being present in other parts of the world in a similar manner? Can you imagine the whole Episcopal Church also being present to the wider world?

There is a billboard in downtown San Francisco that I see on my way to work that says: "Leaders follow leaders." Returning to the survey one final time, you were asked to list political and business leaders you count as friends and/or acquaintances. Your responses are shown in the following summaries.

Political Friends/Acquaintances

President of the World Bank	1
Current U.S. President	3
U.S. Supreme Court Justice	1
U.S. Senators	33
U.S. Congress	41
Secretary of State	7
U.S. Cabinet Member	1
National Security Director	1
Tribal Chiefs	2
Senate Foreign Relations Committee	1
Governors	25
Lt. Governors	2
State Senators	30
State Assembly	12
Attorney General	4
Mayor	36
Judges	5
Chief of Police/Sheriff	4
None listed:	7 (8%)

Business Friends/Acquaintances

- 105 CEOs of large and small firms are considered your friends and/or acquaintances.

- Of these CEOs, 23% are in banking (mainly local); 13% in manufacturing; and 12% in oil and energy.

- The companies of these CEOs include familiar names: Dupont, MCI WorldCom, General Dynamics, Monsanto, Proctor & Gamble, Chase, American Airlines, Cisco, Boeing, Morgan Stanley, Ford, Buick, Pepsico, Merck, ARCO.

- 23% of the 85 bishops polled did not have any CEO contacts.

What is missing from your CEO list is the entire technology (apart from Cisco), venture capital, biomedical, consulting, and investment banking (apart from Morgan Stanley) sectors. And of course, the old Episcopalian staple, JP Morgan, is missing. By the way, we used to be quite good at this. An early founder and patron of Harvard Business School was William Lawrence, Bishop of Massachusetts, and cousin to then President Lowell of Harvard. Which religious groups do you think are at Harvard Business School today?

I invite you to make your own assessments about your network of political and business leaders. What is pertinent to me here is that if you do not know any politicians or CEOs, there is one less religious leader they could potentially have as a friend or counselor. Perhaps they seek out other religious leaders. But what if they do not? Who then ministers to them? You know from your own experience that leadership is extremely lonely.

Three years ago, I was on a panel sponsored by the South American Missionary Society. In the panel, I was privileged to hear the Bishop of Pakistan speak. He urged us not to forget the poor. But he also raised this question: "Why did English missionaries go to Pakistan and elsewhere preaching the gospel to the poor, but then upon returning to England only drink gin and play croquet with the upper classes? Why were they not also preaching the gospel to the rich in their home country?" He then urged us not to forget the rich, noting that one of the richest families in the world, who lives in Buckingham Palace, is also one in the most need of the good news.

Quite apart from *quid pro quo* relationships with corporate leaders, I urge you to consider simple unconditional friendship with rich people. This, after all, was what Jesus did. I have in mind Jesus with the Samaritan woman at the well, engaging in simple mutually self-revelatory conversation, where in the end, both the woman (who found her water of eternal life) and Jesus (who found a good drink) were both mutually transformed and nourished by the encounter. Let us do that. And, let us *not* be too sure that they are the Samaritans and we are Jesus.

THE DESTINY OF THE WEST

In closing, I ask that you reconsider some of the questions and issues with which we have been wrestling. How many of you believe that the United States will be the preeminent power in the next ten years? In the next twenty-five, fifty, or hundred years? What will life be like for your grandchildren? What will be the next area of crisis? Even if the United States and the West remain dominant, who will be the rivals to American influence in the world? If our leaders are pitted in conflict, should our people follow? Who will these people be anyway? Think about your friendships with other religious leaders. Will their communities in other parts of the world be new sources of misunderstanding, hatred, and grief? Are your bonds with other religious leaders from around the world deep and tight enough that you and they might bridge the gap between our respective cultures? If not, do you trust CEOs and politicians to have the vision to work for peace?

We started out by discussing the legacy of the West. Therefore, we must end by examining the corollary: what is the destiny of the West?

What is the West to do in the coming years as it inevitably becomes more prosperous, while other parts of the world grow much poorer? What will the United States do and what will the Episcopal Church do in such a situation? How can we as American Christians in the Anglican tradition become agents for building bridges so that new bonds of affection become the bulwarks against ongoing conflict in the wider world?

This unsettling question about destiny might be ignored if the United States were some third-rate power, but it is not. Answers to the question about the destiny of the West thus cannot be left to an uncritical dependence on nationalism.

Nationalism, like any human attribute, is both positive and negative (or, in theological language, sinful). Positively, nationalism allows human beings the grace to go beyond their individual selves by sacrificing for a community. But nationalism also has the unfortunate sinful effect of pitting one community against another. Nationalism, and its corollary patriotism, are not sufficient to guide us into the future.

Our collective history as human beings is pointed towards ongoing globalization. But that globalization has to go beyond economics. It needs to be a new *oikonomia*—a new ecumenism and a new economy for the common household of our collective humanity. This *oikonomia* must not only generate wealth, it must alleviate poverty; it must not only honor the ambitions of the able, but the hopes of the marginal; it must not only give us a common economic or political framework, but must honor the diversity of cultures; it must not only forward our own Western self-interests (to believe otherwise is to be naïve), it must also honor the hopes and humbleness of others (to believe otherwise is to be myopic). We in the West must imagine such an *oikonomia*, and sacrifice to make it a reality. Not to do so is to lose our legacy.

QUESTIONS FOR THE ECONOMICS OF GLOBALIZATION PRESENTATION

Dear Bishops and Spouses,

Please fill out this short survey. We will share some of the results of this during Saturday's presentation on globalization. Thank you.

Yours truly
The Rev'd Leng Lim

Personal Data:
Province: 1 2 3 4 5 6 7 8 9
Gender: Male Female
Race, Ethnic or Cultural identification:
Citizenship:
Bishop or Spouse:

Questions for Consideration:

1. Who are the CEOs you know as acquaintances and/or friends? Please list them by their company and industry only. No personal names.

2. Who are the political leaders (elected or appointed) you know as acquaintances and/or friends? Please list them by their titles. No personal names.

3. Who are the religious leaders from non-Christian and non-Jewish traditions whom you know as acquaintances and/or friends? Please list them by religion and title. No personal names.

4. What countries, other than those in North America and Europe, have you lived or worked in? For how long?

5. What countries, other than those in North America and Europe, have you traveled or vacationed in? For how long?

6. What are the causes for the success of American and European cultures and economies? Please check all that applies.
    a. Luck
    b. Slavery
    c. Colonization
    d. Science
    e. Inherent attributes of American and European cultures. Identify attributes.
    f. Government and law
    g. Christianity
    h. Capitalism and free markets
    i. Other

7. Globalization has benefited me and my family. Yes. No. Unsure.

8. Globalization has benefited the Church. Yes. No. Unsure.

9. Globalization has benefited the USA. Yes. No. Unsure.

10. Globalization has benefited the world. Yes. No. Unsure.

11. Economic doctrine states that this is a world of scarcity, but that human needs are unlimited. Do you believe this to be true or false?

12. The most important issue facing my ministry is:

13. The most important issue facing the Church is:

14. The most important issue facing the world is:

NOTES

[1] *Human Development Report 1999* (New York: UNDP/Oxford University Press, 1999), 1. Also available at: www.undp.org/hdro/report.html

[2] Ibid.

[3] Ibid., 2.

[4] Jared Diamond, *Guns, Germs, and Steel: The Fate of Human Societies* (New York: Norton and Company, 1999).

[5] It was in St. Andrew's Cathedral that Anglican Archbishops Moses Tay of Southeast Asia and Emmanuel Kolini of Rwanda irregularly consecrated in January 2000 "missionary bishops" Charles Murphy and John Rogers for the Episcopal Church, USA.

[6] Anthony Wild, *The East India Company* (London: Harper Collins, 1999), 11.

[7] Willis Harman, *Global Mind Change* (New York: Institute of Noetic Science, 1998), 157.

[8] *Human Development Report 1999*, 1.

[9] These results are in total numbers rather than percents.

[10] I have lived in the United States for 18 years. I love this country and its culture. It has blessed me with so much, and I have tried to return in kind with service to its people. But, whether it has been in the inner cities, or in the hallowed halls of the Ivy League, my one singular complaint—actually, more like a hurt and chagrin—is this lack of curiosity about the rest of the world among those born in the United States. Americans sometimes remind me of my ancient Chinese ancestors—self-contented and happy to be isolated.

A few days after September 11, I had conversations with some of my international friends who live here in the United States. And we said, "It's finally happened." Many Americans find this sentiment to be astounding, not unlike President Bush's incredulous comment: "How-can-they-hate-us, don't-they-know-who-we-are?" I do not intend to get into the reasons for the hate among various people for the United States—some of it is reasonable, a lot of it is spurious—because the validity of these reasons are not the issue. The issue is the incredulity at our reaction, for it bespeaks an American disconnection with the world.

5

MISSION IN THE MIDST OF SUFFERING

THE "BLEAK IMMENSITY" OF HIV/AIDS, A SOUTH AFRICAN PERSPECTIVE

DENISE M. ACKERMANN

FRAGMENTS FROM THE LIVES OF TWO WOMEN OF FAITH

"**W**hen I was pregnant my partner left me. Perhaps he was afraid that I was HIV because he was. I only found out just before my baby was born. I was given nevirapine. I have lost two jobs. First I was a domestic worker and then I worked in a laundry. The laundry boss forced all the staff to be tested. I knew it was against my constitutional rights, but what could I do? So I was dismissed unfairly. Ten days ago I was attacked on my way home by two youngsters. They had knives and they made me take off all my clothes. "A man has to have sex when it is raining," the one said. But I fought hard and in the end they left me. I told them that I had not seen their faces, so they did not kill me. But today I am so, so happy. I have just heard that my baby is negative. My child will have a life. God is good." Thembisa, a 26-year-old Xhosa woman.

"He married me when I was only 18. He knew he was positive. I did not know until my baby was tested. Then I found out that I was also positive. I knew it was him. He married me because I was a virgin. He believed that if he slept with a virgin he would be cured. I walked out. Now I counsel women who are HIV positive. There is life after infection." Boniswa, a 35-year-old AIDS counselor.

A "BLEAK IMMENSITY"[1]: HIV/AIDS IN SOUTH AFRICA

Speaking about HIV/AIDS in my context is fraught with apparent anomalies. It should be quite straightforward. Clinically speaking, HIV/AIDS is a sexually transmitted disease. The fact that it can also be spread by the transfusion of infected blood or blood products is incidental. As our pandemic escalates, these means of transmission play an ever-decreasing role. The AIDS virus is a weak virus that cannot survive exposure to the environment. HIV/AIDS can only continue if the causal pattern of sexual behavior is present. In the normal course of events, people who do not exhibit such patterns of sexual behavior run no risk of contracting AIDS. Unlike pandemics of past times, which spread by means of droplet infection, AIDS isn't easy "to catch."[2] As I said, it seems quite simple. Yet the AIDS pandemic in South Africa is a complex mixture of issues. Gender inequality, attitudes towards human sexuality, the scarring and fragmentation of large sections of society, our history of migrant labor and uprooting of communities exacerbated today by increased poverty, unemployment, and denial by the state, are all part of the South African AIDS story.

The statistics are a nightmare.[3] According to the joint United Nations Program on HIV/AIDS (UNAIDS), in 2000 there were approximately 40 million people living with HIV/AIDS of whom 26 million were in sub-Saharan Africa. "In the past decade 12 million people in sub-Saharan Africa have died of AIDS—one-quarter being children."[4] In South Africa there are approximately 1,500 new infections a day.

UNAIDS reported in June 2000 that 4.7 million (that is one in nine) South Africans are living with HIV/AIDS.[5] In the previous year, this agency had reported that 19.94 percent of fifteen year olds in South Africa were infected with HIV/AIDS.[6] According to the Medical Research Council of South Africa (October 2001), 40 percent of deaths occurring in the year 2000 of people between the ages of 15 and 40 were due to AIDS-related diseases. If the pandemic continues unchecked, 10 million South Africans will have died from AIDS-related diseases by 2010. In Gauteng and KwaZulu/Natal, one in three mothers visiting antenatal clinics is infected. Approximately 5,000 infected babies are born every month. "There are no longer *any* South Africans who do not know someone or of someone who has died of AIDS or is living with HIV."[7] Over the next ten years, 35 percent to 46 percent of medical insurance's expenditure will be directed towards coping with AIDS-related diseases. Our fragile economy will buckle under the ravages of AIDS in the work force; productivity and growth rate will decline.[8] According to the International Labor Organization (ILO) increased absenteeism due to HIV/AIDS is exacting an enormous toll in the work place.[9] The ILO estimates that 15 percent of our civil service is HIV positive. The South African Teachers Union has conducted its own research. According to its statistics, ten teachers are dying a month. Soon we will have close on half a million AIDS orphans to care for, while the United Nations estimates that a possible 40 million children worldwide will be orphans by 2010, largely due to AIDS.[10] We are, in the words the General Secretary of the United Nations Kofi Annan, facing "a tragedy on a biblical scale."[11]

Addressing an AIDS Conference in Maputo, Mozambique in 1990, assassinated African National Congress stalwart Chris Hani spoke prophetically when he said:

> We cannot afford to allow the AIDS epidemic to ruin the realization of our dreams. Existing statistics indicate that we are still at the beginning of the AIDS epidemic

in our country. Unattended, however, this will result in
untold damage and suffering by the end of the century.[12]

Given this calamitous reality, it is beyond understanding
that certain South African politicians can still prevaricate
about the causes of AIDS and the efficacy of treatments; that
they conspire to keep silent about its ravages and place political agendas and power games above the lives of citizens, the
majority of whom voted them into power.[13] This state of
affairs prompted Dr. Mamphela Ramphele, former vice
chancellor of the University of Cape Town, to say that "no
coherent management strategy [has] yet [been] developed
by the Government." This failure, she stated, "results not
from lack of expertise in South Africa, but in its disregard by
those in Government, with tragic consequences." She
concluded that the South African government's position on
AIDS was "nothing short of irresponsibility, for which history
will judge it severely."[14] Dr. Malegapuru Makgoba, president
of the Medical Research Council of South Africa said recently:
"History may judge us, the present Africans, to have colla-
borated in the greatest genocide of our time by the types of
choices—political or scientific—we make in relation to this
HIV/AIDS epidemic."[15]

In the face of the current pandemic, one must ask: How
can the church of Christ be empowered to accomplish its missionary task in circumstances of such suffering? Attending
endless funerals every weekend is a numbing task. It is more
than numbing when the Body of Christ itself feels an ampu-
tation each time one of its members fills a coffin. There are
no dividing lines between the Body of Christ and some other
reality "out there." The reality of the suffering world is ours.
We too are infected. The church has AIDS. We are reminded,
"When one suffers, all suffer together with it...." (1 Cor
12:26a). To be in communion with one another means to
share the cup, both its bitterness and its sweetness. The Anglican Communion is the suffering Body of Christ, seeking to be
God's hands in the world. The question is "How?"

Certain assumptions undergird the views expressed in this paper. The first is that mission is driven by an ethic of care and hope. If the context in which I find myself is full of wonderful opportunities for me, but is hell on earth for my sister, it is a wretched place for both of us. The task of mission is to identify the sources of wretchedness and lay bare the contradictions in society so that change can come about. The second is that mission is in solidarity with those who suffer, are poor, outcast, stigmatized, exploited, sick, and alienated. This is how I understand Christ's mission. The third is that mission is a "laboratory of freedom."[16] It holds before the world the possibility of being free. Anyone who joins the church must be able to sense that they are entering the home of the free—freedom from exclusion, stigmatization, exploitation, freedom from idolatry, and from servitude to popular ideologies. Lastly, mission should model a new style of life—a life which is open to the love of God as seen in the life of Jesus Christ and which is permeating the world through the work of the Holy Spirit. These assumptions flow from my conviction that the Reign of God, in its "becoming," has many dimensions. It is about our well-being in every aspect of our lives, personally, socially, politically, and spiritually.

In this paper I would like to touch on seven interrelated propositions for discussion which may offer clues on how to set about mission in the midst of suffering. I have no blueprint for the Anglican Communion's global mission. I can only offer these propositions for debate drawn from my experience of living in South Africa. I hope they may help us as we tackle the present global task of mission.

TWO FURTHER VIRUSES: SEXISM AND POVERTY—CHALLENGING THE CHURCH

Teresa Okure, an African theologian, startled her listeners at a theological symposium on AIDS held in Pretoria in 1998, by saying that there are two viruses more dangerous than the

HIV virus because they enable this virus to spread so rapidly. The first virus is the one that assigns women an inferior status to men in society. According to Okure, this virus fuels the sex industry in which young women, themselves the victims of abuse, become infected with HIV and then pass it on to others, even to their babies. This is the virus that causes men to abuse women. This is the virus that is responsible for the shocking fact that in many countries in Africa the condition that carries the highest risk of HIV infection is that of being a married woman. The stories of Thembisa and Boniswa bear witness to the truth of Okure's remarks.

The second virus, which enables the HIV virus to spread at a devastating rate, is found mostly in the developed world. It is the virus of global economic injustice, which causes terrible poverty in many parts of the developing world. Capitalist market economies are thrust on societies that are not geared for them, as are structural adjustment programs designed to meet the requirements of the developed world. Global economic systems disrupt traditional societies, displace economic and educational infrastructures, as well as the market demands of such systems, and make access to prevention and treatment of disease difficult and expensive. It is no coincidence that ninety percent of people infected with HIV/AIDS live in the developing world.

Undoubtedly the HIV virus causes AIDS. But it does not act alone. In southern Africa, HIV/AIDS is in reality a pandemic that has everything to do with gender relations and conditions of poverty. South Africa is a society in which cultural traditions of male dominance, bolstered by a particular understanding of the place of men in the Christian tradition, has resulted in continued inequity for women. Poverty, both in the rural areas and in the informal settlements surrounding our cities, is a further grinding reality. Mahatma Gandhi cautions us:

> To the poor man God dare not appear except in the form of bread and the promise of work. Grinding pauperism cannot lead to anything else than moral degradation. Every human being has a right to live and therefore to find the wherewithal to feed himself.[17]

Understanding the unholy alliance of sexism and poverty should be at the heart of all HIV/AIDS programs and is indeed key to the church's mission in a context such as ours. Of course HIV/AIDS has devastating consequences for *all* South Africans, regardless of age, race, class, or HIV status. But for South African women the AIDS pandemic is particularly perilous.[18] While it is cutting a deadly swathe across the educated classes in the 20- to 40-year-old age group, its greatest impact is on the most vulnerable members of society: *the poor, the marginalized, and the displaced.* This makes HIV/AIDS a crisis for women and children, particularly those who are poor in the rural areas and those who struggle to survive in shacks on the outskirts of our cities.[19] Quoting from UNAIDS (1997), Vicci Tallis points out that "almost four-fifths of all infected women live in Africa; in sub-Saharan Africa, there is a ratio of six women to five men infected; in the 15- to 24-year-old age group the risk of HIV infection for young women is even more disproportionate, with young women out-numbering young men by a ratio of 2:1."[20]

Women who have little or no education and/or who live in traditional male-dominated relationships, have scant access to information on HIV/AIDS and generally lack the skills and the power needed to negotiate safer sex. Tallis continues: "According to UNAIDS (1997) studies in Africa and elsewhere [show that] married women have been infected by their husbands (as their only sexual partner). Simply being married is a major risk for women who have little control over abstinence or condom use in the home, or their husband's sexual activities outside the home."[21] Strategies to deal with HIV/AIDS have failed these women because they insist on preventive behavior which they, the women, have little power to implement. Research on teenage girls found that many experienced their first sexual encounter as coercive. In the province of KwaZulu/Natal, seventy-two percent of teenage girls attending clinics related that they had refused to have sexual relations with their partners, but were usually unsuccessful at doing so and that attempts at refusal could result in physical abuse, termination of the relationship, or financial hardship.[22] Furthermore, women who are HIV positive are at the receiving end of prejudice, social ostracism, and violence.

HIV/AIDS is nourished by silence in South Africa. Breaking the silence about one's status can be life threatening. Gugu Dlamini became South Africa's first AIDS martyr when, in December 1998, she was stoned to death for speaking out about her HIV status. The dark mystery that lies at the heart of the pandemic in this country is the stubborn multilayered silence or what is called "the denial" by professionals. Suzanne Leclerc-Madlala, a medical anthropologist, comments that this silence "has much to do with heterosexual power, sexual life ways, the structure and meanings of which are contoured by what is often termed 'culture.'"[23] Wrestling with the stubbornness of the silences around HIV/AIDS in our part of the world, Leclerc-Madlala states:

> [W]ell-documented social science studies...point to high levels of premarital activity, extramarital relations and sexual violence, making African societies, taken as a whole, more at risk for both STDs and HIV/AIDS than those in other parts of the world. In many communities women can expect a beating, not only if they suggest condom usage, but also if they refuse sex....[24]

What emerges from present research into HIV/AIDS in sub-Saharan Africa, is the fact that the role of men needs to be addressed, particularly the attitudes and behaviors that are sexually irresponsible and that result in a certain death sentence not only for themselves, but also for millions of women and children. Given the powerful role of men in society, HIV/AIDS interventions and strategies targeting men will have a substantial impact on reducing the vulnerability of women to HIV. The theoretical and practical implications of the growing awareness of men's role in the HIV/AIDS pandemic are now being tackled by social scientists on our continent.[25] Heavily male institutions such as the military, sports clubs, and trade unions are being focused on for HIV prevention.[26]

HIV/AIDS is compelling South Africans to face the realities of gender inequity and poverty and how the two are a lethal combination. Saying this does not imply that I am negating the importance of other strategies for dealing with HIV/AIDS, such as advocating closed sexual relationships, the use of preventive measures, the need for appropriate treatment such as post-exposure prophylactics, AZT, or nevirapine for pregnant mothers. I am simply saying that the issue of gender relations, when related to poverty, lies at the very root of the matter.

To speak good news into a situation such as the one I have sketched means having both mind and a heart open to the relationship between gender oppression and poverty. Indeed, HIV/AIDS challenges our theologies and our practices as the Body of Christ. It raises questions such as: How can a more profound understanding of Christian traditions that have resulted in the distortions of gender relations become part of Christian mission? How can Christian mission recapture the intensity of "bread and gospel"?

I find myself thrown back on the creeds. To what extent do I practice what I confess? What does it mean to confess to being the "one, holy, catholic and apostolic" church in the midst of this HIV/AIDS crisis? If we are truly *one*, we are the church with HIV/AIDS. People living with HIV/AIDS are found in every sector of society and every religious denomination. We are all related; what affects one member of the Body of Christ affects us all. We are all living with HIV/AIDS. There is no "us" and "them." We dare not forget that inclusion, not exclusion, is the way of grace. If we are *holy,* we are not living some superhuman mode of existence. "Holiness does not require a transcendence of our human condition, but a full utilization of our condition toward the concrete reality of love."[27] Holiness is not withdrawal from the smell of crisis, sickness, or poverty, but engagement, often risky, in situations where God is present. If we are *catholic,* we are in solidarity because we are connected, in communion, with those who are suffering and who experience fear of rejection, poverty and death. If we are *apostolic,* we stand in continuity with the church in its infancy and we strive to live as Ignatius of Antioch put it, "in the manner of the apostles." This means that we are true to the heart of our teaching, that we are zealous for the Word, and that we continuously examine the ideals of the early church and measure ourselves against them. This is nothing new. It is simply a call to put the words of the creed into practice. Is this not a secure foundation on which to base our mission in contexts of suffering?

The mission of the church in situations of suffering requires a profound knowledge of cultural patterns of oppression, of the causes of poverty and women's oppression, as well as a willingness to translate our creeds into life-giving and just actions.

THE POWER OF NARRATIVE

Human beings cannot survive without a narrative of identity.[28] Telling stories is intrinsic to claiming one's identity and in this process finding impulses for hope. For those living with HIV/AIDS there is a need to claim and to name their identities in order to move away from the victim status so often thrust upon them. Narrative has a further function.[29] Apart from claiming identity and naming the evil, narrative has a sense-making function. The very act of telling the story is an act of making sense of an often incomprehensible situation, of a suffering and chaotic world in which people wrestle with understanding and in so doing seek to experience relief.

The stories of people living with HIV/AIDS are not only stories of suffering. They are also stories of triumph, of resistance, and of hope as the stories of Thembisa and Boniswa so clearly show. These stories need to be heard in our communities of faith. Churches can offer a supportive and empathetic environment for storytelling in the search for meaning. "The self-narrative is an individual's account of the relationship among self-relevant events across time, a way of connecting coherently the events of one's own life," writes Joan Laird.[30] Stories, she continues, are "to be thought of as narratives within the narrative."[31] The stories of people living with HIV/AIDS are individual tales within the meta-narrative of the pandemic. Hearing and engaging with these stories in communities of faith has the potential to draw members into relationship with one another across barriers of race, class, and most importantly, across the barriers that stigmatize people living with HIV/AIDS. We all have stories to tell. As our stories intersect, they change. We become part of one another's stories. In this process, we are all changed. Hearing and telling stories begins a process of openness, vulnerability, and mutual engagement that challenges stigmas, ostracization, and the loneliness of suffering, and can lead to acts of engagement, affirmation, and care. Narrative has the power to break the silences surrounding this crisis and to give it a human face.

The real meta-narrative is *the* story of our faith: the story of the ministry, suffering, death, and resurrection of Jesus Christ. The intersecting of our life stories with the story of Jesus is our ultimate hope.

Mission in the midst of suffering is a two-way endeavor—hearing the stories of suffering and triumph and re-telling THE story of suffering and triumph.

EMBODIMENT

The HIV virus enters, lurks, and then makes forays into the immune system until ultimately it destroys the body. This pandemic is all about bodies. Our social reality is an embodied reality. In Elaine Graham's words, "The effects and dynamics of power, truth, reason, good and evil never exist as transcendent ideals; they remain to be embodied, enacted, performed in human communities as forms of bodily practice."[32] Our bodies are more than skin, bone, and flesh. Our bodies encompass the totality of our human experience, our thoughts, our emotions, our needs and memories, our ability to imagine and to dream, our experiences of pain, pleasure, power, and difference, as well as our beliefs and our hopes. Ethicist Christine Gudorf reminds us that the body is synonymous with the self. "The mind is not over and against the body but rather is part of it, as are the emotions."[33] Our bodies are, in fact, the intricate tracery of all that is ourselves. Again in Graham's words, "...embodiment is more than an 'issue' exciting our compassion; rather, it points us to the performative, incarnational nature of all theology. Bodily *praxis* is the agent and the vehicle of divine reality and the faith practices of the Body of Christ are 'sacraments' of suffering and redemption."[34]

Unfortunately, "...in spite of doctrines of incarnation, resurrection, and *imago dei*, and theories about the ingestion of the very body of Christ during the mass, both the Catholic and Protestant churches, perhaps especially during some of the modern centuries, have conceived their principal domain as that of the soul and its salvation," writes William LaFleur.[35] The issue of the body challenges centuries of separating the soul and body, the mind and emotions in some or other specious hierarchal order. For women, the body is at the center of political, social, and religious struggles. This is hardly surprising as the female body has been the subject of ridicule, adulation, envy, discrimination, abuse, and stigma.

The question of stigma is particularly relevant to persons suffering from HIV/AIDS. Ignorance, prejudice, stereotypes, issues of power and dominance all conspire to stigmatize sufferers and in so doing to label them and distort their true identities. You simply become "an HIV positive," a statistic whose identity is now subsumed in your status. This denies the active, meaningful, and contributing lives led by increasing numbers of HIV positive people. Erving Goffman's influential theory of stigma points to the link between stigmas and assumed identities. He asserts that stigmas are specially constructed relationships.

> Historically, stigmas were imposed on individuals in the form of physical marking or branding to disgrace them. In modern societies, however, stigmas arise through social processes of interaction whereby individuals are marked or segregated because of an attribute they possess or because of something discrediting known about them. Hence stigmatized identities emerge though interpersonal interactions rather than as a psychological reaction to events.... The mere existence of stigma ensures that social interactions between stigmatized and non-stigmatized persons are usually uncomfortable, tense, and frustrating.[36]

Goffman's work on "stigmatized identities" refers to the disabled. Yet, it strikes profound cords in our context. As I have pointed out, women who are known to be HIV positive are stigmatized by a large section of South African society. Fortunately, within the body of people living with HIV/AIDS there is an increasing band of people who are slowly gaining power by defining their experiences and claiming their reality, speaking out, and breaking the silence around the disease. There is also a new brand of social activism emerging in South Africa, as individuals march in the streets demanding affordable treatment for HIV/AIDS.[37]

In summary, when, on the one hand, the body is seen merely as a vehicle for the soul or, on the other, as a trap to ensnare, it has been maltreated, vilified, and abused. This is an important clue for the mission of the church. Bodies are at the center of this crisis: sick, poor and too often female bodies. The gospel is not disembodied Good News—it speaks in the sight of suffering and the smell of death.

Embodied mission enters into places of exclusion and does not shy away from the smell of sickness and death, as it takes up the challenge to be God's hands in this world.

ETHICAL CODES

In South Africa today there is much talk, and very necessary talk, about abstinence, prevention, and medication in the face of the HIV/AIDS crisis. Roman Catholics say abstinence is the only answer. Anglicans say yes, but if you must, use condoms. There is very little being said, however, about the moral and ethical issues raised by the HIV/AIDS pandemic. So far the churches have not grasped this nettle. The recognition that the church is a community of sexual human beings[38] is slow in coming and centuries of ignoring any matter related to human sexuality is merely feeding the silences around HIV/AIDS. It simply is not good enough merely to preach fidelity and abstinence in sexual relations. This message cannot be heard, understood, or followed as long as it is communicated without a properly constructed debate on what constitutes a moral community. Moral choices and moral accountability, and a community in which women are respected as equal partners in the church itself, are essential to this debate.

What makes a moral community? Christian ethics are communal ethics. How people live with one another, and our faithfulness to God are two sides of the same coin. The people of Israel received the law, according to Rowan Williams, "when God had already established relations with them, when they were already beginning to be a community bound by faithfulness to God and to each other."[39] Williams continues:

148

> When the Old Testament prophets announce God's
> judgment on the people, they don't primarily complain
> about the breaking of specific rules (though they can
> do this in some contexts) or about failure to live up to
> a moral ideal; they denounce those actions that signify
> a breaking of the covenant with God and so the break-
> ing of the bonds of faithfulness that preserve Israel as a
> people to whom God has given a vocation.[40]

In the New Testament, Paul deals with ethical dilemmas
(for example, Rom 14 and 15, 1 Cor 10) by arguing that any
decisions taken should be guided by the priority of the other
person's advantage, by avoidance of judgmentalism, and by
acceptance of one another and thus by the ultimate imperative
of building the Body of Christ more securely. For Christians,
ethical actions flow from involvement in community with
God and with one another. Actions that promote justice and
love are actions for the good of the Body of Christ.

How does the shaping of moral community begin?
Bernard Brady in his book *The Bond of Community* has a chapter entitled "You don't have anything if you don't have stories." He writes: "Narratives form and inform our values, our
dispositions and how we 'see the world.'"[41] It is indeed possible to argue that narrative is *the* medium of moral communication. What is certain is that narrative is at the heart of
our faith, a narrative that "sets up the conditions for the possibility of the moral life."[42] Once the stories of our source
book and our traditions interact with our own stories, moral
consciousness, the ability to distinguish the "is" from the
"ought" and the choices this involves, can be nurtured.
Acquiring moral agency does not separate "being" from
"doing," or character from decision making and action. To
be a member of the Body of Christ means "*the formation and
transformation of personal moral identity in keeping with the faith
identity of the community.*"[43] A moral community is one in
which right relationship is both the goal and the praxis of
achieving that goal. The main task of a moral community is to
nurture the moral capacities of its members, by storytelling, by

involvement in the work of justice and charity, affirmed by our liturgical practices. In this way the community becomes one of moral deliberation and praxis. "In both Jewish and Christian traditions, faith's truth is finally a 'performative' one."[44] It becomes real when it is embodied. Moral truth and a way of life go hand in hand.

"Ethics is the human edge of thinking," says William Schweiker.[45] Borrowing from Schweiker, the place to start is with the question of the goodness of existence. "Is life good? Is it good to be, or better to die? How do we account for innocent suffering?"[46] Understanding the dilemmas facing those who suffer means understanding what is valued, and what moral spaces people inhabit. Related to this is the question of difference. Pluralism and diversity are our reality. Those involved in the mission of the church should see themselves as "travelers and interpreters of diverse moral worlds rather than trying to catch the human spirit through the spheres of one culture," Schweiker reminds us.[47] The church's mission is in essence about life, about the challenge of the moral life to become better. This is not simply a personal matter; it is also a social one because the real goal is the transformation of the world.

In their book, *Bible and Ethics in the Christian Life,* Bruce Birch and Larry Rasmussen tell the story of Dom Helder Camara meditating in the middle hours of the night about the attitudes of the rich toward the poor and then writing a poem. This poem speaks to those of us in the church who are not HIV positive and who may be tempted to feel virtuous about our status.

> I pray incessantly
> for the conversion
> of the prodigal son's brother.
> Ever in my ear
> rings the dread warning
> "this one [the prodigal] has awoken
> from his life of sin.

When will the other [the brother]
awaken
from his virtue?[48]

Mission in the midst of suffering requires an ethic of care that is unafraid to ask the difficult questions and to seek answers in communal moral praxis.

A LANGUAGE FOR MISSION

We need an appropriate language for mission in the midst of suffering. I suggest that the ancient language of lament offers a point of departure for mission in such circumstances. It also offers the body of the church the opportunity to say: "We are suffering; we stand in solidarity with all who suffer; we lament while we believe that there is hope for all in the Good News." In situations of suffering, lament is in fact a necessary precursor to spreading the Good News.

What is lament?[49] Lament is a form of mourning. But it is more. It is somehow more purposeful and more instinctive than mourning. Lamenting is both an individual and a communal act that signals that relationships have gone awry. While lamenting is about past events, it also has present and future dimensions. It acknowledges the brokenness of the present because of injustice. It instinctively creates a link between healing and mourning that makes new, just relationships possible in future. Lament should be generous and not grudging, explicit not generalized, unafraid to contain petitions and confident that they will be heard. Lament is not utilitarian. It is as primal as the child's need to cry. The cry of lament, while ostensibly wrought from the human heart in situations of suffering, is filled with enigmatic energies, unbearable urges, moments both profane and sacred. Lament is more than railing against suffering, breast-beating, or a confession of guilt. It is a coil of suffering and hope, awareness and memory, anger and relief, desire for vengeance, forgiveness and healing.[50] It is our way of bearing the unbearable, both individually and communally. It is a wailing of the human soul, a barrage of tears, reproaches, petitions, praise, and hopes that beats against the heart of God. It is, in essence, supremely human.

Once the wail is articulated, the lament usually takes on a structured form. This does not mean that lament should be tamed or domesticated, but rather that it happens in spaces that are contained by liturgical boundaries and rhythms. Lamenting, however, remains risky speech. Walter Brueggemann acknowledges this, saying that it is "dangerous, restless speech."[51] It is risky because it calls into question the structures of power, it calls for justice, and it pushes the boundaries of our relationships with one another and with God beyond the limits of acceptability. It is a refusal to settle for the way things are. It is reminding God that the human situation is not as it should be and that God as the partner in the covenant must act. Its "...questions to God are really questions about the power and presence of God."[52] Lament is never an end in itself. It is undergirded by the hope that God not only can but that God *will* hear the cries of the suffering and the penitent and *will* act with mercy and compassion.

For the language of mission to speak into the moment, we can learn from the powerful witness of Israel in the psalms. The psalms express Israel's relationship with God with an undimmed quality which has come to us through the ages, expressing the rawness of suffering as well as trust and hope in God. In Brueggemann's words: "Israel unflinchingly saw and affirmed that life as it comes, along with joy, is beset by hurt, betrayal, loneliness, disease, threat, anxiety, bewilderment, anger, hatred, and anguish."[53] Israel also saw that lament and praise go hand in hand. On the one hand, the psalmists almost assault God with facts about the human condition. On the other hand, they reveal trust and confidence that God will deliver them.

Lament occurs in different spheres and is not limited to the religious sphere of life. Human beings lament experiences of death and destruction, injustice and suffering, guilt and shame. We lament privately and communally. We lament in our faith communities and outside them. Just as the shape of lament differs, so do the circumstances which give rise to it.

When the language of lament becomes the language of mission in circumstances of suffering it has a number of grave implications. First, it has important implications for the political and social witness of the church and the impact of its message. The credibility in society of the church as an institution that claims to be an inclusive, caring community is in doubt if the church is not seen to lament injustice while working for the common good. In sub-Saharan Africa the struggle against the legacies of colonialisms are translated into wars, famine, corruption, and oppressive governance that are ravaging a continent in which there are, at present, an estimated 20 million refugees and roughly 34 million people infected with HIV/AIDS. Why are we not lamenting? Lamenting can be politically subversive and therefore dangerous as it is never about the preservation of the status quo.

Second, the language of lament can enrich our liturgies. Some people shy away from lament as it feels too emotional, too uncontained, even threatening. Yet I have seen lament at work in St George's Cathedral in Cape Town where, after the end of apartheid, people faced one another across the racial divide, told their stories, wept, and joined in prayers of petition and praise. Then I understood why so many prayers of praise are impoverished. Too often praise is not praise that emerges from grappling with radical doubt about God's presence in the world and our disquiet about suffering. It is not praise that is compelled by the belief that God can be worshiped despite the reality of human suffering. It is not praise that is wrought from trust, despite continuous questioning. It is not praise that knows that many questions are unanswered, but still continues to assault divine silence with tears and petition.

Third, in situations of suffering, healing and lament are intimately related. Pastoral care is part of our mission. Painful memories, experiences of exclusion and stigmatization cannot be healed if they are suppressed. They need to be told and when words fail, the psalms offer a valuable resource for lament. They honor people's pain and offer hope. Hope is nurtured in community. When the community of faith joins in lamenting, the suffering person feels that her pain is validated. The locus of pain is shifted from the inner world of private suffering to the outer world of the community of faith in a potentially cathartic movement. The desire for vengeance is often the only option for the powerless. Christians can, when lamenting, however, remind themselves that the principle of retaliation has to be renounced because it is beyond our ability to deal with justly. Our understanding is too partial and ultimate justice is God's.

Finally, the practice of lament can contribute to a more intimate and authentic relationship with God. We live in a world of displaced people, of war, terrorism, exile, devastated communities, abuse, sickness, and poverty. These situations raise legitimate questions about God, about justice, and about God's presence and power in a suffering world. Is God's justice and care for us reliable and, if so, where is it? There is much cause for lament, yet its loss stifles our questions about evil in the world. Instead, we settle for a God sugarcoated with a veneer of religious optimism, whose omnipotence will "make everything right in the end." Religious optimism is deeply different to a life of faith that is unafraid to examine suffering, but is nonetheless grounded on hope. Religious optimism prefers to sanitize God by removing God from the ugliness of evil and suffering. This is a God whom we dare not approach with our genuine grief and with whom we are in a relationship of eternal infantilism. Prayers of lament which are direct, truthful about suffering, which name the unnamable to God, are powerful in their potential to heal our doubts, address our lack of trust, and restore our faith in God's power to act on our cries.

Lament offers mission an authentic voice that names the suffering and holds to the hope that God is faithful and trustworthy, come what may.

AN ESCHATOLOGICAL SPIRITUALITY

Mission in the context of suffering is founded and nurtured on an eschatological spirituality. To rephrase what I mean, let me ask the question: What could the bearer of the Good News say to someone who is infected with HIV or who is dying of AIDS?

I suggest that the place to begin is to affirm that God is a lover of life, so much so that life continues into eternity. Certainty about this comes from the promise of the resurrection of the body. Hope is the key to questions about life and death. Not "pie in the sky when you die" kind of hope, which is nothing more than the thin skin of religious optimism, but creative, imaginative, expectant, and risky hope, maintained only with struggle. Hope is demanding, because we have to live our lives in such a way that that which we hope for can come about. This kind of hope takes our confessed belief in "the life everlasting" as not only something for one day when I die, but also as a confession of how I will live my life this day, in this moment. It is the kind of hope that enabled Dietrich Bonhoeffer, when he took leave of a fellow prisoner in Flossenbürg concentration camp and went to his execution, to say: "This is the end—for me the beginning of life."[54]

Life, death, and resurrection all belong together—they make up the whole of life. Resurrection cannot be reduced to "life after death" alone. When John (1 Jn 3:14) writes "We know that we have passed from death into life, because we love one another," he stresses that love is passionate about life, that we must say a hearty "Yes" to life, life that leads to death. What the resurrection of the body means is the subject of theological speculation; resurrection talk, however, remains body talk according to our creeds. Resurrection does not mean a deferred life—something we put off until after we die. In Jürgen Moltmann's words: "I shall live *wholly* here, and die *wholly*, and rise *wholly* there."[55] Eternal life is all of me, all of everyone, all of creation, all healed, reconciled, and completed. Nothing will be lost. Christian faith is shaped by the experience of the dying and the death of Christ, and by his resurrection. The process of the resurrection of the dead begins in Christ and continues in the Spirit "the giver of life," and will be completed in the raising of all the dead.[56] So, I would say to the person dying of AIDS, "Death is not your end. *Every life remains before God forever.*" To be raised to eternal life means that nothing has been lost for God, "…not the pains of this life, and not in moments of happiness."[57] Thus death both separates and unites. "Eternal life is the final healing of this life into the completed wholeness for which it is destined."[58]

Unfortunately, there are Christians who believe that AIDS is God's punishment for sin. In her interesting book *AIDS and its Metaphors*, Susan Sontag says, "Plagues are invariably regarded as judgments on society.…"[59] We are very quick to link any sexually transmitted disease with sin as if there are no innocent victims. Insensitive zealousness has resulted in persons dying of AIDS being told: "Your sin has caused your death." I am cautious, even suspicious of this language of fear. Despite those terrifying medieval pictures of judgment tempting women and men to seek comfort and salvation in the arms of the church, people have not stopped sinning. The mere mention of HIV/AIDS raises fear. It seeps into places where we did not know it before: fear of sexuality, fear of bodily fluids, fear of the communion cup, as Sontag comments, "fear of contaminated blood, whether Christ's or your neighbor's."[60] (Not surprisingly, Nietzsche commented acerbically on what he called the "holy lie"—the invention of a God who punishes and rewards by holding out the afterlife as some sort of "great punishment machine."[61]) Death can be caused directly by sin. We kill one another. We are destroying our environment. But death is not God's ultimate judgment on us. Admittedly, Christian thinkers like Paul, the old church fathers, and Augustine saw death as punishment for "the wages of sin." James (Jas 1:15) writes that "...then, when that desire has conceived, it gives birth to sin, and that sin, when fully grown, gives birth to death." Undeniably death can be caused by sinful acts.

There are other traditions in Christianity that do not see death as a judgment on sin. Schleiermacher and liberal Protestant theology of the nineteenth century disputed the causal connection between sin and physical death.[62] Moltmann argues that death may be called the "wages of sin" but that this can only be said of human beings. Angels are dubbed immortal but according to Peter (2 Pet 2:4), they sinned! Animals, birds, fish, and the trees don't sin, yet they die. Through human beings, death has been brought into nonhuman creation. Death has been with us from the beginning. God's first commandment to human beings was "be fruitful and multiply." We were mortal right from the beginning. From a pastoral point of view, theological speculation about the relationship between sin and death is not particularly helpful for the person dying of AIDS.

The body is implicated in the process of sin. The very context in which we live is affected by sin. Innocence suffers. Everything that is "born" must die. It is part of our condition. Our responsibility is to live and to die in loving solidarity with that sighing and groaning community of creatures described by Paul (Rom 8:23), all waiting for "the redemption of our bodies"(Rom 8:23).[63] We all need redemption. "The death of all the living is neither due to sin nor is it natural. It is a fact that evokes grief and longing for the future world and eternal life."[64] We all await what Letty Russell calls "the mending of creation."[65]

At the center of our efforts to understand the link between life and death is Christ. For Paul, community with Christ, who is the subject of our hope, extends to the living and the dead. "For to this end Christ died and lived again, that he might be Lord both of the dead and of the living" (Rom 14:9). Moltmann reads this verse as follows:

> I understand this in the following sense: In dying, Christ became the brother of the dying. In death, he became the brother of the dead. In his resurrection—as the One risen—he embraces the dead and the living, and takes them with him on his way to the consummation of God's kingdom.[66]

As we struggle to understand what it means to live hopefully, we are reminded that life remains unfinished. We have tried to live according to the plan for our lives, but we have failed. We are wounded, incomplete, not yet the persons that God intends us to be. We mourn the death of those we love. We grieve precisely because we have loved. Yet, in grief we try to hold on to hope. There is no quick fix for those who suffer. Life in the midst of suffering and death is a constant struggle, it risks moments of despair and loss of trust and it seeks hope even in the darkest places.

An eschatological spirituality which dares to risk, struggle, and hope in the fraught context of suffering enables us to see how our present reality is already in the realm of God's grace and redemption.

THE EUCHARIST

Turning to the church, it is a truism to say that living in right relationship in the Body of Christ is profoundly hard work and not easily achieved. This is apparent in the brokenness of our stories, the suffering of people, and our too-often dubious morality. But failure does not have the last word in the Christian life. Our hope is in Jesus Christ, the embodiment of our faith, whose life, death, and resurrection we celebrate in the Eucharist.[67] Michael Welker reminds us that the Eucharist was instituted "in the night that Jesus Christ was betrayed and handed over to the powers of this world."[68] Its origins do not lie in success or triumph but in the human betrayal of the Son and it is precisely here that we dare to hope. I want to conclude my search for clues with a few thoughts on how the Eucharist links up with the themes that I have already raised and their significance in our present context.

At the outset of this paper, I said that the Body of Christ has AIDS. I see a link between the abused bodies of Thembisa and Boniswa, the violated bodies of women and children, the bodies of people living with HIV/AIDS, and the crucified and resurrected body of Jesus Christ, who we remember and celebrate in the bread and the wine at the Eucharist. Deep inside the Body of Christ, the AIDS virus lurks and, as we remember Christ's sacrifice, we see in his very wounds the woundedness of his sisters and brothers who are infected and dying. Our hope is in Christ who takes the church as his bride, makes it his Body, and through this nuptial act sets before us the possibility of relationships in love that are the antithesis of disordered and morbid expressions of human relationship.

The Eucharist is the bodily practice of grace. Nancy Eiesland writes: "Receiving the Eucharist is a body practice of the church. The Eucharist as a central and constitutive practice of the church is a ritual of membership...the Eucharist is a matter of bodily mediation of justice and an incorporation of hope."[69] Because God chose to live with us in the flesh, sacramentality takes physical reality very seriously.[70] We are bodily partakers of the physical elements of bread and wine, Christ's presence in our lives and in our world. The very bodiliness of the celebration of the Eucharist affirms the centrality of the body in the practice of the faith. "The Supper," writes Welker, "centers on a complex, sensuous process in which the risen and exalted Christ becomes present. The Supper gives Christians a form in which they can perceive the risen and exalted Christ with all their senses."[71]

The celebration of the Eucharist makes the Reign of God present "to us" in the form of Christ's body broken "for us" and Christ's blood shed "for us." Christ invites us to the feast, and he is "both the giver of the feast and the gift itself."[72] In other words, the gift of the Reign of God is quite simply present in the person of Christ himself—Christ crucified and risen. Thus the communion meal mediates communion with the crucified one in the presence of the risen one. It becomes a foretaste of the messianic banquet of all human kind. It is the meal at which all are welcome. In Christ's Body, the Eucharist is *the* sacrament of equality. Only self-exclusion can keep one away. At the communion table, we are offered the consummate step in forging an ethic of right relationship, across all our differences. "We who are many are one body for we all partake of the one bread." This visible, unifying, bodily practice of relationship, with all its potential for healing, is ours. For the Eucharist to have meaning in our lives, we need to feel its powerful pull to the radical activity of loving relationships with those who are different. "The Eucharist involves a commitment (*sacramentum*) to sharing with the needy neighbor, for Jesus said, 'The bread that I shall give is my own flesh; given for the life of the world'" (Jn 6:51).[73]

A covenanted Eucharistic community is a community in relationship with one another and with God. Paul describes us as the Body of Christ, a body that though it has many members, is one body. "If one member suffers, all suffer together with it; if one member is honored, all rejoice together with it" (1 Cor 12:26). It is a body in which the weakest are to be treated with respect for "...God has so arranged the body, giving the greater honor to the inferior member, that there may be no dissension within the body, but the members may have the same care for one another" (1 Cor 12:25). The picture here is one of solidarity in suffering, of mutual support and of a moral community in relationship with one another and with God.

To link up with the previous thoughts on moral community, how we partake of the Meal is deeply significant for how we live as a moral community. "The Eucharist may be understood as nourishment for moral growth and formation,"[74] writes Duncan Forrester. A community with a moral code and a moral identity partaking in a meal of grace, memory and new life, brings resistance to evil and hope for now and tomorrow for the church with HIV/AIDS.

The role of the Eucharist and all that is signified by "we who are many are one, for we all partake of the one bread," is the binding glue for mission in the midst of suffering. In the act of drinking the wine and eating the bread we affirm our oneness in the Body of Christ. We also affirm our trust in Jesus' words (Jn 6:54): "Those who eat my flesh and drink my blood have eternal life, and I will raise them up on the last day."

In conclusion, for the Anglican Communion, HIV/AIDS is our *kairos*. It is a time when the ordinary rhythm of life is suspended. In the words of John Chrysostom, we are a people in danger of being "grazed thin by death."[75] The witness of the church in South Africa, my country, is challenged as never before. So too is the global mission of the church. Will it be a time of doom, or will we find a new unveiling of God's presence and love for us here and now?

NOTES

[1] Wole Soyinka, *Art, Dialogue and Outrage: Essays on Literature and Culture* (New York: Pantheon Books, 1993), 16.

[2] Willem Saayman and Jacques Kriel, "Towards a Christian Response to AIDS," *Missionalia* 19:2, 1991, 154–167.

[3] Figures quoted here are a combination of estimates published by the United Nations health agencies and the National Department of Health. For a global assessment of the AIDS situation, see also: Elizabeth Pisani, "AIDS in the 21st Century: Some Critical Considerations," *Reproductive Health Matters* 15, (8,2000) 63–76.

[4] Alan Whiteside and Clem Sunter, *AIDS: The Challenge for South Africa* (Cape Town: Human and Rousseau, 2000), 44.

[5] *Sunday Times Business Times,* July 2, 2000. See also Whiteside and Sunter, *AIDS,* Chapter 8, "AIDS and the Private Sector," 98ff.

[6] Statistics on HIV/AIDS are continuously questioned and revised. A South African government report on HIV/AIDS, released in March 2001, reports that the infection rate among women younger than 20 decreased from 21% in 1998 to 16.5% in 1999 to 16.1% in 2000. The HIV infection rate in KwaZulu/Natal—still the province with the highest prevalence—increased from 1999's 32.5% to 36.2% in 2000.

[7] Whiteside and Sunter, *AIDS,* 134.

[8] *The World Economic Forum's Africa Competitiveness Report,* released in July 2000, states that 40.77% of South African firms rank HIV/AIDS as having a moderate to major impact on their health care costs and 30.07% say their training costs have increased considerably, *Sunday Times Business Times,* July 2, 2000.

[9] *Cape Times,* October 11, 1999.

[10] Accessed at: www.un.org/millennium/sg/report

[11] Accessed at: www.un.org/news/press/docs/2000

[12] Hein Marias, *To the Edge: AIDS Review 2000* (Pretoria, University of Pretoria, Centre for the Study of AIDS, 2000), 4.

[13] Politicians, who beat a path to the home of dying Nkosi Johnson, a courageous little boy who spoke out about living with AIDS and who pleaded for treatment to be available to sufferers, while they refused to state publicly that HIV causes AIDS or to lobby for effective treatment for AIDS sufferers, speaks of moral turpitude. The recent report (at a cost of R2.4 million or U.S. $300,000) issued by President Mbeki's AIDS advisory panel has done little to resolve any of the key issues that led to the formation of the panel. It has merely given a further platform to dissident scientists to air their controversial view that HIV does not cause AIDS.

[14] Quoted from a speech entitled "Involvement of People Living With HIV/AIDS: How to Make it More Meaningful," given by Justice Edwin Cameron at the Second National Conference for People Living with HIV/AIDS, March 8–10, 2000, Durban.

[15] Quoted from an article entitled "A Sacrifice on the Altar of Expediency" by Sipho Seepe in the *Daily Mail and Guardian*, September 16–21, 2001. Not only South African politicians are parsimonious in their involvement with AIDS. Given the fact that approximately forty million people in the world are now HIV positive or have full blown AIDS, President Bush's first major decision as president of the United States was to deny U.S. aid to family-planning organizations abroad that inform women about medical options that may include abortion as *an* option. As I understand it, the Bush ruling says that clinics abroad will lose U.S. funds if they even discuss abortion with their patients. The results of this decision are nothing short of shocking. Added to this is the shameful action of President Clinton's administration with regard to AIDS. Al Gore pressured the South African government to

abandon a plan to impose compulsory licensing on drugs made by the big international drug companies, so that others could make and sell them far more cheaply. The drug issue in regard to AIDS is a crucial test of the morality of the U.S. government and its understanding of what is happening in the developing world. In 2000, 39 international pharmaceutical manufacturers took the South African government to court to prevent legislation being implemented that would enable the manufacture of cheaper generic drugs in South Africa to curb the HIV/AIDS pandemic. On April 20, 2001, a settlement was reached and the case did not proceed.

[16] Carl E. Braaten, "Mission as Revolution" in Carl E. Braaten and Robert W. Jenson, *The Futurist Option* (New York: Newman Press, 1970).

[17] Tissa Balasuriya, *The Eucharist and Human Liberation* (Maryknoll: Orbis Books, 1979), 145.

[18] For statistics see Quarraisha A. Karim, "Women and AIDS: The Imperative for a Gendered Prognosis and Prevention Policy," *Agenda* 39 (1998): 15–25.

[19] Hilda Adams and Anita Marshall, "Off Target Messages— Poverty, Risk and Sexual Rights," *Agenda* 39 (1998): 87–93.

[20] Vicci Tallis, "AIDS is a Crisis For Women," *Agenda* 39 (1998) 9.

[21] Tallis, "AIDS," 9–10.

[22] Rachel Jewkes, C. Vundule *et al,* "Relationships Dynamics and Teenage Pregnancy In South Africa," *Social Science and Medicine* 52 (2001): 733–744. See also Christine Varga and Lindiwe Makubalo, "Sexual Non-negotiation," *Agenda* 28, 1996, 33.

[23] Suzanne Leclerc-Madlala, "The Silences that Nourish AIDS in Africa," *Mail and Guardian,* August 11–17, 2000.

[24] Ibid.

[25] See C. Baylies and J. Bujra, *AIDS, Sexuality and Gender in Africa: The Struggle Continues* (London: Routledge, 2000); J. Bujra, "Risk and Trust: Unsafe Sex, Gender and AIDS in Tanzania," in P. Caplan, ed. *Risk Revisited* (London: Pluto Press, 2000); K. Carovano, "HIV and the Challenges Facing Men," *Issues Paper 15*, New York, UNDP HIV Development Program; K. Nkosi, "Men, the Military and HIV/AIDS in Malawi" in M. Foreman, ed. *AIDS and Men* (London: Panos Publications/Zed Press, 1999).

[26] See also Janet Bujra, "Targeting Men for a Change: AIDS Discourse and Activism in Africa," *Agenda* 44 (2000): 6–23.

[27] Marjorie Suchocki, "Holiness and a Renewed Church," in L. M. Russell, ed. *The Church with AIDS: Renewal in the Midst of Crisis* (Louisville: Westminster/John Knox, 1990), 115.

[28] Robert Schreiter, *Reconciliation: Mission and Ministry in a Changing Social Order* (Maryknoll: Orbis Books, 1999), 34.

[29] I am grateful to my friend and colleague, Bernard Lategan, for pointing out that the narrative has the further hermeneutical function of sense making, an understanding he attributes to the work of Jörn Rüsen's concept of *Sinnbildung*.

[30] Joan Laird, "Women and Stories: Re-storying Women's Self-Constructions" in M. McGoldrick, C. M. Anderson and F. Walsh, eds. *Women and Families: A Framework for Family Therapy* (New York/London: W. W. Norton, 1991), 430.

[31] Ibid., 133.

[32] Elaine Graham, "Words Made Flesh: Embodiment and Practical Theology," paper read at the International Academy for Practical Theology's Biennial Conference, Seoul, Korea, 1997.

[33] In Anne B. Gilson, "Embodiment" in L. M. Russell, and J. S. Clarkson, eds. *Dictionary of Feminist Theologies* (Louisville: Westminster/John Knox Press, 1996), 82.

[34] Graham, "Words Made Flesh."

[35] William R. LaFleur, "Body" in M. C. Taylor, ed. *Critical Terms for Religious Studies* (Chicago: University of Chicago Press, 1998), 41.

[36] Nancy Eiesland, *The Disabled God: Toward a Liberatory Theology of Disability* (Nashville: Abingdon, 1994), 59–60.

[37] Here I have in mind the Treatment Action Campaign headed by the intrepid Zackie Achmat who is HIV positive and who refuses to take anti-retroviral drugs until they are available to all who need them in South Africa.

[38] Peter Brown has documented the variety of ways in which Christians in late antiquity found sexuality a problem. See: *The Body and Society: Men, Women and Sexual Renunciation in Early Christianity* (New York: Columbia University Press, 1988).

[39] Rowan Williams, "On Making Moral Decisions." Unpublished address to Lambeth Plenary Session, Canterbury, July 22, 1998.

[40] Ibid.

[41] Brad V. Brady, *The Moral Bond of Community: Justice and Discourse in Christian Morality* (Washington: Georgetown University Press, 1998), 1.

[42] Ibid., 22.

[43] Bruce B. Birch and Larry L. Rasmussen, *Bible and Ethics in the Christian Life* (Minneapolis: Augsburg, 1989), 45.

[44] Ibid., 137.

[45] William Schweiker, *Power, Value, and Conviction: Theological Ethics in the Postmodern Age* (Cleveland: Pilgrim Press, 1998), 3.

[46] Ibid., 4.

[47] Ibid., 4–5.

[48] Birch and Rasmussen, *Bible and Ethics in the Christian Life*, 47.

[49] See also the following articles by me on lament: "Lamenting Tragedy from the Other Side" in James R. Cochrane and Bastienne Klein (eds.), *Sameness and Difference: Problems and Potentials in South African Civil Society,* (Washington D.C., The Council for Research in Values and Philosophy, 2000); "Tales of Terror and Torment: Thoughts on Boundaries and Truth-telling," *Scriptura,* 63, 1997, 425–433; "On Hearing and Lamenting: Faith and Truth-telling" in H. R. Botman and R. M. Petersen (eds.), *To Remember and to Heal: Theological and Psychological Reflections on Truth and Reconciliation* (Cape Town: Human and Rousseau, 1996); "'Take up a Taunt Song': Women, Lament and Healing in South Africa" in Leny Lagerwerf (ed.) *Reconstruction: The WCC Assembly Harare 1998 and the Churches in Southern Africa* (Zoetermeer: Meinema, 1998).

[50] Walter Brueggemann, "The Shape for Old Testament Theology: Embrace of Pain." *The Catholic Biblical Quarterly* 47: 400, describes lament as "a dramatic, rhetorical, liturgical act of speech which is irreversible." It articulates the inarticulate. Tears become ideas.

[51] Ibid., 401.

[52] Patrick D. Miller, *They Cried to the Lord: The Form and Theology of Biblical Prayer* (Minneapolis: Fortress Press, 1994), 133.

[53] Walter Brueggemann, "From hurt to joy, from death to life," *Interpretation* 28 (1974), 4.

[54] Jürgen Moltmann, *The Coming of God: Christian Eschatology,* tr. M. Kohl (Minneapolis: Fortress Press, 1996), xi.

[55] Ibid., 67.

[56] Ibid., 69.

[57] Ibid., 71.

[58] Ibid.

[59] Susan Sontag, *AIDS and its Metaphors* (New York: Farrar, Straus and Giroux, 1989), 54.

[60] Ibid., 73

[61] Friedrich W. Nietzsche, *The Will to Power*, tr., W. Kaufmann and R. J. Hollingdale (New York: Random House, 1967), 90.

[62] For an explanation of these views, see Moltmann, *The Coming*, 87 and 89ff. for a discussion of Karl Barth's adaption of Schleiermacher's views:

> Schleiermacher, and with him modern Protestant theology, distinguished strictly between person and nature; and he restricted himself to the religious and moral experiences of the human person....With these presuppositions it is quite logical that Schleiermacher would have declared death *per se* to be neither evil nor a divine punishment but the natural end and temporal limit of the finite existence of men and women. It is only a God-consciousness deranged by sin that will experience this natural death subjectively as an evil, and fear it as a punishment. Death is not caused by sin, but it is through sin that it acquires spiritual power over human beings.... Liberal Protestant tradition developed Schleiermacher's position further. The underlying exegetical assumption was that the biblical traditions are talking about death both literally and in a transferred sense. In the transferred sense, "death of the soul" means a breach of fellowship with God, while "eternal death" is its loss. These experiences in the God-consciousness must be uncoupled from physical death. The consequences of sin are spiritual disintegration, lack of inner peace, moral corruption, and fear of eternal damnation. To derive physical death from this source is nonsensical. Physical death cannot be put down to religious and moral causes.... Liberal Protestant teaching concludes that the death of the soul and eternal death follow upon sin; but it removes the death of the body from this cohesion, because it distinguishes strictly between person and nature. (87–88)

[63] Moltmann, *The Coming*:

> The modern separation between person and nature (as in Schleiermacher) or between covenant and creation

> (as in Barth) does neither justice to human nature nor to the community of creation. It is an expression of the anthropocentrism of the modern world, an anthropocentrism destructive of nature.... The patristic church's doctrine of physical redemption was more comprehensive in its cosmic dimensions. (92)

[64] Ibid., 92.

[65] Letty Russell uses this term in many of her works to denote the eschatological implications of the Reign of God.

[66] Moltmann, *The Coming*, 105.

[67] See Michael Welker, *What Happens in Holy Communion?* tr. J. F. Hoffmeyer (Grand Rapids: Eerdmans, 2000), 56–59. Welker argues that the supper is more than a "thanksgiving."

[68] Ibid., 43.

[69] Eiesland, *The Disabled God*, 112.

[70] Susan A. Ross, "God's Embodiment and Women," in C. M. La Cugna, ed. *Freeing Theology: The Essentials of Theology in Feminist Perspective* (San Francisco: Harper and Row, 1993), 186.

[71] Welker, *What Happens*, 18.

[72] Moltmann, *The Coming*, 250.

[73] Duncan B. Forrester, *Truthful Action: Explorations in Practical Theology* (Edinburgh: T. & T. Clark, 2000), 96.

[74] Ibid., 95.

[75] John Chrysostom in *de Virginitate* 14.1, quoted from Peter Brown, *The Body and Society: Men, Women and Sexual Renunciation in Early Christianity* (London: Faber and Faber, 1986), 6.

6

ENCOUNTERING DIFFERENCE IN A PLURAL WORLD

A PENTECOST PARADIGM FOR MISSION

CHRISTOPHER DURAISINGH

This essay is born of a passionate longing for the renewal of the church and the building up of the people of God for their participation in the mission of God in a world that is both increasingly globalized and fragmented. For I believe that an un-missionary church is not the church, the body of Christ broken for the healing of the world. This paper is also an expression of a desire to see that the church does not domesticate mission as one of its many activities; for mission essentially is not a function of the church, but rather the church is a function in the ongoing mission of God. "Mission does not come from the church; it is from mission and in the light of mission that the church has to be understood."[1]

The church's mission is primarily a responsive one to the mission of God, as it discerns the movement of the Spirit in the world and seeks to follow the Spirit. Hence a re-visioning of the church's mission requires discernment of the *missio Dei*, the mission of God, as the first step. A re-visioning of the mission of the church thus does not begin with an *a priori* discussion on the nature and function of the church, but rather with a holistic understanding of the presence and work of the Triune God in the world at large. Considering the nature of the church before considering the mission of God in the world that God loves, and where God in Christ is redemptively present, is placing the cart before the horse.

If by the mission of the church we mean essentially the credible and tangible mediation of the liberative presence of God in Jesus Christ in the midst of the historical ambiguities of our time, then any reflection on the nature of mission can be responsible and relevant only when such thinking is rooted in the concrete realities of the real world. God works in and through the vicissitudes of history. It is in the midst of the broken conditions of our day-to-day life that the redemptive presence of God in Jesus Christ breaks through. Hence, any re-visioning of mission necessarily first involves an analysis of the conditions of the reality of the world today. What, then, are some of the characteristics of these days in which we are called to witness to God's liberative love in Jesus Christ?

THE WORLD CONTEXT

Today, more than ever before, the world cries out for credible signposts to show that human community is still possible in the midst of all that divides us. The anguish across this great nation since the tragic events of September 11, the fears expressed in so many ways as the country became vulnerable to terrorism as no one could ever imagine before, the consequent crowded churches, the peace marches on university campuses, the daily bombings of Afghanistan, the "War Room" syndrome of the media—all these are expressions of this longing for some form of a "domination-and-fragmentation free" human community in the midst of our racial, ethnic, cultural, and religious differences. Behind it all lays a deeper crisis in understanding and dealing with difference and diversity. Whatever else the significance of these events may be, they certainly serve as a window into how we handle difference, respond to the "other," and negotiate plurality at times of crisis.

But increasing diversity and the consequent conflict and fragmentation are significant hallmarks of our times in almost every corner of the earth. There is no reversal to this process. Remember that almost a hundred years ago the well-known journal *The Christian Century* came into publication. It shared the optimism of Christian leaders in the West, like John R. Mott, that the whole world would be evangelized in one generation. But note what happened by the end of the twentieth century. There was an unprecedented revival and growth in all major non-Christian religions of the world. Most of them have become world religions and "missionary," with very well-established international communication machinery. Religious pluralism is a fact of life in every country in the West. Temples and mosques mark the landscape of this country. As Diana Eck, both through her major research study on pluralism and in her recent book, *The New Religious America*,[2] demonstrates in no uncertain terms, that, "the United States is the most religiously diverse nation in the world." The subtitle of the book is provocative: *How a "Christian Country" Has Become the World's Most Religiously Diverse Nation.*

September 11 is also a powerful reminder that in the face of diversity, religious traditions themselves have become ambivalent, with power both to heal and destroy. Certainly, religions have provided the power to embrace those who are different, as was seen in the heroic acts during days immediately following the horror of September 11. But it is also the case that the rhetoric of the Taliban, and those who rally the United States for war against the Taliban, has consistently made *instrumental use* of religious identities, symbols, and resources. Around the world, narrow ethnic, linguistic, and nationalistic interests are fueled by religion, at times

173

with demonic consequences, as in the case of Osama bin Laden. Fundamentalism, intolerant of those who are different, manifests itself in almost all religious traditions, making the very nature of religion ambivalent.[3]

It is at times like this that we need to hear again the famous dictum of Max Muller, the German pioneer of comparative study of religion, which says something to the effect: The one who knows only one religion knows none. Those who know only one culture, one way of life, know none, not even their own. In the history of the world, those who know only one religion or culture have done barbaric deeds, as the Christian crusades, the Holocaust, and the events of September 11 remind us.

Difference, in and of itself, is not bad. In fact, diversity has been and can be a source of blessing. The World Council of Churches has consistently recognized diversity within the church as a rich blessing bestowed upon it by the Holy Spirit. The Yale missiologist, Lamin Sanneh, suggests, "For all of us pluralism can be a rock of stumbling, but for God it is the cornerstone of the universal design."[4] In recent times, however, the expanding plurality of cultures, values, and norms has led to competitive violence, and, as a result, diversity has become conflictual. We need to explore why this is so.

Let us look at the broader world scene. We may discern two opposite, yet interrelated, forces in operation. On the one hand, through the *centripetal forces* of globalization, the world's cultures are increasingly thrown open to each other. A process of deterritorialisation leads to an undermining of nation-states and democracies in a drive toward turning the globe into one large consumerist collective. Heads of some multinational corporations talk about themselves as the engineers of a new world-culture, a secular *oikoumene*, as it were. MTV, Macintosh, and McDonald's are just a few agents of the global forces of media, technology, and the market, tying the world together by entertainment, communications, information, and commerce. In many ways peoples in different parts of the world, particularly in the West or in "free trade zones" such as in South East and East Asia, find this trend significant for their growth. But the integrative power of the centripetal drive is felt by others, particularly in the Third World and non-Western contexts, as a threat to local cultures and the uniqueness of particular life styles. The impact of market and media is perceived by the already-marginalized masses as excluding more and more people from the benefits of globalization. Further, the centripetal force of media, technology, and the market has also brought about unprecedented migration from the South to the North, thus accentuating diversity in the North and the consequent conflicts. In many ways, the pressures of globalization divide and exclude as much as they unify and include.

On the other hand, the world is witnessing an ever-increasing struggle for particular cultural, ethnic, or religious identities. The *centrifugal forces* of narrow group identities, blood and belonging, and primordial ties of language, religion, and race seem to fragment societies everywhere. We witness across the world armed intra-state conflicts across ethnic lines. Ireland, Sri Lanka, Rwanda, and Kosavo are but a few examples. In all parts of the world, we find a search for ethnic roots and tradition, a stress on cultural uniqueness, an insistence on difference, and an assertion of a group's rights, often at the expense of other groups. In many instances, conflicts are fueled and even legitimized by an instrumental use of religions, including Christianity. Hate groups sustained by the religious right multiply like mushrooms in the United States. In other parts of the world, inter-ethnic and intra-state conflicts are exacerbated by religious tensions. A few years ago, when he was the President of the European Council of Churches, Dean John Arnold of Durham Cathedral described the context for the mission of the church in Europe with the haunting words: "Instead of the Europeanization of Ulsters, I see all around me the Ulsterization of Europe."[5] How true! Whatever else may be the problem with Samuel Huntington's description of the world, he is right in insisting that the battlegrounds of tomorrow shall be the cultural fault lines of today.[6]

What is important, however, is to remember that these twin forces, the centripetal force of globalization and the centrifugal forces of ethnic, religious, and cultural identities operate in tandem and feed upon each other. It is often the case that the centrifugal force of fragmentation is strengthened by its violent response to the centripetal trend and uses the logic and media of globalizing process to sustain and spread itself. In the words of Benjamin Barber:

> Ironically, a world that is coming together pop culturally and commercially is a world whose discrete subnational ethnic and religious and racial parts are also far more in evidence, in no small part as a reaction to McWorld.... The more "Europe" hoves into view, the more reluctant and self-aware its national constituents become. What Gunter Grass said of Germany—"unified, the Germans were more disunited than ever"—applies in spades to Europe and the world beyond: integrated, it is more disintegral than ever.[7]

The catchy titles of several recent books bring out the point in a telling manner. For example, *The Balkanization of the West* by Stjepan G. Mestrovic[8] is a daring description of the centrifugal forces that lead to the fragmentation of the Western world into increasingly smaller and hostile units, often sustained by cultural, linguistic, and religious fervor. George Ritzer's *The McDonaldization of Society*[9] is a significant sociological study of the process of globalization, of which McDonald's is, perhaps, the most obvious manifestation. Benjamin R. Barber's *Jihad vs. McWorld* is an early and convincing description of the double and interacting phenomena of how the "the planet is both falling apart and coming together" and what it means for cultures, both local and global.

The world is thus caught between twin forces—one of intense integration and the other of divisive fragmentation.

In a sense ours is not an age of a "new world order" but rather one of intense social and cultural uncertainty and conflict in the context of an overwhelming and almost over-powering economic integration of the world. These twin forces together destroy genuine pluralism and democratic ways of negotiating difference. The centripetal force destroys authentic differences and local identities by seeking to homogenize diversity; and the centrifugal force has the same effect by insisting on the uniqueness and the exclusive rights of one's own at the expense of the rights and identity of others.

Certainly there is a genuine human need for integration, the need to be included in, or united with, a larger whole. Similarly, there is also the need for uniqueness, for being different, and to insist upon one's particularity. But when these human drives work against each other, when the centripetal and centrifugal drives are not kept in creative tension so that both integration and uniqueness may be held holistically and in tandem, then there is no adequate way of negotiating plurality. The assimilative drive toward integration and the competitive drive of the diverse, together, make plurality highly problematic. Combined they seem to tear human communities apart. The result is a world of uncertainty, due to the fear of either losing the identity of a people in a larger whole, or being fractured along the lines of competing claims. As Barber rightly warns us: "Unless we can offer an alternative to the struggle between Jihad and McWorld, the epoch on whose threshold we stand—postcommunist, postindustrial, postnational, yet sectarian, fearful, and big-oted—is likely also to be terminally postdemocratic."[10]

This uncertainty drives many to turn to religious traditions searching for identity and stability. Marc Gopin suggests that we see two "very different possible futures" emerging from such a turn to religions and traditional cultures at this point in time. On the one hand, "religion's visionary capacity and its inclusion of altruistic values has already given birth to extraordinary leaders, such as Gandhi, King, Dalai Lama, and Bishop Tutu...inspired to work for a truly inclusive vision that is multicultural and multireligious."[11] On the other hand, this turn to religion has also led to a disintegration of society, painfully apparent in the mass murders, the tortures, and "the religious financial support" of brutal regimes as well as of the events of September 11. The events of that day cannot be dismissed simply as the act of some mad men, nor can we understand it as though it has nothing to do with any religious commitment, even if perverted. Rather, it is an extreme way of using misplaced religious fervor to destroy a way of life and a value system that one has come to demonize in the light of what one understands as his/her religion or truth. The events of September 11 were a dastardly way of dealing with difference that threatens one's beliefs and values. In many ways, both the demonic act of destruction and a number of the immediate responses to the tragedy are indications of an inability to handle difference and negotiate plurality. Both the attacks and the responses reflect an inability to hold in creative tension the centrifugal and centripetal drives of human communities, a failure to hold together the human need for both integration and uniqueness. On both sides of the equation, healthy pluralism is the casualty. In this context, then, the basic human predicament is how to encounter diversity and negotiate pluralism without succumbing to either domination or fragmentation. *It is this human predicament that is the locus of the* missio Dei *today.*

How may we be faithful to God's design of enriching human communities through healthy diversity, of cultivating a posture of permanent openness to the other, and of celebrating the plurality of cultures and traditions that exist in the world no matter how strange and unsettling they might be?

It is important to note at this juncture that a central element of the gospel imperative is for a permanent openness to the other, the stranger, and the alien. Hospitality to strangers and recognition of "the other," the resident alien, is intrinsic to the biblical story of God's love in Christ. Kosuke Koyama argues convincingly that the gospel is stranger-centered at its core. An inclusive love for "the other" is at the heart of the biblical faith and is the defining characteristic of the early church's understanding of the person and work of Christ.[12] Koyama offers a timely reminder that for any theology to be authentic it must be constantly challenged, disturbed, and stirred up by the presence of strangers. In the Hebrew Scriptures, the idea of *ger*, the stranger, the resident alien, is central to the life of the people of Israel. The way the people of Israel dealt with the diverse strangers among them became the litmus test for their obedience to God, for they were constantly reminded that they themselves were strangers. Similarly, was it not Plato who suggested that the measure of a civilization is the manner in which it treats the strangers and those who are different? And today, several contemporary Western thinkers like Gadamer, Habermas, Rorty, and Levinas, each from a very different standpoint, suggest that in our historical situation "it is all the more imperative to try again and again to foster and nurture those forms of communal life in which dialogue, conversation, *phronesis*, practical discourse, and judgment are concretely embodied in our everyday life."[13]

MISSION AS RECONCILIATION

In a context where both globalization and fragmentation threaten the very search for authentic human community, it is imperative that a central aspect of the church's mission be our witness to God's bringing into being a reconciled human community across all that divides us. No wonder that the theme "waging reconciliation" comes to us as an urgent call. Does not the Book of Common Prayer state, in no uncertain terms, that "the mission of the Church is to restore all people to unity with God and each other in Christ."?[14] Yet, it is the stark and painful reality of our times that, both in the church and in the world at large, diversity itself has become a central problem threatening the very life and unity of both the Body of Christ and the very fabric of human community.

Reconciliation is at the core of most of the religious traditions of the world. In fact, as Catherine Keller puts it well: "Religion true to its name activates connection. It 'ties together,' binding up the wounds of breaking worlds. It is the bridging, bonding process at the heart of things. There is no reason not to call this process Love: the *Eros* that seeks to get things together, no matter what."[15] Such a religion, however, if developed and defined in separation from all else, can become "the bearer of disconnection."

It is not surprising, therefore, that the Canberra Assembly of the World Council of Churches envisioned the nature of the mission of the church primarily in terms of God bringing into being a reconciled community of communities in Christ Jesus.

> The reconciliation brought about by the cross is the basis of the mission of the church. A reconciled and renewed creation is the goal of the mission of the church. The vision of God uniting all things in Christ is the driving force of its life and sharing.[16]

In fact, the purpose of the Ecumenical Movement has been defined not simply as calling the churches to the goal of visible unity of the church in one faith and in one eucharistic fellowship. Rather, the unity of the church is seen primarily as a sign and instrument for the unity of humankind, the breaking down of barriers between people, and the promotion of one human family in justice and peace. It is strange, however, that sustained attention has not been given to the question regarding what the richness of the diversity of peoples in a variety of cultures and traditions could mean for the mission of the church or the understanding of the *oikoumene*. As a result there is an ecclesio-centric view of the world and a "churchification" of the *oikoumene*.

The previous General Secretary of the World Council of Churches, Philip Potter, has suggested that the only way to recapture the vision of God's purpose for the *oikoumene* is to discover it as the reconciled humanity through a universal dialogue of cultures, affirming the distinct identity of each and yet bringing them into a mutually enriching encounter. I am convinced that we are at a point in ecumenical-mission thought in which we are called to recognize that the central paradigm for mission is God's act of gathering up all things and reconciling all peoples in their rich diversity in Christ. Reconciliation of alienated identities in Christ is the principal motif, the controlling vision, of our mission thinking and practice. St. Paul says, in no uncertain terms, that the ministry of the church is that of reconciliation, (2 Cor 5:18–20). The Pauline vision in Ephesians and Colossians develops further a similar theme (Eph 1:9, for example). Can a missionary understanding of God, drawing diverse and often conflicting identities into the *oikoumene* and uniting them within the one household of God, function as a critical principle for the church's mission and evangelism in the new millennium?

Here again, one is reminded of Philip Potter's powerful description of the purpose of the ecumenical movement:

> The whole burden of the ecumenical movement is to cooperate with God in making the *oikoumene* an *oikos*, a home, a family of men and women, of young and old, of varied gifts, cultures and possibilities, where openness, trust, love and justice reign.[17]

The fact that many member churches of the World Council of Churches around the world have committed the first decade of this century as a decade for overcoming violence and building community further highlights that reconciliation is a valid and adequate paradigm for our mission thinking and practice today.

THE CHALLENGE OF "THE OTHER"

But overcoming violence and working toward reconciliation of people across plural cultures and religions demand taking "the other" seriously. For it is only through an engaged encounter with the other, those whose difference is disturbing in many ways, that one comes to a more informed and textured understanding of the traditions to which both belong. It is not the mere fact of plural cultures, but rather the experiencing of the *demand* upon me of those who are different, and the challenge they pose to my own pre-judgments, that result in a decentering of my self. The other is the one who beckons me to change, who breaks open my boundaries.

It is important to clarify the use of the term "other" in this presentation, albeit, rather tentatively. Ofelia Schutte has given us a helpful definition of the other:

> The other is not the one who passively confirms what I am predisposed to think about her; she is not the one who acts as the mirror to myself or the one whose image justifies my existing ego boundaries. If that were the case, the other would only be a stand-in for the self's narcissism. Just the contrary; the other is that person or experience which makes it possible for the self to recognize its own limited horizons in the light of asymmetrically given relations, marked by sexual, social, cultural, or other differences. The other, the foreigner, the stranger, is that person occupying the space of the subaltern in the culturally asymmetrical power relation, but also those elements or dimensions of the self that unsettle or decenter the ego's dominant, self-enclosed, territorialized identity.[18]

But such a call and commitment to the other stands against the spirit of the long-held, Western cultural tradition that often tends to reduce, absorb, or appropriate what is taken to be the other into the same. When this happens differences disappear.

The colonial logic about the other is still alive and well in many quarters. It is a logic and language of sameness, unity, universality that "masks the violent reduction of the alterity of the other into more of the same."[19] An essentialist description of reality and valorizing the homogenous over the diverse seem to be significant features of much of Western thought and culture. For can it not be argued that the dominant tendency in Western metaphysical and theological traditions has been to privilege and valorize unity, harmony, totality, and thereby to denigrate, suppress, and marginalize multiplicity, contingency, and particularity?[20]

Humans have found many ways of resisting otherness and reducing that which is different into more of the same. Several technologies of encountering and minimizing the challenge of alterity are used.[21] Robert Schreiter has helpfully pointed to a number of them.[22] Making use of his insights, rather freely for my purpose, let me identify some ways, or mechanisms by which we engage difference in unhealthy ways.

First, many tend to gloss over difference, holding that differences will disappear or will not matter if one gets to know the other more closely. Here is a mechanism of denying or dominating the other by *homogenizing* the one who is strange and thereby problematic or threatening. Homogenizing is a technique of constructing the other as though there is nothing unique or distinct about it. It seeks to dismiss that which is strange, disturbing and, at times, threatening. Homogenizing is a strategy that many whites and "white-likes" adapt to those who are racially other in order to blunt and avoid the challenge that the other offers. How often do we hear from such individuals that they are "color-blind" and "all people are the same?"

Secondly, there is a mechanism by which one seeks to *pluralize* difference. It acknowledges that there is no human being like any other. All are different in some respect. Therefore, difference is a fact of life and does not really matter for inter-human relationship. Pluralizing difference is an intellectual equivalent to the popular psychological assertion,

"I'm OK, you're OK, and there is no problem." It is a way of covering up diversity, not by denying it, but by removing the cutting edge of challenge and contestation that come with it.

A third way that many deal with difference is by *romanticizing* it. The otherness is constituted as exotic in nature, attractive, and fascinating. The other is reduced to an object of curiosity, a collectable, as it were, something to be "had" like "ethnic food" in the United States. My personhood does not matter. I become an object. Robert Young describes this way of dealing with the other as the "colonial desire" akin to the British colonial gaze upon their subjects in India.[23] The male gaze that dominates and constructs the woman primarily in terms of her body is yet another example of this oppressive mechanism of otherness. The other is not only made less threatening but is turned into a "serviceable" other for one's interest and use.

The fourth mechanism is almost the opposite of the third; it is an attempt to *demonize* the other. The other is constructed as inferior, polluted, or simply evil. He or she is a threat to one's wholeness and hence must be avoided or better yet, expunged. White people's fear of people of color is an example of its simplest form. Extreme forms include racial profiling in the United States or "ethnic cleansings" that we have witnessed in recent times in Rwanda and former Yugoslavia.

A fifth type of relationship to the other may be described as a desire to *colonize* the other. The other is inferior and needs to be raised up and educated to a higher level. Such a mechanism is found in the "civilizing" project of the colonial masters and has manifested itself as "white man's burden" in the colonies. It is also the same mindset that leads some heterosexuals to feel that "curing" gay men and lesbians is their calling. These are not simply innocuous expressions of a "teacher- or healer-complex." Rather, they are dangerous strategies to dominate the other, the one who differs in gender, race, or sexual orientation, thus making him or her less threatening.

These mechanisms of excluding the other and dealing with the threat of plurality arise out of a centered, essentialist mindset, as manifested in Euro-centrism for example. Since some of the same features of thought in the "centered, essentialist mindset" also characterize the world caught in conflict between the centripetal and centrifugal forces described above, it may be useful to consider such a mindset more closely. By identifying a few of the characteristic features of an essentialist mindset, I believe, it may be possible to consciously subvert that very thought form and promote a healthy way of encountering the other and negotiating a plural world. No amount of persuasion to take the other seriously would succeed as long as the basic habits and patterns of thought that lie behind exclusionist strategies are still in effect.

First, both the centrifugal and centripetal forces deny their own historical particularities and therefore tend to universalize and essentialize their concepts, values, and beliefs as valid for all. For example, within the globalization process, the Euro-American standpoint—its notions of liberal democracy, for example—becomes the singular defining categorical scheme for adjudicating all other forms of inter-human polity. This standpoint becomes the singular touchstone of all other viewpoints. Many post-modern thinkers warn us that at the core of the Western tradition lies the search for something unitary and fundamental that can provide a stable center on which to hang all our understanding, and, in the light of which, boundaries and exclusion can be erected. It is a search for a single meta-narrative. In this sense, much of modern thought is *essentialist*. It reduces reality into autonomous, simply located substances, as in Newtonian metaphysics. In a similar way, the struggle for the survival of the particular identity of a local movement—such as the Islamic fundamentalism represented by persons like Osama bin Laden or Christian fundamentalism, for that matter, is now claimed to be the only universally valid way of being. My suspicion is that a careful analysis of much of the rhetoric of any form of religious, cultural, or political fundamentalism would reveal a universalistic mindset that seeks to valorize one's own position and thereby denigrate, suppress, and marginalize, or even eliminate, that which is particular and different.

Secondly, when a particular standpoint, a position, is described in essentialist terms, it is easy to bifurcate reality and organize everyday life and discourse in terms of binaries, such as white/black, civilized/uncivilized, the West/the rest, for example. Further, the binary thinking that undergirds the modern mindset necessarily leads to a hierarchical ordering of reality and to an erecting of borders in the name of authenticity and purity. Binary thinking also privileges the first or the dominant term in any oppositional construct, such as white people over people of color, male over female, and the North over South. Recent feminist theories have explored extensively how those who are in power seek to maintain their essentialized identities, power, and privilege by constructing the world in oppositional terms. These theories also reject the consequent hierarchical organization of reality and relationships. While rejecting identities as unified and fixed, they advance a view of reality that is multiple, unstable, historically situated, the products of "differentiation and polymorphous identifications"[24]

Thirdly, when reality is bifurcated and identities are defined primarily in oppositional terms, it is not difficult to draw boundaries around one's own experience or context and exclude the other and all that is different. These boundaries are made impermeable in order that the other might be effectively kept out. Such logic leads to the exclusion of the other. Thus the global market, by its very nature, excludes. The "one world" that it promises is a world of exclusion for millions. As Christopher Kurien, a well-known Indian economist, powerfully puts it:

> There is only one thing it respects—resource power;
> there is only one code it understands—intensity of
> resource power; there is only one thing it aims at—con-
> trol over more resource power. Guided by this motive
> and propelled by this logic,…it confers profits and pros-
> perity on a few who have the resource power to be
> included on its aggressive designs…but excludes them
> (those who have no resources) from all its favours. . . To
> millions and millions on our little planet whose daily
> lives have been disrupted and whose livelihood has
> been disturbed by it,…it is a very dangerous reality
> indeed.[25]

Similarly, forces that seek to exclude those who are different also seek to silence them. As was seen on September
11, and in recent times in Rwanda and former Yugoslavia,
and in many other parts of the world, the final step in this
exclusionary process is the elimination of voices that are different. No wonder it was the symbols of market, military
might, and the seat of democratic power that were chosen as
targets for silencing by the terrorists on September 11.

In the light of the above observations, we may sum up by
saying that when the human need for uniqueness and integration, as manifested in the centrifugal and centripetal
forces of globalization, operate in opposition to each other,
then the following seem to result:

- a *centering* and *essentializing* of one's self, one's nation,
  market, values, norms, and so forth, in such a way that
  they are taken to be universal and true;
- a *bifurcation of reality* where the non-dominant are conceived in oppositional terms;
- an *erecting and maintaining of borders* that exclude the
  other;
- a *silencing* or even eliminating the voice of the other.

It is in this context, then, that we are called to reflect
upon the nature of the mission of the church as the reconciliation of peoples across all that divide them. I submit that
an adequate understanding of the practice of mission today

involves: *a de-centering of selves, a courageous border crossing, and empowering of multiple, even contesting, voices within a shared communion.* Mission as reconciliation becomes an embracing of the other in the place of exclusion—a new relationship with God, with each other, and with creation that is free of domination and fragmentation in the perspective of the reign of God. It is my belief that the life and witness of the Christian community provide us insights into such a three-fold mission demanded of us today.

THE PENTECOST PARADIGM

There are several powerful images in the Bible that give us some clues as to how we may deal with diversity and nego-tiate life in a plural world. First, there is the image of Babel, the classic paradigm for the centripetal force of globaliza-tion and integration that tends to destroy difference. It is the symbol of the human quest for the monological, the search for a single language and unitary truth by which the rest can be interpreted and assimilated.

The very language of those who want to build the tower is oppositional in intent, against God, against other humans, and against creation. It values the unitary and homogenous. It orders reality hierarchically. It cannot tolerate being at the margins. It celebrates self-sameness. It is the symbol of dom-ination and possessive power over everything else.

Then, for example, there is the tendency manifested in the post-exilic tradition during the time of Ezra, where the passion for the unique identity and exclusive particularity of Israel as a covenant community leads to what we may call today ethnic cleansing. Clear boundaries are erected; lines are drawn; outsiders (those who are culturally and religiously other) are clearly identified. In preserving itself as a sacred community and a holy people, Israel lost its compassion for those who were different, racially, culturally, and religiously. Thus the Biblical records remind us of the dangers of both the centripetal and centrifugal forces—the quest for assimilation as in Babel, and the self-centered desire for exclusive identity in the post-exhilic tradition.

The Bible, however, has yet another powerful paradigm of negotiating diversity. It is that of the Pentecost—the day when, through the operation of the Holy Spirit, the quests for integration and uniqueness are drawn together so that diversity in communion and harmony is affirmed. The narrative in Acts 2 takes care to hold the terms "each" and "all" in creative tension. Each hears in his or her native tongue and thus monologic traditions are overturned; vernacularization takes place. All cultures and languages are affirmed, yet none becomes the norm. Pentecost both destigmatizes each culture and relativizes all cultures at one and the same time, thereby bringing about a communion of diversity. All are included and yet each is decentralized. The Spirit brings about not a homogenized, safe, and secure uniformity but a differentiated and costly unity of all people, Jews, Arabs, and people from many nations.

Perhaps the most powerful image of the Pentecost story is the richness of diversity. As the story of Pentecost opens, the first thing that strikes us is the fact of a milling crowd, of masses of people, a sea of humanity, in the narrow streets of Jerusalem. They come in different colors and speak different languages. They include Arabs and Libyans, Romans and Iranians, a microcosm of the then-known world. In the experience of Pentecost, the gospel is heard in the interwoveness of the plurality of peoples, in cultures in collision.

Ours is an era of immigration, particularly from the former colonies to the colonizers' metropolitan centers. The biblical image of Pentecost tells us that in the midst of the reality of immigration, and all the promise and pain that it entails in our postcolonial times, the Spirit lives. The meaning and content of the gospel story is to be found in the interwoveness, the intermingling of the plurality of peoples. Therefore diversity is not something of which we are to be afraid; for the Spirit breaks forth in the midst of color, contrasts, and plurality. It is in the midst of diversity that the gospel is made known as the transforming power of God bringing into being the new. The Pentecost story, however, is not simply a celebration of diversity, for those who respond to the Spirit then are drawn into a communion in and through their differences. They have *koinonia,* a common sharing, of their diversity as the basis for mutual enrichment. As they mutually share their differences, the vast varieties of people come to know and witness to what the author of Ephesians later calls, "the multi-colored wisdom of God."

I believe that there are three significant lessons for our times as we seek to deal with diversity and negotiate in a plural world. *Pentecost points to a de-centering of centers and identities that exclude, a courageous crossing of borders, and a promotion of a multi-voiced, polyphonic community.* Let me briefly turn to each of these.

A Call for a De-Centering of Selves

First, an authentic way of dealing with pluralism calls for a de-centering of individual and collective identities constructed as totally autonomous and self-sufficient. Consider again the story of Pentecost. The story is set against the disciples' earlier question of whether the kingdom of Israel will be restored and their identity would be affirmed. But Jesus' response foreshadowed the reality that when the Spirit does come upon them, they will be dispersed, their collective existence will be de-centered, and they will go to the ends of the earth. Their identities from now on are to be defined in terms of their plural locations and the diverse peoples among whom they would go to witness. A centripetal quest is responded to with a promise of centrifugal dispersal. There is no central place, no single language, and no single authoritative seat of power, not even Jerusalem. The disciples come to learn that baptism itself is a sign of an alternative identity, of a new and inclusive humanity that replaces exclusivist ways of defining oneself. Baptism decenters identities defined either purely in terms of *polis*, i.e. the nation-/city-state to which one belongs, or in terms of *blood*, i.e., one's ethnic and kin relationships.

I am increasingly convinced that one of the major obstacles for a healthy way of dealing with difference is the pervasive habit of thought, or a mindset, shaped by the Enlightenment. The Enlightenment has given us the notion of the human self, or one's particular group, as a bounded and autonomous entity. Is it not a major element of Western cultural logic that the self is autonomous, self-contained, integral, self-sufficient, often monologically defined? Aristotle's understanding of individuals as independent, unchanging, and enduring subjects provided the basis for much of Western thought regarding the separative self. Augustine inherited Aristotle's philosophical construct and Thomas Aquinas fine-tuned it.

The thought pattern that shaped much of Christian theology until the modern period defined substance in general, and self, in particular, as that which needed nothing but itself in order to exist. Within Christian theology, God was conceived as the wholly Other, in no need of anything outside of "Himself," and related to creation only externally. All these led to a theological framework that was not conducive for an authentic encounter with the other or negotiating plurality in an authentic way.[26] When, consciously or unconsciously, we share this habit of thought, and hold that the human self is separate and in full possession of its own capabilities, anything outside of the self appears to be potentially threatening and therefore must be overcome or made serviceable to our well-being.

This autonomy obsession of the individualistic and possessive self often leads to a dominating relationship over all other beings, particularly those who are different. Is it not the case that much of Western polity and inter-human relationships are shaped by the treacherous Lockean notion that the pursuit of individual comfort, security, and growth is paramount? Locke further argues that such a pursuit will indirectly enrich the life of everyone else. I submit, however, that as long as individuals and groups are taken to be internally independent, separate, unified, and fixed, then they can have only "external" relations with others. "Oneness" will be victorious over multiplicity, self-identity over difference, and sameness over diversity. Many recent feminist theorists have powerfully established that there is an unmistakable correlation between domination and a kind of disembodied, abstract, and transcendent form of self. The same disembodied self further leads to a notion of knowledge as being applicable everywhere and to everyone.[27] Or, as Jane Flax states, the colonial logic demands that "only to the extent that one...group can dominate the whole can reality appear to be governed by one set of rules, be constituted by one privileged set of social relations, or be told by one story."[28] Such a mindset, such a habit of thought, needs to be de-centered if we are serious about discovering healthy ways of living with plurality.

American pragmatists like G. H. Mead have attempted to overthrow such a habit of thought and insisted that the human self is co-owned, shared, and jointly shaped. Humans are dialogically brought into being. They are relational, social selves. Anthropologists like Clifford Geertz also point out that the notion of the autonomous self is peculiar to the Western Enlightenment tradition. Many non-Western cultures are collective cultures in which nurturing relationships and loyalty to others are supreme social values. Selves in these cultures are not egocentric, self-contained, or nonporous. They are socio-centric. They are "dividual" and relational. As an African proverb puts it: "We participate, therefore I am." Contrast this to the Cartesian dictum: *Cogito ergo sum* (I think therefore I am), or a possible modern consumerist equivalent, "I possess, therefore I am!"

It appears that those who have been able to negotiate diversity in a healthy way seem to have a sense of their selves as "an act of grace" and "*a gift of the other.*" They celebrate the "other" as the one who contributes to their becoming. Their relationship to others and all else is internal. The spirituality of Paul seems to imply the formation of such a de-centered self. He says that he is crucified with Christ. No longer is it he who lives, but it is Christ who lives in him (Gal 2:19–20). Paul recognizes one's self as a gift from Christ as the one who stands for God and humans, the representative other. It is in connection with the other that one comes to be and has fuller life. My self is connective.

The interplay of the terms "each" and "all" in the Pentecost story is yet another example of the sort of de-centered self that we are describing here. Similarly, at the end of the second chapter of the Book of Acts, we are given a powerful description of a *community of relational selves,* socially formed, and sharing all things in common.

It appears, therefore, that a prerequisite for learning to live with diversity and encountering difference in a wholesome manner is a *conversion* from the Enlightenment notion of a private, monological, and separative self to the self as co-constituted relationally and dialogically with others. In this sense, mission as reconciliation begins with a call to conversion from selves centered on themselves. Such requires a prophetic critique of a culture that supports and is, in turn, shaped by self-sufficient and egocentric selves. While a monologic definition of the self is the heartland of domination, relational selves, dialogically formed selves, open up reality as connective and liberative. As Keller puts it,

> The more diversity I take in, the more I feelingly connect—and the roomier is my individual character. But such a composite subjectivity...surely unhinges any traditional notions of a subject.... the subject-superject arises from the endless breadth of its connections to the world.[29]

The leading Japanese Buddhist thinker, Maso Abe, argues that individual self-centeredness often leads to national and/or religious self-centeredness. He demonstrates that the logic behind all these forms of centrisms is the same.[30] For at the core of them lies the search for something unitary and fundamental that can provide a stable center on which to hang all our understandings; and in the light of which boundaries can be erected and exclusion effected. Self-centeredness is characterized by a search for a single meta-narrative. It reduces reality, and selves in particular, into autonomous simply located substances, as in Newtonian essentialist metaphysics. But a decentered understanding of self and reality sees each entity or self through its social location and its multilayered relationship to others. Everything has meaning only as it is located both in its particularity—such as by race, class or gender—and within a densely woven web of relationality. Therefore, no single self, nation, religion, or race can be privileged over others, whatever their economic or political power.

It is urgent that those who are committed to encountering pluralism in ways that promote reconciliation and build community across differences must seriously challenge the Enlightenment model of the egocentric self, or nation, or religion. The separative self needs to be exposed as a lie and an illusion. The boundaries that the separative self erects against other selves, or one community or nation erects against another, must be transgressed. This leads to the second imperative of the Pentecost paradigm.

A COURAGEOUS BORDER CROSSING

Monological or egocentric selves, as we saw above, are constructed oppositionally. Identity of an individual or community is defined by differentiating oneself from what one is not. Each is seen as sharply atomized, this from that, you from me, God from the world, and so on. This differentiation quickly turns into sharp distinctions, distinctions that lend themselves to opposition and confrontation. As David

Hardy puts it:

> Through long habits instilled into western patterns of thought by figures of the past, we are inclined to think in terms of dualities. Whenever, therefore, we need to identify something, we do so by differentiating it from what it is not. We tend therefore to see everything as sharply atomised, this from that, you from me, God from the world, and so on. These differentiations quickly turn into sharp distinctions, and the distinctions into oppositions or confrontations: and it soon seems paradoxical to suppose that there is some fundamental unity between those which/who have been disjoined. [31]

In order to preserve one's identity, non-porous borders are erected and maintained. The logical consequence is that differences can no longer be tolerated.

The Acts of the Apostles portrays Peter in a similar situation bounded by borders of race and religion; his attitude to a gentile Cornelius is shaped by his sense of pollution by contact with those different from him and his community. Yet as the power of Pentecost operates, he is given the strength to cross borders and discover that God has no favorites. How then can we learn to cross borders hitherto impermeable? First, we must realize that no cultural or religious border is impermeable. As Richard Bernstein argues convincingly, "There is no horizon which is ontologically closed.... There are always the linguistic and imaginative resources within any horizon that can enable us to extend our horizon...." [32]

In other words, we can come to understand what we believe to be alien and strange if we have the willingness to cross our self-imposed boundaries in order to engage the other. Despite the argument of postmodern radical relativism and its notion of incommensurability of plural identities and cultures, behind our cultural, linguistic, and even national borders there is a significant connectedness of our diverse identities and histories in these postmodern times. Certainly, in these days the coordinates of all our borders are continuously defined and redefined in terms of our interaction with each other. Many identities are hybrid and in constant flux.

One of the factors behind many a contemporary nationalist conflict or ethnic cleansing is the inability of a people to move beyond their own background, or ethnic, or cultural boundaries. We need to remind ourselves that it was the ideology of the incommensurability of races and cultural horizons that motivated the demonic destruction of hundreds of thousands by the Third Reich. Hence, rupturing the spatial and temporal boundaries of our histories and crossing borders are urgent imperatives for our communities of faith in a conflictual and plural world.

Of course, the fear of border crossing leads some to cling to the security of searching for universals by which all particulars can be comprehended. Trans-historical and transnational perspectives beyond and outside of the relational matrix of particularities are simply not available. Often what is taken to be a universal is none other than the specific point of view or narrative of a particular group, generally of those in power, now ascribed to have universal significance or to function as a meta-norm. What is needed, therefore, is a rejection of both the postmodern radical relativism and its notion of incommensurability of cultures on the one hand, and the Enlightenment claims for an all-encompassing and ahistorical meta-framework, on the other.

Instead, as in the case of Peter, we need to speak of the continuous formation and reformation of personal and communal borders through courageous acts of border crossings. Since the boundaries of today are no longer boundaries of territory, but rather boundaries of difference, they are constantly in flux. Following a God who continuously shifts our borders, we are called to transgress them as they shift.

Such a border crossing is similar to what John S. Dunne refers to as the phenomenon of "passing over and coming back." Describing new interfaith relationships as "the spiritual adventure of our time," Dunne says:

> Passing over is a shifting of standpoint, a going over to
> the standpoint of another culture, another way of life,
> another religion. It is followed by an equal and opposite
> process we might call "coming back," coming back with
> new insight to one's own culture, one's own way of life,
> one's own religion.[33]

Here there is no fusion of borders such that our individual or group identities become lost. Nor is there a border diffusion or dissolution. Rather there is a crossing over and a returning so that the coordinates of one's identity may now be redrawn in a much richer way due to the gift from the other.

In a dialogical context across difference, it is important that one does not bypass the elements of "strangeness" or possible contestation. Nor can one subsume difference under an already familiar category to oneself. The temptation to search for quick agreement and consensus must be resisted. For, as "Lyotard's debate...makes it clear, the rationality of consensus is only a few steps from the desire for one system, one truth—in sum, one rationality—to dominate human civilization. In its extreme, the will to one truth has yielded the totalitarian Reign of Terror."[34]

Such a border crossing is costly because it demands of us a rejection of commonly accepted modes of oppositional thinking and binary habits of thought. Border crossing is risky because it calls us to be liminal, to stand at the threshold. All threshold existence is threatening, but it is only when we step across the threshold that we may creatively discover the new. Victor Turner speaks convincingly of the power of such a crossing over. He states, "*Communitas* breaks through the interstices of structure, in liminality; at the edges of structure...possibly because it transgresses or dissolves the norms that govern structured and institutionalised relationships and is accompanied by experiences of unprecedented potency."[35]

In Isaiah 19:23–24, the prophet envisions such a border crossing. The vision speaks of an impossible possibility.

Three former enemies now cross borders and walk back and forth to each other over a highway built by God. But for Israel it was costly. Israel had to give up its privileged position and learn to be on par with Egypt and Assyria. It had to give up its special name as "my [God's] people" in relationship with others who have been hitherto called the gentiles. But the prophet speaks of this border crossing as though it is God's dream and purpose for humanity. The mission of the church today, I submit, is building such a highway over which people of diverse cultures, religions, and races can cross borders for both integration and enrichment of their particular identities. Such an act will, indeed, demand from the church a critical examination and renunciation of theologies that exclude and missionary practices that maintain impermeable boundaries between Christians and the people of other faiths.

While such a costly border crossing is not possible by our own resources, it is possible—and it has been so in the history of the church—in the power of the Holy Spirit; for the gift of the Spirit is the love that overcomes all alienation. This gift of the Spirit is what Whitehead calls, "the cosmic Eros." It is "'the divine element in the universe' luring all things toward each other…Eros is a name for that unlimited desire that drives beyond the fixed bounds of all separations."[36]

TOWARD MULTI-VOICED AND POLYPHONIC COMMUNITIES

If we look back at the story of the early church after the Pentecost, it appears that the Spirit did not leave the believers only with border crossings. Certainly such crossings brought out newer dimensions of integration or wholeness and helped redraw the coordinates of identities. But the Spirit demanded more. The Spirit led the disciples to the formation of a community where every form of difference could be articulated, where contestation was possible. Those whose voices had not been heard previously were now empowered to speak. Very early in the life of the church the concerns of the marginalized, Greek widows for example, became a factor in the structural alteration of the community and its ministries. The stories of those who were silenced were now heard, and, in the light of those stories, theology was recast. The experience of the "gentiles" thus became a decisive factor in determining the future of Christian life and mission.

The first council in Jerusalem is a case in point. The council is set in a context of intense conflict as early Christians encounter difference of ethnicity, culture, and tradition. The powerful "Judaizers" have their say. Yet, at the center of it all are the stories of those who are outside the Jewish community, the gentiles. Truth is shared not in propositional terms, but as a common sharing of a variety of stories in the life of the Spirit. It is in the voicing of these stories that a multi-voiced community comes into being. For storytelling suggests the creative invention of a multiplicity of voices. It is significant to note that feminist literature places a great emphasis on the act of voicing. Because it is by constructing and telling stories about themselves that women (and oppressed people in general) constitute themselves as subjects and create community. No wonder Carol Gilligan's ground-breaking text on the moral development of women has the title *In a Different Voice*. Similarly, in his book *God of the Oppressed*, James Cone points out the power of storytelling, voicing, in the act of empowerment and community building. He says:

> Indeed, when I understand truth as story, I am more likely to be open to other people's truth stories. As I listen to other stories, I am invited to move out of the subjectivity of my own story into another realm of thinking and acting. The same is true for others when I tell my story…. Indeed it is only when we refuse to listen to another story that our own story becomes ideological that is a closed system, incapable of hearing the truth.[37]

Cone warns that community itself is at stake and domination of one group by another is the result when we believe that our own stories are the only valid truth. He says, "When people can no longer listen to other people's stories, they become enclosed within their own social context, treating their distorted visions of reality as the whole truth. And then they feel that they must destroy other stories, which bear witness that life can be lived in another way."[38]

Thus the Pentecost paradigm places before us an authentic way of dealing with difference and negotiating plurality. The Pentecost vision is the intentional creation of a community, a space, where the "other," who has been silenced for so long, can now be heard on his/her own terms. It is a space where monologues give way to dialogues and the co-construction of the self and others takes place within a shared communion. It is a space that safeguards differences and yet builds up a common sharing. Such a dialogical and multi-vocal relationship is possible because the selves involved in it, as we have seen above, are not self-sufficient, discrete, and bounded individuals, but rather are permeable, open to the other, and in process of being co-constituted with the contributions of others.

This implies that we have many different voices in and through which we speak, think, and hear others—and in and through which we relate to the world. "We are 'the voices that inhabit us.'"[39] Every relationship is mutual and multi-voiced, genuinely promoting verbal or cultural exchange, so that all those involved in the relationship are changed or enriched. Here, Mikhail Bakhtin's notion of the polyphonic nature of discourse is significant. Bakhtin insists that each voice exists only in dialogue with other voices. As he puts it, "Utterances are not indifferent to one another, and are not self-sufficient; they are aware of and mutually reflect one another."[40]

The many voices of *heteroglossia* offer a richness of thinking, knowing and experiencing that informs our understanding of ourselves and all that is around us. It is thus through this multi-voicedness that we are constituted as social selves. The absence of multi-voicedness leads a community to a single, dominant mode of discourse where definitions of truth are static, exclusive, and universal.

I use the term "multi-voiced" and not the more familiar term "multicultural" primarily to indicate that the space— the community we are envisioning here—is not simply the inclusion of more representatives from diverse groups. Rather, the multi-voiced community actively fosters a setting where pluralities of voices are heard, their diversities and contestations are expressed, and they actively participate in decision making. Voicing thus implies the exercise of power.

In a multi-voiced community, therefore, power sharing is critical. But such a community is possible only when the dominant group is willing to give up inherited structures of power and privilege. Much will be demanded of those who commit themselves to creating such dialogical and multi-voiced spaces, especially in the midst of a predominantly monological world.

Liberating dialogue among diverse communities demands a willingness to abandon the false security of one's own self-identity and a readiness to cross over the boundaries of cultural experiences and traditions. It calls for a willingness to move beyond our limited and finite horizons, our theological and ideological comfort zones. The fifth world conference on Faith and Order of the World Council of Churches, held in 1993 in Santiago de Compostela, emphasized the need for *metanoia* and *kenosis* in authentic ecumenical dialogue. In powerful words it called all who are committed to ecumenical dialogue to a life of openness and risk taking.

> As we strip ourselves of false securities, finding in God our true and only identity, daring to be open and vulnerable to each other, we will begin to live as pilgrims on a journey, discovering the God of surprises who leads us into roads which we have not travelled, and we will find in each other true companions on the way.[41]

201

The same openness and risk is necessary for the realization of a genuine multi-voiced community.

Mission towards a multi-voiced community, witnessing to truth as stories, will necessarily involve the radical vulnerability that Jesus demonstrated. It calls for a genuine "incarnate presence" before the other, and within the cultures and religious heritage of the people around us. *Witness from within* is the only proper mode of evangelism worthy of a God who does not control history from *without,* but rather enters into our history, suffers with it, and transforms it by participating in it fully. As the well-known Asian theologian, C. S. Song, puts it,

> Christian mission in essence should be a love affair of the church with other human beings with whom God has already fallen in love.... It is Christian believers building with them a community in the power of God's love. If this is what Christian mission is, then Christian mission is God's mission.[42]

Often the practice of mission tends to forget this central affirmation. Mission, in essence, is an expression of God's pain-love demonstrated in Jesus Christ to all human beings already loved by God. Mission in the mode of vulnerable love is necessarily dialogical, a genuine listening and responding to stories of God's love from others, however strange they may sound. Song thus challenges us to seriously examine the nature and style of our mission and missionary policies.

> Christian mission has been very much a truth affair of Christians with the world.... All in all, a truth affair is a judgmental affair. It judges, and is not to be judged. It conquers, and is not to be conquered. Union of contradictions, opposites, and polarities is not its particular interest.... Truth, despite its lofty claims, is limited in its power to unite the "ununitable"; love, despite its humble and soft appearance, is unlimited in its power to unite the "ununitable."[43]

One thing is certain: only when we are led by the pain-love of the crucified Christ, the same pain-love that gives life to all and voice to the voiceless, will we become authentic witnesses to the power of the risen Christ. It is only through Christ's compassionate solidarity and love that the reconciliation of all with God and each other, and the drawing of all of creation into God's embrace, are accomplished. Witnessing to this fact in a plural world is our call and our reward.

SOME PRACTICAL CONSIDERATIONS

What then are the implications for our mission thinking and practice in the context of pluralism and at a time of increasing globalization and fragmentation, a time of centripetal and centrifugal forces in collision? Let me raise a series of questions and concerns that need to be explored if we seek to engage in mission as reconciliation in our plural world today.

A theology of mission and mission policies grounded in the priority of the *missio Dei* will recognize and celebrate the plurality of religious traditions as a gift of the Holy Spirit for the enrichment of the church's life and witness. A significant mission policy therefore will be to seek ways of ensuring the authentic identity and freedom of various religious communities in the neighborhood of the church. Can the money and energy of churches be made available for providing space for worship and witness of peoples of other faith? Is setting aside time and resources to educate Christians in local communities for genuine dialogical relationship with people of other faiths seen as an integral part of our missionary obedience today? Since sustained exposure to the worship life and festivals of people of different faiths may lead to a genuine celebration of plurality, can training for such exposure be part of mission education?

What role should courses in world religions and cultures other than one's own play in ministerial formation and seminary studies? Can any one be deemed competent to minister in a multi-ethnic and multicultural local parish without adequate exposure to, and training in, cross-cultural exchange and inter-faith relations? The implications of these questions for theological curricula, and even the General Ordination Examination, are enormous.

A brief word about encountering the religiously other is in order at this point. Mission as reconciliation is clearly a sharing, with humility, of what we know as God's love in Jesus Christ. We must witness to what we have found in Christ with an attentive and open posture. But such listening and speaking need not take place only within specifically religious settings.

It is often the case that witnessing as neighbors takes place as we share our common humanity in normal life situations and as we face problems together. Often common action for social change leads peoples of different faiths to share their deep convictions about God and the human condition. Dialogue at a deeper level, however, cannot be honest unless Christians give clear testimony to their experience of God's love in Christ with humility and love. As the San Antonio conference of the World Council of Churches Commission on World Mission and Evangelism puts it:

> We cannot point to any other way of salvation than Jesus Christ; at the same time we cannot set limits to the saving power of God.... We are well aware that these convictions and the ministry of witness stand in tension with what we have affirmed as God being present in and at work in people of other faiths; we appreciate this tension, we do not attempt to resolve it.[44]

The report continues, that we ought to "recognize that witness and dialogue presuppose a two-way relationship. We affirm that witness does not preclude dialogue but invites it, and that dialogue does not preclude witness but extends and deepens it."[45]

An urgent mission task is to explore what "living in this tension" means in practical terms at the local parish level?

What would holding witness and dialogue in tandem and in tension imply for our mission policies and practice? What resources are needed to educate women and men to engage authentic dialogue in their daily lives with those who are different in culture or religion? How can we create safe spaces and genuine community for people of different faiths to encounter each other without dogmatism or neutralizing convictions?

Several years ago the Council of Churches in Britain and Ireland identified the following four principles as essential for any encounter between people of different faiths. The Interfaith Network in Britain, including representatives of all major religions, has further adopted these principles as part of its "Code of Practice for Faith-Sharing." I list them below in the belief that they are equally applicable for developing human relationships across any form of diversity:

1. Dialogue *begins* when people meet each other.
2. Dialogue *depends* upon mutual understanding and mutual trust.
3. Dialogue *makes it possible* to share in service to the community.
4. Dialogue *becomes* the medium of authentic witness.[46]

In closing, let me briefly suggest some key needs that churches and individual Christians must consider as we seek to promote authentic Christian witness across cultures and religions. We must fulfill the following if we are to seek, and be faithful to, God's "multi-colored wisdom" in a plural world:

- the need to take concrete steps to promote greater sharing of gospel experiences and insights across churches from different cultures both from within and outside a given country/region;

- the need to create space and programs where people from diverse cultures, races, and religions in a given neighborhood may interact, share, and learn with and from each other for mutual enrichment;

- the need for concerted multi-faith education at all levels in the church from the local congregation to the curricula of theological faculties;

- the need to develop a language to speak and express diversity adequately in order for Christians to learn from and communicate meaningfully across cultures;

- the need to cultivate a "polysymbolic" spirituality, i.e., a spirituality of empathy and imagination that opens one to be shaped by a plurality of insights and symbols;

- the need for a "both/and" attitude as an alternative to an "either/or" thought form;

- the need to become aware that "monological" definitions of truth, values, and norms have the power to oppress, marginalize, and destroy;

- the need to equip Christians to engage in dialogical relationships with those who are different, both within the local congregation and in the neighborhood;

- the need to be aware when and how the misuse of power and privilege operate in inter-confessional and intercultural dialogues and find ways of overcoming imbalance of power among them, thus making possible a more authentic sharing;

- the need for greater attentiveness to God/truth as mystery that we are called to "stand under";

- the need to discern genuinely plural options and possibilities in any situation and therefore to learn to accept liminality;

- the need to discover that it is in liminality, at the thresholds and margins of the known and comfortable, that God's creative and reconciling action breaks into the world.

Notes

[1] Jürgen Moltmann, *The Church in the Power of the Spirit* (New York: Harper and Row, 1977), 10.

[2] Diana Eck, *The New Religious America: How a "Christian Country" Has Become the World's Most Religiously Diverse Nation* (New York: HarperCollins, 2001).

[3] The conflicts fueled by religions around the world are so many that a recent book by Scott Appleby dealing with the theme has the title, *The Ambivalence of the Sacred: Religion, Violence and Reconciliation* (Lanham, MD: Rowman & Littlefield, 2000).

[4] Lamin Sanneh, *Translating the Message: The Missionary Impact on Culture* (Maryknoll, NY: Orbis Books, 1989), 27.

[5] From the author's notes of an unpublished address by John Arnold given at the Mission Conference of the European Council of Churches in Santiago de Compostella, Spain in 1991.

[6] Samuel Huntington, *The Clash of Civilizations and the Remaking of the World Order* (New York: Simon & Schuster, 1996).

[7] Benjamin R. Barber, *Jihad vs. McWorld* (New York: Random House, 1995), 11.

[8] Stjepan G. Mestrovic, *The Balkanization of the West* (London: Routledge, 1994). Since then, many new texts on the theme can be identified such as Michel Maffesoli's, *The Time of the Tribes* (London: Sage Publications, 1996).

[9] George Ritzer, *The McDonaldization of Society* (Thousand Oaks, CA: Pine Forge Press, 1993); see also his *The McDonaldization Thesis* (Thousand Oaks, CA: Sage Publications, 1998). William Greider's, *One World Ready or Not* (New York, New York.: Simon and Schuster, 1997) is yet another in the same genre.

[10] Barber, 20.

[11] Marc Gopin, *Between Eden and Armageddon* (Oxford: Oxford University Press, 2000), 4.

[12] Kosuke Koyama, "Extend Hospitality to Strangers: A Missiology of Theologia Crucis," *International Review of Mission* vol. LXXXII, no.327 (July/October 1993), 283–295.

[13] Richard Bernstein, *Beyond Objectivism and Relativism* (Philadelphia: University of Pennsylvania Press, 1985), 229.

[14] The Book of Common Prayer (New York: Church Hymnal Corporation, 1979), 855.

[15] Catherine Keller, *From A Broken Web: Separation, Sexism and Self* (Boston: Beacon Press, 1986), 219.

[16] Michael Kinnamon, ed., *Signs of the Spirit, Official Report Seventh Assembly* (Geneva: World Council of Churches, 1991) 100.

[17] Quoted in Josef Smolik, "One Aspect of Philip Potter's Ecumenism," *Communio Viatorum*, Vol. XXVIII (1985), 67f.

[18] Ofelia Schutte, "Cultural Alterity: Cross-cultural Communication and Feminist Theory in North-South Contexts," in: Uma Narayan and Sandra Harding, eds., *Decentering the Center: Philosophy for a Multicultural, Postcolonial, and Feminist World* (Bloomington: Indiana University Press, 2000), 48.

[19] Richard Bernstein, *New Constellation, The Ethical-Political Horizons of Modernity/Postmodernity* (Cambridge, MA: MIT Press, 1992), 71.

[20] Ibid., 58 ff.

[21] Sue Golding, *The Eight Technologies of Otherness* (London: Routledge, 1997).

[22] Robert Schreiter, *Reconciliation: Mission and Ministry in a Changing World Order* (Maryknoll, NY: Orbis Books, 1992), 52–53.

[23] Robert Young, *Colonial Desire: Hybridity in Theory, Culture and Race* (London: Routledge, 1995), especially Chapters 6 and 7.

[24] Ella Sohat and Robert Stam, *Unthinking Eurocentrism* (London: Routledge, 1994), 49; I am indebted to Stam and Sohat's useful way of identifying the marks of polycentric thinking, see in particular pages 46–49.

[25] Christopher Kurien, "On Earth—A Dangerous Reality," in *Cultures in Dialogue: Documents From a Symposium in Honour of Philip A. Potter* (Geneva: World Council of Churches, 1983), 17–18.

[26] See: Joreg Rieger, *God and the Excluded* (Minneapolis: Fortress Press, 2001). This is a recent critique of models of self and the other as well as the concepts of God that particularly exclude people at the margins. There are some excellent critiques of notions of the egocentric and self-sufficient self. See: Catherine Keller, *From a Broken Web* and Susan Hekman, *Moral Voices, Moral Selves* (Pennsylvania: The Pennsylvania State University Press, 1995). By and large, much of feminist theory provides a sustained critique of such a mindset.

[27] For example, see:

Loraine Code, *What Can She Know? Feminist Theory and Construction of Knowledge* (Ithaca, NY: Cornell University Press, 1991).
Patricia Collins, *Black Feminist Thought,* Revised edition (London: Routledge, 2000).
Linda Alcoff and Elizabeth Potter, eds., *Feminist Epistemologies* (London: Routledge, 1993).
Catherine A. McKinnon, *Toward a Feminist Theory of the State* (Cambridge, MA: Harvard University Press, 1989).

[28] Jane Flax, *Thinking Fragments* (Berkeley: University of California Press, 1990), 28 as cited in E. Sampson, *Celebrating the Other* (London: Harvester Wheatsheaf, 1993), 10.

[29] Keller, 186.

[30] Maso Abe, *Buddhism and Interfaith Dialogue* (Honolulu, Hawaii: University of Hawaii Press, 1995), Chapter 5.

[31] David Hardy, "The Future of Theology in a Complex World," in Hilary Regan and Alan J. Torrance eds., *Christ and Context* (Edinburgh: T&T Clark, 1993), 22.

[32] Richard Bernstein, "The Hermeneutics of Cross-Cultural Understanding," in: Anindita N. Balslev, ed., *Cross-Cultural Conversation* (Atlanta: Scholars Press, 1996), 35.

[33] John S. Dunne, *The Way of All the Earth: Experiments in Truth and Religion* (New York: Macmillan, 1972), ix.

[34] Schutte, 50.

[35] Victor Turner, *The Ritual Process* (Ithaca, NY: Cornell University Press, 1989), 128.

[36] Keller, 156–157.

[37] James Cone, *God of the Oppressed* (New York: Seabury Press, 1975), 102–104.

[38] Ibid, 103.

[39] Gary S. Morson, *Mikhail Bakhtin: Creation of a Prosaics* (Stanford, CA: Stanford University Press, 1990), 213.

[40] Cited in Robert Stam, *Subversive Pleasures: Bakhtin, Cultural Criticism, and Film* (Baltimore: John Hopkins University Press), 231.

[41] Thomas F. Best and Gunther Gassmann, eds., *On the Way to Fuller Koinonia* (Geneva: WCC, 1994), 234.

[42] C.S. Song, *Tell Us Our Names* (Maryknoll, NY: Orbis, 1984), 108.

[43] Ibid., 106.

[44] Fredrick R. Wilson, ed., *The San Antonia Report: Your Will Be Done—Mission in Christ's Way* (Geneva: World Council of Churches, 1990), 32.

[45] Ibid.

[46] Kenneth Cracknell, *Towards a New Relationship: Christians and People of Other Faith* (London: Epworth Press, 1986), 114 ff.

7

RESTORATION, RECONCILIATION, AND RENEWAL IN GOD'S MISSION AND THE ANGLICAN COMMUNION

IAN T. DOUGLAS

As Christians, any discussion of mission in this time of globalization and crisis must be set within the context of our common life in the Body of Christ. To this end, I want to consider our participation in God's mission as members of the Anglican Communion in a time of radical change and transition both in the church and in the world. To begin with we will look at how understandings of mission have changed in the last half century. We will then consider the profound transformation in both demographics and power that have occurred in the Anglican Communion during the same period. Having laid out the terrain of these changes in mission thought and in Anglicanism, I will suggest that, rather than reacting to the tumultuous times in which we live, we are called to a deeper engagement in God's mission, to be renewed in God's mission for the sake of a hurting world.

MISSION IN A TIME OF CHANGE

Mission in nineteenth and first half of the twentieth centuries made sense. Mission during this period, what mission scholar David Bosch has described as "Mission in the Wake of the Enlightenment," was something that Christians in Europe and North America did "over there, to other people."[1] Conversion of "the heathen" through the spread of churches and the advance of Western "civilization" went hand in hand. The abuses (and contributions) of missionaries and the close connection between mission and imperialism in Africa, Asia, Latin America, and the Pacific are well documented and need not be rehearsed here.[2] Suffice it to say that throughout the nineteenth century and for the first half of the twentieth century, the Western churches had their missions, *missiones ecclesiarum* (churchs' missions). These missions, as dependent outposts of European and North American Christianity, usually in some "far off" part of the world, sought to extend church models and cultural world-views of the Enlightenment.

In the middle of the twentieth century, significant shifts in the theological and ecclesiological terrain of an emergent global Christianity began to shake the ground of missiological thought. Quakes occurred and fissures opened up between older, established models of mission and new understandings of mission in the emerging post-colonial, post-modern world. Discussion in ecumenical councils turned from the role of the churches' missions to wrestling with the nature of the mission of the church, the *missio ecclesiae*.[3] Mission was seen less as something done by voluntary associations of Christians, often as a side interest of the churches, and more as the central calling of the church. These theological shifts led individuals such as Emil Brunner to state: "The Church exists by mission as fire exists by burning," and Stephen Neil to proclaim: "The age of missions is at an end; the age of mission has begun."[4]

The predominance of this ecclesiocentric view of mission in the immediate post-World War II era was short lived. While the International Missionary Council promoted the coterminous nature of church and mission, individual theologians and missiologists were beginning to look beyond the church for the locus of God's action in the world. Increasingly, the church was seen as being an agent, at best, or extraneous, at worst, to God's salvific intervention in the wider struggles of the world. The *missio ecclesiae* (the mission of the church) was to give way to the *missio Dei* (the mission of God).

Johannes Hoekendijk led the charge against prevailing church-centered definitions of mission. He criticized such as leading to a form of evangelism whose goal was to maintain and extend the bridgehead of the Western Enlightenment church. Hoekendijk said:

> To put it bluntly, the call to evangelism [the call to mission] is often little else than a call to restore "Christendom," the *Corpus Christianum*, as a solid, well-integrated cultural complex, directed and dominated by the Church. And the sense of urgency is often nothing but a nervous feeling of insecurity, with the established Church endangered, a flurried activity to save the remnants of a time now irrevocably past.[5]

In short, Hoekendijk argued that "Evangelization (mission) and *churchification* are not identical, and very often they are each other's bitterest enemies."[6] Hoekendijk wanted to move mission from an ecclesiological to an eschatological point of departure. For him, the goal of evangelism, the goal of mission, was not to extend the church as the *Corpus Christianum* but rather to participate with God in God's new creation, to work for God's *shalom*, God's *salaam*. Hoekendijk was the first of his generation to suggest that it was God's mission in the world to bring about God's *shalom*, God's Kingdom, God's reign.

Most missiologists today would affirm that the mission of God, the *missio Dei*, is God's action in the world to bring about God's reign. The Trinitarian God, Creator, Redeemer, and Sanctifier, has effected a new order, a new *shalom*; one in which all of creation can find new life and new hope. Whereas some earlier proponents of the *missio Dei* eschewed the role of the church in God's mission, today's mission thinkers affirm that the church, as the Body of Christ in the world, does have a crucial role to play in the salvation work of God. The church is called and uniquely empowered by the Holy Spirit to participate with God in God's mission of justice, compassion, and reconciliation. Our Presiding Bishop, in his jubilee call, has continuously lifted before the Episcopal Church our participation in God's mission, or as he puts it, "God's project" as the *reason d'etre* of the church.

Although the church has a unique and crucial role in God's plan of salvation, it does not have, however, exclusive rights on participation with God in God's mission. Thus, many advocates of the *missio Dei*, especially missiologists from religiously plural contexts, see the possibility of cooperation with people of other faiths in God's universal mission. The South Indian theologian, S. J. Samartha, emphasizes:

> In a religiously plural world, Christians, together with their neighbors of other faiths, are called upon to participate in God's continuing mission in the world. Mission is God's continuing activity through the Spirit to mend the brokenness of creation, to overcome the fragmentation of humanity, and to heal the rift between humanity, nature and God.[7]

In these difficult times, following the death and destruction of September 11, it is particularly important that we as Christians recognize and lift up our commonality with the other great Abrahamic faiths, especially Islam, in God's project of mending the brokenness of creation and healing the rift and fragmentation within humanity.

Participating with God in the healing of the world is at the heart of God's mission, is at the heart of our common calling as Christians. Our Catechism thus affirms: "the mission of the Church is to restore all people to unity with God and each other in Christ."[8] The Episcopal Church has gone on record stating that the mission of God, as manifested in the church as the Body of Christ, is no less than the eschatological restoration and reconciliation of all people to unity with God and each other in Christ. The mission of God, the mission of Jesus, and the mission of the church is one of restoration and reconciliation.

God's mission, manifested in Jesus and empowered by the Holy Spirit, is thus not static but a centrifugal force of movement outward.[9] Jesus demonstrated in word and deed that the reign of God, realized in the sending of God's son, must continue to expand to the ends of the earth. "As you have sent me into the world, so have I sent them into the world." (Jn 17:18) Two by two, Jesus' disciples are sent to bear his mission, God's mission, in the world. Being sent in God's mission has as much efficacy for the baptized today as it did in apostolic times.

For over a century and a half, the Episcopal Church has affirmed that baptism incorporates the faithful into the mission of God. The General Convention of 1835 proclaimed boldly that the church was to be first and foremost a missionary society. All Episcopalians, by virtue of baptism and not voluntary association, are members of the Domestic and Foreign Missionary Society.[10] Participation in God's mission, God's project, therefore is at the heart of the baptismal call. Baptism is thus a commission, co-mission, in God's mission. The imperative is clear; we are all called to God's work of reconciliation.[11]

THE ANGLICAN COMMUNION IN A TIME OF CHANGE

Bishops who attended the Lambeth Conference in 1998 might recall some of the surprises and learnings they encountered at that global meeting of Anglican bishops. For the first time, many church leaders from the industrialized West had to wrestle deeply with the reality that the Anglican

Communion is no longer a Christian community primarily identified with Anglo-American culture. We in the West can no longer rest in the economic and political privilege of colonialism or the theological/philosophical paradigms of the Enlightenment. We are being pushed to recognize that the Anglican Communion is moving into a post-colonial, post-modern reality, no matter how much that might challenge us or scare us.[12]

Up until the summer of 1998, however, most Anglicans in the West could pretty well ignore these radical shifts in the Communion and thus avoid the hard questions of identity, authority, and power. In a similar, yet more extreme manner, up until September 11, 2001, most United States citizens could pretend that we were insulated from the pains and evils of the world. Our cultural, economic, and political hegemony shielded us from deeply engaging the realities of our increasingly multicultural and plural church; just as, in case of the hijackings, it shielded us from the realities of death and destruction caused by militarism, terrorism, or economic injustice.[13] I am afraid that, already, the symbolism of the terrorist targeting of the Pentagon and the World Trade Towers is lost on those who call for revenge and retribution.

But Lambeth 1998 signaled a turning point for Anglicanism. (Just as September 11 marks a turning point for the United States.) In debates over international debt and/or sexuality, it became abundantly clear at Lambeth '98 that the churches in the Southern Hemisphere, or the Two-Thirds World, would not stand idly by while their sisters and brothers in the United States, England, and other dominantly Anglo contexts set the agenda. Whether aided by some in the West who stood to gain ground in sexuality debates by siding with bishops in Africa, Asia, Latin America, and the Pacific, or not, it became abundantly clear to all that a profound power shift is occurring within Anglicanism. Old understandings of identity based on shared Anglo, cultural, economic, and political hegemony are being pushed aside by a radically multicultural Anglican Communion. Anthems of Titcomb and Tallis sung by boy choirs in chapels at Cambridge and Oxford can no longer hold us together. Even bishops taking tea with the Queen during Lambeth is not what it used to be.

The changes in contemporary Anglicanism, from a white, predominantly English-speaking church of the West to a church of the Southern Hemisphere, embodying vast differences of culture, geographies, and languages, are consistent with the changing face of Christianity over the last four decades. Anglican mission scholar, David Barrett, has documented that in the year 1900, 77% of the 558 million Christians in the world lived in Europe or North America. Today only 37% of the close to two billion Christians live in the same area. Barrett further predicts that in less than three decades, in the year 2025, fully 71% of the projected 2.6 billion Christians worldwide will live in Asia, Africa, Latin America, and the Pacific.[14]

If we consider the church in Africa south of the Sahara, specifically, the numbers are equally astounding. In 1960 after 150 years of Western missionary activity the number of Christians in Africa were approximately 50 million. From 1960 until 1990, the Christian population in sub-Saharan Africa increased from 50 million to 300 million. That change represents a five-fold increase in one fifth of the time; and population increase alone cannot explain this incredible growth.

What are we to make of this transformation in the global Body of Christ? In particular, how has our own little corner of the Christian tradition, that Body of Christ that traces its origins to the Holy Catholic Church first rooted in the British Isles and now known as Anglicanism, been transformed into a truly global Christian community of difference? Let us briefly consider the history.

For the majority of the nineteenth and the first half of the twentieth century the Anglican Communion (as it existed) was dominated by Western churches, chief among them were the Church of England, the Episcopal Church in the United States, and the Anglican churches in Canada and Australia. Each of these four autonomous Anglican churches supported and controlled their own missions around the world with the Episcopal Church's three biggest mission fields being China, Japan, and Liberia. From the 1850s to the 1960s, mission was thus inextricably linked to Western colonialism and imperialism. This was especially true for the established Church of England, for wherever the crown went so too did the church. If you look closely at a map of today's Anglican Communion you will find that the majority of Anglican churches lie in areas of the world that at one time or another were territories of either England or the United States.

All of this began to change in the 1960s. As colonies in Africa, Asia, Latin America, and the Pacific struggled for political independence from their former masters, mission fields in the same regions sought ecclesial independence from the older, sending churches in England and the United States. Over time the missions grew into fully autonomous Anglican churches in their own right and the number of churches in the Anglican Communion multiplied. With this change, Anglicans began to search for new ways of coming together, new ways of relating one to another as the Body of Christ.

The Anglican Congress of 1963, held in Toronto, Canada, was a watershed for the contemporary Anglican Communion. This meeting of Anglican lay people, priests, and bishops from every corner of the Globe embraced an influential and far-reaching vision: "Mutual Responsibility and Interdependence in the Body of Christ" (MRI). MRI proposed a radical reorientation of mission priorities and stressed mutual responsibility for mission between all Anglican churches as equal partners. It stated in part:

> In our time the Anglican Communion has come of age.
> Our professed nature as a worldwide fellowship of
> national and regional churches has suddenly become a
> reality.... The full communion in Christ, which has
> been our traditional tie, has suddenly taken on a totally
> new dimension. It is now irrelevant to talk of "giving"
> and "receiving" churches. The keynotes of our time are
> equality, interdependence, mutual responsibility.[15]

Unfortunately the vision of MRI remains a goal to be achieved rather than a reality that is lived. The real question for Anglicans today is how does this mutual responsibility and interdependence play itself out in a community of 38 equal, and autocephalous churches? What are the challenges prohibiting us from realizing the vision of the 1963 Anglican Congress? I believe that there are two large forces, one political and economic, the other philosophical and theological, that stand in the way of the Anglican Communion's genuine embrace of mutual responsibility and interdependence.

The first force prohibiting our living into the vision of a mutually interdependent community in Christ is the ongoing legacy of colonialism. As I have mentioned, the Anglican Communion, as we have known it for the majority of its history, has been intimately connected to Western colonialism. Unfortunately, we are not yet free from the vestiges of colonial power plays and/or new colonial abuses. When we in the West give to, or hold back money from, "partner churches" in the Southern Hemisphere, based upon our needs and desires, or when brother bishops and archbishops from around the world take it on themselves to set up alternative polity structures in the United States as a means to support so called "orthodox" believers, these actions run counter to the spirit and commitments of MRI. Like it or not, colonialism dies hard.

The second major force that hinders our embrace of the new Anglican Communion lies in the philosophical and theological roots of modernity. Whether we mark the beginning of the Anglican Communion in 1784 with the consecration of Samuel Seabury as the first bishop of an Anglican church outside of the British Isles or with the first Lambeth Conference of Bishops in 1867, the Anglican Communion, *per se*, as a family of churches is only about 200 years old. As such, the Anglican Communion is a thoroughly modern phenomenon, with modern understood as the age of modernity, the last 500 years, the Age of Enlightenment.

The Anglican Communion has historically traded on the power of Enlightenment thought as much as it has on the power of Western colonialism. Up until very recently, most Anglicans relied upon philosophical and theological constructs of the Enlightenment that value either/or propositions, binary constructs, and dualistic thinking. Anglicans formed in Enlightenment thought pride themselves on being able to figure things out, to know limits, to be able to define what is right and what is wrong, who is in and who is out. Modern man (and I use this non-inclusive term deliberately) values clear lines of authority, knowing who is in charge, a hierarchical power structure. Pluralities and multiple ways of seeing the world are an anathema to modernity and thus to many who have been in control in the Anglican Communion for most of its history.

But all of this is changing as the majority of Anglicans today are located in places where the constructs of Enlightenment thought have less efficacy. I do not mean here that sisters and brothers in the South and those who are more free from the constrictions of modern thought are less educated or caught in a world of superstitions, as some might posit. Rather the majority of Anglicans in the world today are able to live in multiple realities, both the Western Enlightenment construct as well as their own local contexts. It is important to emphasize here that marginalized people in the West, especially women, people of color, poor people, gay and lesbian individuals, have always lived multiple realities— their own particularities and that of the dominant culture. It is only those in power, historically, white, financially secure, heterosexual, ordained males in the West, who have the privilege of believing and acting as if there is only one reality, ours. The movement within Anglicanism from being a church grounded in modernity and secure in the Enlightenment, to a postmodern or extra-modern reality is as tumultuous as the shift from colonialism to a post-colonial reality.

The transition in the Anglican world from colonialism to post-colonialism and from modernity to postmodernity is terrifying, especially for those of us who historically have been the most privileged, most in control, most secure in the colonial Enlightenment world. The radical transition afoot in the Anglican Communion is terrifying for it means that we in the West, especially, dare I say it again, people like me—white, male, heterosexual, well educated, financially secure, clerics—will no longer have the power and control that we have so much enjoyed. As a result we are anxious, confused, lost in a sea of change.

The movement from being a colonial and modern church to that of a post-colonial and postmodern community in Christ, with its concomitant specter of loss, is vigorously countered by those who have been historically the most privileged in the Communion. Various attempts to reassert control, regain power, put Humpty Dumpty back together again, are dominating inter-Anglican conversations at this point in history. There is not space in this paper to explicate in detail these attempts to reassert power by the historically privileged, but let me briefly mention two reactions to the changing face of Anglicanism that I see emerging, both of which I believe are un-Anglican.

The first reaction is a rise of new confessionalism. There is an increasing desire from some among us to articulate clear definitions of what it means to be an Anglican today. Such individuals look for security in a kind of confession like our Lutheran and Presbyterian sisters and brothers have. I see new attempts in various corners of the church, especially in the West, to raise the Thirty-Nine Articles or even the Chicago-Lambeth Quadrilateral to be the defining statements of what Anglicans are, and are to believe. Driven by fear, insecure individuals in these changing times are trying to nail down Anglican theology and beliefs. Armed with clear doctrinal definitions and limits, the same folk will then be able to count who is in and who is out. Control is reasserted and ambiguity is overcome.

The second reaction to these changing times can be seen in attempts to construct a new central structure of authority for the Anglican Communion, what I call a new curialization. There are those who believe that without a clear, central authority structure, a curia (such as the one our Roman Catholic sisters and brothers have) the Body of Christ, the church catholic, will fly apart in a disorganized mess. And so, some try to imbue bishops and primates with new kinds of authority and responsibility for the unity of Anglicanism. Recent commission documents and study papers like the "Virginia Report" of the Inter-Anglican Theological and Doctrinal Commission and the paper on "The Role and Purpose of the Office of Primate and the Meeting of Primates," prepared for the eleventh Primates Meeting, look toward the primates, and especially the Archbishop of Canterbury, as being primarily responsible for inter-Anglican common life and decision making. Lambeth 1998, specifically Resolution III.6 on "Instruments of Anglican Communion," provided the primates, for the first time ever, enhanced responsibility for pan-Anglican doctrinal and moral matters and unheard of extra-metropolitical authority to intervene in the life of Anglican provinces locally.[16]

Whether confession or curia, catechism or conference, constitution or council, the fearful are looking for easy answers. But easy answers based on a shared Anglo heritage will no longer hold the Anglican Communion together. In these changing times we must not put our hope in either tighter doctrinal definitions or a more centralized international authority structure. Instead, a new commitment to God's project, a renewal in God's mission, is needed if we are to remain in communion across the colors and cultures, nations and nationalities that Anglicanism now embodies.

REACTION OR RENEWAL IN CHANGING TIMES

So far, I have attempted to sketch out the profound changes we in the church are experiencing today, both changes in mission thought, and changes in demographics and power dynamics within the Anglican Communion. I have emphasized that some who are most afraid of these changes, who feel they have the most to lose, are vigorously trying to fight what God is about in our world and our church by seeking security in a new confession or a new curia. Both of these are reactions to where we are today. What would it look like if, instead of being reactive to the changes, we saw them as an opportunity to be renewed in God's mission, an invitation to go deeper into God's project? This, then, is the choice we have before us today as Anglican Christians. Are we going to react to the changes out of fear or are we going to seize the moment as a possibility for renewal in God's mission?

These two choices, reaction or renewal, were vividly laid before the Communion when the Primates, or "heads" of the churches in the Anglican Communion, met together in Kanuga, in March 2001. For many, especially those whom I would characterize as reacting to the changes in the world and in Anglicanism, the 2001 Primates Meeting was to be the final showdown where the American Episcopal Church would be chastised, once and for all, for its "revisionist" positions on women's ordination and human sexuality.

Arriving in North Carolina, the primates found themselves invited into an intimate and retreat like setting at the Kanuga Conference Center. Unlike the Primates Meeting in Orporto, Portugal, in 2000, the gathering of Archbishops and Presiding Bishops would not be accessible to press and outside influences. It was only without the influence from outside observers and activists that the primates could enter into a deep place of honesty, sharing, and communion with God and one another. Much credit for the depoliticization of the 2001 Primates' Meeting needs to be given to the President of the Meeting, Archbishop of Canterbury George Carey. Archbishop Carey knows that there are forces at work in the Anglican Communion that seek to construct a dividing line between churches and dioceses within Anglicanism. As Archbishop of Canterbury, he takes seriously the historic role of his See as a point of unity for Anglican Christians.

It was the Archbishop of Canterbury, early on in the Kanuga Primates Meeting, who called the Archbishops and Presiding Bishops not to react out of fear, but to be renewed in God's mission. He very easily could have advanced a proposal that sought to put in place processes to ostracize one or another church in the Anglican Communion. Likewise, as president of the meeting, he also could have chosen to ignore such a proposal altogether, making believe that all is well and good in the family of churches. By all reports, the Archbishop of Canterbury chose to do neither.

Early in the meeting, Archbishop Carey called the primates together for a fireside chat about the proposal. At his invitation, the primates shared their diverse perspectives and it was clear that there was not unanimity on what it means to be a faithful Anglican today. Under the careful leadership of Carey, however, consensus did emerge that the primates, and the whole Anglican Communion, needed to find a different way of being together than the exercise of party politics that set churches and individuals over against one another. The primates had come to the precipice of division and chose not to jump into the abyss of schism.

Differences between the primates and between churches in the Anglican Communion did not magically disappear at the fireside hearth that evening at Kanuga. What did occur, however, was an invitation and an expectation to go deeper into the meaning of communion, to go deeper into God's mission. The primates were called to become a church made up of, paraphrasing Archbishop Rowan Williams of Wales, "solidarities not of our own choosing, where none can say, I have no need of you."

As the meeting progressed, the primates prayed together, walked together, and talked together. They heard stirring testimonies about the struggles of Christians around the world to live with faith and integrity in the face of crippling poverty, political instability, religious persecution, and the scourge of the HIV/AIDS pandemic. In his presentation to the Kanuga meeting, the Rev. Gideon Byamugisha from Uganda, himself HIV positive, put a face to the devastating disease and forced the primates to move beyond rhetoric and disembodied pronouncements to genuine action. And it was in the movement from talk about the church to action for the world, that a new way of being together for the primates, and perhaps even for the whole Anglican Communion began to emerge. It was in the movement from talk about the church to action for the world that the primates moved from reaction in fear to renewal in mission.

By the end of the Kanuga Primates' Meeting, the heads of the churches of the Anglican Communion had chosen common action in God's mission over doctrinal disagreements and sentiments of schism. Eschewing the previous practice of issuing a communiqué or statement, the primates instead offered a pastoral letter calling Anglicans the world over to prayer and action. The letter describes how the primates had heard stories of the freeing good news of Jesus Christ in the face of pain and persecution in such diverse places as Iran, Congo, Sudan, India, and Zimbabwe. Encountering these realities as genuine brothers in Christ led the primates to conclude: "coming close to these and many other situations, we have discovered the unity among us, and we call on all Anglicans to discover the same closeness through prayer and action."[17]

"Through prayer and action," maybe here are the seeds of a new Anglicanism, a renewed and reconciled community in God's mission. For the first time ever, the primates took two bold and deliberate steps coming out of Kanuga. They specifically challenged Anglicans worldwide to pray during the days between Ascension and Pentecost for growing unity in the Anglican Communion, for those enslaved by poverty or wealth, and for those living with HIV/AIDS. This "Call to Prayer" was followed with an "Action Plan" that laid out specific tasks before the Communion in general, and the primates in particular.

In calling for prayer and direct action to confront death-dealing realities of the world, such as economic globalization and the HIV/AIDS pandemic, the primates who met in Kanuga last March not only succeeded in avoiding division in the Communion, but also actually challenged the church to a new level of pertinence and accountability beyond our inner-ecclesial squabbles. "The Call to Prayer" coupled with the specifics of the "Action Plan" saved the church from our self-preoccupations while turning us inside out for the world for which Christ died. Kanuga 2001 was a sign of renewal in God's mission.

Some of these Action Plan initiatives have already begun to bear fruit. In August 2001 church leaders from Africa and other parts of the world came together in Johannesburg, South Africa, for an All Africa Anglican Conference on HIV / AIDS. This unprecedented gathering challenged secular and religious leaders to commit themselves to fight against the scourge of HIV / AIDS. Their prophetic words rang true to God's mission in the world:

> We are living with AIDS. As the body of Christ, confronted by a disaster unprecedented in human history, we share the pain of all who suffer as a result of AIDS. Faced by this crisis, we hear God's call to be transformed. We confess our sins of judgment, ignorance, silence, indifference, and denial. Repenting of our sin, we commit ourselves to: breaking the silence in order to

end all new infections; educating ourselves at every
level within the Church; confronting poverty, conflict
and gender inequalities; ending stigma and judgment,
and holding ourselves accountable before God and the
world. Only then can we live out the Good News of the
all-embracing love of Christ.[18]

Lest we think that renewal in God's mission is only occurring among the primates or African church leaders of the
Anglican Communion, I would like to name two other
examples of the Spirit challenging the church, specifically
the Episcopal Church, USA, to new levels of faithfulness and
engagement in God's mission. These two examples of renewal
in mission, both of which are primarily lay led, testify to the
reality that the movement of the Holy Spirit in mission is not
confined to old categories or battle-lines, but rather they
expand previous definitions and classifications creating new
constituencies and allies for action.

The first example is the emergence of the Episcopal Partnership for Global Mission (EPGM). This network of over
fifty mission-related organizations in the Episcopal church,
including congregations, dioceses, voluntary agencies, and
missionary societies, as well as legislative and executive bodies of the church such as the Standing Commission on
World Mission and the Executive Council, is perhaps one of
the most diverse and eclectic gatherings of American Episcopalians. From the Episcopal Divinity School to the South
American Missionary Society, from the Daughters of the King
to Trinity Wall Street, these fifty agencies have covenanted
around a common theology of mission, and share resources
and information in order to bolster the Episcopal Church's
world mission efforts. Episcopalians associated with the
EPGM have been able to lay aside the seemingly divisive
issues that others use to divide us from one another. Looking beyond ourselves we have been reconciled one to another as we discovered new solidarities and oneness in our common calling in God's mission in the wider world.

A second example is the increasing commitment in our church to fight against the persecution of individuals for their religious beliefs. In particular, Episcopalians have begun to join hands across theological and ecclesiological divides in order to fight for justice and peace in Southern Sudan. Individuals who otherwise have profound differences on such issues as human sexuality, such as Louis Crew, founder of the gay and lesbian organization in the Episcopal Church known as Integrity, and Diane Knippers, executive Director of the conservative, Washington-based organization, The Institute for Religion and Democracy, are working in common to fight against the tragedy of war, religious persecution, and ethnic cleansing in Southern Sudan.

What is going on here? Is there a divine plan to the seeming inconsistencies and incongruities developing in Anglicanism today? Are we witnessing the birth of a new Communion with an emerging ecclesiology built upon solidarity and service to God's mission? I believe so with all my heart and soul. Whether we are primates, clergy, or lay people, we Anglicans today are called to move beyond reactive positions that divide us from one another within the body of Christ. Rather, given the suffering and pain of the world, God is calling the Anglican Communion to live beyond ourselves for the sake of those who are not of our fold. *Living for others and not for ourselves* will require us to recognize and live into the post-modern and post-colonial reality that we are not all the same, that real differences exist, and that the world is a wonderful plurality of peoples and contexts. *Living for others and not for ourselves* means that we in the West need to own our culpability in the last two centuries of colonialism that profited some of us at the expense of the wider world, and then repent of such sins. *Living for others and not for ourselves* will call us to a deeper level of commitment and service to God's mission of justice, compassion, and reconciliation. *Living for others and not for ourselves,* we will discover new life in the risen Christ. The common witness of the primates in Kanuga, the African leaders at the AIDS Conference in Johannesburg, the work of the Episcopal Partnership for Global Mission, and Louis Crew and Diane Knippers for justice in the Sudan, are signs of a new church and a new Anglican Communion. Let us, as Christian leaders today, not be afraid of the changes and turmoil we are experiencing. Instead, let us live for others and not for ourselves by going forward boldly in God's mission to restore all people to unity with God and each other in Christ.

NOTES

[1] David J. Bosch, *Transforming Mission: Paradigm Shifts in Theology of Mission* (Maryknoll, NY: Orbis Books, 1991), 262–274. Part of this first section has appeared in: Ian T. Douglas, "Baptized into Mission: Ministry and Holy Orders Reconsidered," *Sewanee Theological Review* 40 (no. 4, Michaelmas 1997): 431–443.

[2] For an overview of the Episcopal Church, USA and its foreign mission history see: Ian T. Douglas, *Fling Out the Banner: The National Church Ideal and the Foreign Mission of the Episcopal Church,* (New York: Church Hymnal Corporation, 1996).

[3] The meetings of the International Missionary Council in Whitby, 1947, and Willingen, 1952 were particularly concerned with the missionary nature of the church.

[4] Stephen Neill, *A History of Christian Missions* (New York: Penguin Books, 1964), 572.

[5] Johannes C. Hoekendijk, "The Call to Evangelism," *International Review of Missions* 39 (April 1950): 163.

[6] Ibid., 171.

[7] S. J. Samartha, *One Christ—Many Religions: Towards a Revised Christology* (Maryknoll, NY: Orbis Books, 1995), 149.

[8] The Book of Common Prayer (New York: The Church Hymnal Corporation, 1979), 855.

[9] Johannes Blauw, *The Missionary Nature of the Church* (Grand Rapids, MI: Eerdmans, 1974).

[10] *Journal of the Proceedings of the Bishops, Clergy and Laity of the Protestant Episcopal Church in the United States of America in a General Convention 1835* (New York: Swords, Stanford and Company, 1935), 130–131.

[11] With the development of a centralized national program of education, social, service, and missions in 1919, the Domestic and Foreign Missionary Society became the incor-

porated appellation for the "national church." Today the name remains the legal title for the corporate work of the Episcopal Church in the United States.

[12] A fuller discussion of these issues, from which this section is drawn, is found in: Ian T. Douglas, "The Exigency of Times and Occasions: Power and Identity in the Anglican Communion Today," in Ian T. Douglas and Kwok Pui Lan, eds. *Beyond Colonial Anglicanism: The Anglican Communion in the Twenty-First Century* (New York: Church Publishing Inc. 2001), 25–46.

[13] For a discussion of the politics of hegemony in the Anglican Communion see: Ian Douglas, "Radical Mutuality Still Out of Reach: Lambeth Analysis" *The Witness* 81 (no. 11, November, 1998): 24–27. Hegemony is defined as: preponderant influence or authority, especially of one nation over others.

[14] David B. Barrett, "Annual Statistical Table on Global Mission: 2000," *International Bulletin of Missionary Research* 24 (January 2000): 24–25.

[15] E. R. Fairweather, ed., *Anglican Congress 1963: Report of the Proceedings*, (n.p.: Editorial Committee of the Anglican Congress, 1963), 118.

[16] See Resolution III.6 on "Instruments of the Anglican Communion" in: *The Official Report of the Lambeth Conference of 1998*, (Harrisburg, PA: Morehouse Publishing for the Anglican Communion, 1999), 398–399.

[17] "A Pastoral letter and a Call to Prayer." The Primates of the Anglican Communion, 8 March, 2000, Anglican Communion News Service #2410.

[18] "Our Vision, Our Hope: The First Step," Communique from the All Africa Anglican Conference on HIV/AIDS, Johannesburg, South Africa, 22 August 2001, Section 2, Anglican Communion News Service #2601.

CLOSING REFLECTIONS BY THE PRESIDING BISHOP

COMMUNITY OF BISHOPS
September 26, 2001

FRANK T. GRISWOLD

And not only that, but we also boast in our sufferings, knowing that suffering produces endurance, and endurance produces character, and character produces hope, and hope does not disappoint us, because God's love has been poured into our hearts through the Holy Spirit that has been given to us. (Rom 5:3–5)

I have been pondering this text, and it keeps coming back to me. It is elusive. I'm not exactly sure, in the deepest sense, what Paul was expressing of his own experience. It is an ascetical, mystical text and it invites us to ponder that progression: suffering produces endurance, endurance produces character, and character produces hope, and hope does not disappoint us because the Holy Spirit has been poured into our hearts.

The events of the last days, and indeed some of the seasons in the life of this church, have been and are times of suffering. But suffering—as we've heard from so many of our speakers in the last week—is a process of purification, a narrow door through which one passes in union with Christ to a new place. We are shaped and formed and, in a very deep way, conformed to the pattern of Christ, through the reality of suffering. Not that we seek it, and not that we romanticize it. It is simply an element in our lives that we tend to discount and deny quite often until we find ourselves in it. Suffering can be public. Suffering can also be intensely personal and hidden. And yet, if we live it in union with Christ, it doesn't destroy us, but in a very paradoxical way it breaks us open. It makes us real. It takes us beyond the suffering into the realm of character, by way of endurance.

I don't think we've spent nearly enough time pondering that Pauline grace: endurance or patience. We often rush desperately to some kind of resolution, when in fact we simply have to endure and live through a situation and face the reality of what it costs us. As a nation we are now at that place. We don't know exactly what's coming, but we have to live it in such a way that we keep our focus on Christ. And, in that way endurance leads to character—the fuller realization of whom we are called to be in grace and truth—and that opens the way to hope.

We as a House of Bishops have been at this Pauline reality for a decade. In 1992, it was decided that we would meet in Kanuga in the spring in addition to our regular autumn meeting. For the first few years of this new pattern there were murmurs and protests, with bishops thinking they couldn't give that much time, or that they were far too busy in the life of their dioceses. Now, happily, meeting twice a year has become a norm. There is absolutely no way we can become a community of wisdom if we don't actually come together often; an annual meeting was simply insufficient.

Over the last decade, in a variety of ways, we have been trying to practice the ascetical disciplines of reconciliation. We are far from perfect. There is still among us a great deal of sinfulness that needs to be confessed and worked through. But my feeling is that our trajectory is the right one. And, as I take soundings from you, year by year, there is a general sense that though certain realities continue to afflict us and keep us from perfect reconciliation, still the movement is in that direction and bit by bit, step by step, we are incarnating the very thing we seek to proclaim to others. And, obviously, if it doesn't exist among us, our proclamation is false and shallow.

Certainly the events of the September 11 have turned us from self-preoccupation to a more public stance. Our focus is not primarily on us and our internal struggles. Our focus is now on the world around us, and particularly this nation in relationship to other nations as we enter into what our President is calling a "war on terrorism." This is a war that must be fought, not simply because we have been attacked, but because terrorism is so all-pervasive in this world and touches so many lives and so many countries.

At the same time, I think it is very important for us to wage reconciliation. Waging reconciliation is our particular way of participating in the war on terrorism. We support our nation in its efforts. We pray for the President and all his advisors, and the members of Congress that they may be wise and prudent in their decisions. We pray, of course, for all those in the military service, particularly our chaplains. I've seen a number of chaplains since the events of September 11 and experienced some of their fragility and wonderment at what lies ahead. That is replicated on a much larger scale on the part of those who serve in the armed forces. In a very special way we need not only to pray for them, but also to give them our active support and encouragement.

So, as a House of Bishops we have moved with a kind of a divine logic we weren't even aware of. I think we enter into this *kairos* moment in some sense prepared by our own struggles, by our own efforts to be a community of reconciliation, living the dynamic of conversation, conversion, communion, and commitment. That work goes on; obviously we must continue to attend to our life as the community of faith for the sake of the world so that our proclamation is authentic in terms of the life we lead.

Now, however, we also are called to turn our focus very much to the world around us. This conference, of course, was planned without any knowledge of the context in which we would find ourselves. Globalization is exactly the topic we needed to consider. And I'm so grateful to our several speakers for the way in which, with a wonderful consistency, they've built on one another. Instead of being tugged and pulled in seven different directions by winning presentations, all of which would have their own integrity, the fact that there has been an integration has been extremely helpful to all of us.

Now, we move forward at a number of levels. A frame for me, in addition to the passage from Romans, is the notion in the Spiritual Exercises of Ignatius of Loyola of *Deus Operaius*, a laboring God. God labors in creation. God labors on behalf of creation. The whole notion of laboring God and our participation in God's labor is absolutely fundamental to the Spiritual Exercises of Ignatius and is the dynamic out of which all Ignatian active apostolic spirituality springs. It is something we could do well to think about.

The understanding of God's labor, God's work, comes to us not only from Ignatius of Loyola, but is absolutely fundamental to the Gospel of John. If you take the theme of work, God's work: "my food is to do the will of the one who sent me to accomplish his work" (Jn 4:34). "Father I have glorified you on earth by completing the work you gave me to do" (Jn 17:4). On the cross Jesus cries: "It [the work] is finished" (Jn 19:30). And he says to his disciples: "We must work the works of the one who sent me" (Jn 9:4).

So the whole notion of God's project, God's work, God's mission, is absolutely fundamental to our life as persons of the gospel. It comes to us from Scripture and it comes to us from the ascetical tradition of the church. But entering into that work, being co-laborers with God on behalf of creation, involves a number of things. Certainly it involves conversion.

We must ask: where do I resist reconciliation in my own life? Where do I live with interior divisions? Where do I cling to divisions between me and others with all sorts of self-justifications? Where am I being called to let go of some of my fully formed judgments with respect to others so that I can enter into a new kind of relationship?

Conversion is not easy. We are ministers of that conversion to one another, but I think we are fooling ourselves if we simply leap to some kind of noble ministry of reconciliation without looking at the personal cost. And the personal cost is to let something go. It is a form of "green martyrdom" in the Celtic tradition, looking within ourselves and asking, "What do I have to take leave of in order to enter into freedom with respect to those around me?" This is not just so that we can be cozy and loving, but for the sake of the world, because when reconciliation occurs between people it releases an energy that is larger than their own relationship. There is a force that can go forth beyond them into the world. We want to become rooted and grounded in that force.

So I look at waging reconciliation on a number of levels. First, the personal level: what needs to happen within me? Where am I in my companionship with Christ? Am I willing to join Christ in Christ's ongoing work, the work of Abba? Where do I stand in need of conversion? We show one another in wonderful ways what those areas are.

Then there is the interpersonal—and I would say that this community is a very good laboratory of interpersonal reconciliation. We might ask: Who do we need to talk to? Who do we need to be honest with? Whose reality do we have to make room for alongside our own? How do we move from either/or to both/and? I've stressed this over the last couple of years as integral to quantum thinking, moving from Newtonian either/or to the quantum both/and. I think of some words of Thomas Merton, "It is not a question of either/or but of all in one, of wholeness, wholeheartedness and unity which finds the same ground of love in everything."

It is that common ground of love, the love of God poured into our hearts by the Holy Spirit, that then gives us the capacity to make room for difference, to honor it, to respect it, to rejoice in it, not to be threatened by it or need to beat it into some subjection to our own view of what reality is.

So conversion: a personal conversion, an interpersonal conversion, and then we look at ourselves institutionally. And certainly part of this time we've spent together is looking at ourselves as part of the Anglican Communion in relationship to other parts of that community that are very different from ours. I am very glad that David Gitari [The Most Rev. David Gitari, Archbishop of Kenya] made the sacrifice of time and the difficulty of travel to be with us. There are lots of other useful things he could have done. I'm very grateful that he has been the embodiment of difference that represents that larger Communion in our midst. I'm very grateful to you for being here, David.

And then there is the whole ecumenical dimension, which has been touched on in a variety of ways. I'm hoping that as we move ahead Chris Epting [The Rt. Rev. Christopher Epting, Deputy for Ecumenical and Interfaith Relations] and others can help us frame some of our conversations that need to take place across the lines of religion. Our focus has been on other Christian bodies, other ecclesial communities, and I think we've neglected those larger conversations that involve other religious traditions. They are much needed and we have to make amends and begin some of those conversations very quickly.

So, we look at these levels: personal, interpersonal, institutional, and then there is the world around us, which so many of us find daunting. It's easy to live within our little ecclesial world. We have a certain authority. We know the rules. We have the costumes. People know how to address us, which is very consoling. Then you find yourself in the corridors of power—as we like to say—and someone says, "Hi, Reverend," and you think, "Reverend...I am at least the

Right Reverend, don't they realize that I am more than simply a local pastor?" and that begins to make us feel uneasy.

I think we often feel impotent and used in public realms. Part of the conversion that needs to occur within us is to take seriously the fact that our ministry as bishops in the church of God carries with it a public aspect that we neglect at our peril. Jesus was not afraid to appear before leaders and we should not be either. Maybe some of the disciplines that have been put forward by those of us who are more confident in this area might be an encouragement to the rest of us to step forward.

My own experience has been that people are grateful, the leaders are actually grateful when you appear. So I think it's extremely important to step forward into the world. Don't underestimate your capacity to make a difference in the public realm. That may mean the letting go of certain reticence, the letting go of a perspective of yourself as a religious leader safely immured in the confines of your cathedral. It may not be a physical cathedral, but a kind of psychological cathedral where you know what to do and how to do it, and you feel somewhat confident. This is tiptoeing out into a new realm, a new area, and that too is an area of conversion.

A number of you have put down ideas for concrete action and I want to tell you what I've done. I've asked Arthur Walmsley [The Rt. Rev. Arthur Walmsley, Bishop of Connecticut, retired] to convene, as soon as possible, a small group to take counsel about next steps. I hope the group will include someone like Richard Parker, some bishops, some economists, and others with particular expertise, members of our church who have never been called upon to be part of the public life of the church or policymaking. I've asked Arthur to take the various concrete recommendations that you've made—some are cosmic, of course, and some are very specific and highly doable, like a day of fasting, and working with some of the staff people at the Episcopal Church Center who already are involved in some things that are relevant to your concerns—and to pull together a very concrete plan that can be set before us no later than our Spring meeting of the House of Bishops. There are so many ideas that are worth taking seriously.

I do think that we've been given some resources, in the papers and in what we have heard from one another, that give us a whole new way of thinking about ourselves globally and in relationship to other parts of the world. I also think that just digesting what you've heard over the past few days gives you a word to speak that you should not be shy about speaking. So don't underestimate the fact that you've received something; digest it and let it be the word that flows out of you to your community and the world.

APPENDIX 1

PRAYERS FROM THE COMMUNITY EUCHARISTS

THE RT. REV. GERALYN WOLF
Bishop of Rhode Island

THURSDAY, SEPTEMBER 20, 2001

Let us bend the knee of our hearts, offering our prayers to God, the all-merciful One, in whose arms the tears of the world are embraced, responding to each petition by saying, Christ, have mercy.

That we may testify to the reconciling love of Christ, whose cross bids us to share in the painful and sacrificial work of transformation and renewal; for this we pray.

That we may be broken and healed by the eucharistic meal, dividing our bread that others may eat, sharing our wealth that others may increase their own, claiming our vulnerability that we may find our place among the community of nations; for this we pray.

That wisdom's grace may descend upon our President, his advisors, and leaders throughout the world, that our response to tragedy be tempered, and that patience may prevail amidst calls for action; for this we pray.

That all who mourn may be comforted in their affliction, and to all who have died, may they be received into God's heavenly home, where there is no death, neither sorrow nor crying, but the fullness of joy with all your saints; for this we pray.

That in this community of bishops and spouses, we may be awake to the feelings and experiences that we bring to this gathering, and find in each other a source of God's blessing; for this we pray.

May God, whose feet lead us into the ways of peace, guide us now as we continue our prayers either silently or aloud.

The people add their own petitions.

FRIDAY, SEPTEMBER 21, 2001

In the fear of the Lord, let us turn from evil, and offer our prayers with a humble heart trusting in God's saving grace. The response to each petition is, "Christ, have mercy."

For the courage to move outside of comfortable expressions of ministry, following Jesus into places of discontent, where the poor know his embrace, and the sinner his forgiveness; let us pray to the Lord.

For our children, that they may walk in the path of our spiritual ancestors, receive the faith proclaimed today, and offer the Word to generations to come; let us pray to the Lord.

For the leaders of the nations of the world, especially George, our President, Frank, our Presiding Bishop, and all whose words and actions echo in the global family, that they may seek divine wisdom in the midst of human frailty; let us pray to the Lord.

For the forgiveness of our sins—our pride and hypocrisy, our greed and prejudice—that in recognizing our painful shortcomings we may be vulnerable to the transforming hands of Jesus; let us pray to the Lord.

For innocent victims of ageless religious disputes, especially in Northern Ireland, the Middle East, and on our own soil, that religious rightness be turned into mutual dependence in God, whose definition no one can capture; let us pray to the Lord.

In thanksgiving for rescue workers who continue to seek the living, for caretakers who comfort those who mourn, for those who love well and bring love into the world; let us pray to the Lord.

In the spirit of St. Matthew, whose gospel has for centuries instructed the church, lead us now as we continue our prayers and petitions.

The people add their own petitions.

SATURDAY, SEPTEMBER 22, 2001

Creator of the world, open our eyes to see the beauty of water, wind, and sky, and help us to be guardians of your earthly treasures; for this we pray.

Word of Life, rend our thoughts and bend our hearts that we may see your truth not in our wisdom, nor in our power, but in our foolishness and the shame of your cross; for this we pray.

Spirit of peace, descend upon our President and his advisors, that they may make wise and tempered decisions, choosing reflection over immediacy, and the wisdom of the nations over a unilateral response; for this we pray.

God, the all-merciful One, whose name is blessed, be with Frank, and the community of bishops, that the riches of our work may be gathered and shared with the rest of church, and find a hearing in our national life; for this we pray.

Gracious God, call to the ordained ministry young women and men of various races and cultures, that your gospel be proclaimed through many voices, and your church extended through their ministry; for this we pray.

Jesus, the Comforter, be with those who mourn, bring eternal rest to those who have died; to the sick bring your healing grace, and in your mercy transform all our wounds into sources of love; for this we pray.

Holy Paraclete, come and free us from the bondage of our sins—our complacency in speaking for the poor, our collusion with wealth, our sense of entitlement and all that alienates us one from another—that as we choose conversion we may experience forgiveness; for this we pray.

Through the gift of prayer that God has given to us let us continue to intercede on behalf of ourselves and others.

The people add their own petitions.

MONDAY, SEPTEMBER 24, 2001

We have been anointed with the Spirit of God, to proclaim good news in the midst of captivity, to see through blindness, and so offer our prayers through the poverty of our spirit, that we can respond to each petition by saying, "Christ, have mercy."

Hold our fractured lives in your hands, that our brokenness may reflect the Body of your Son, spent and given for the redemption of the world, and make us instruments of your peace in the midst of an uncertain future; for this we pray.

Make us a people yearning for transformation of vision: that we may see beyond personal necessities, reach beyond cultural experiences, love and be loved by people whose lives will make us whole; for this we pray.

Awaken us to the cries of desperation from people throughout the world, especially women and children suffering from poverty, abuse, HIV/AIDS, and let us be horrified by their lament; for this we pray.

Keep us vigilant in prayer for our enemies, for terrorists at home and abroad, and all who seek to extinguish the light of justice and freedom; for this we pray.

Challenge our spirits by your message of hope, that mustard seeds of faith will move every barrier that keeps us from being your one, holy, catholic, and apostolic church; for this we pray.

Send your Holy Spirit upon those who mourn the death of loved ones, and those who grieve for human loss throughout the world, and to all who have died grant eternal rest; for this we pray.

In thanksgiving for our fellowship, the arms of support that uphold us in times of doubt and the strength that overcomes our individual weaknesses; for this we pray.

Let us join with the prayers of the baptized throughout the world, as we continue our petitions either silently or aloud.

The people add their own petitions.

TUESDAY, SEPTEMBER 25, 2001

May the Spirit of God dwell within us, and give us the yearning to pray on behalf of others.

For the church: for George, Archbishop of Canterbury; Frank, our Primate; and David, Archbishop of Kenya, that with them we may call the church to a rededication to mission, opening ourselves to the breadth and depth of the Anglican Communion throughout the world; let us pray to the Lord.

For George, our president; for the leaders of the nations of the world; and for all in positions of public trust, that decisions may be tempered by wisdom; and action with patience; let us pray to the Lord.

For the courage and intention to support groups whose fears have intensified at this time: those of the Muslim faith, those of Arab and Middle Eastern descent, and children and young people, that we, who do not wear their face, may support their human dignity and legal rights; let us pray to the Lord.

For an enlargement of the church through the witness of the religious life, that we may have a renewed sense of simplicity in the midst of abundance, fidelity in an age of lost promises, and obedience to God's voice in the chatter of our time; let us pray to the Lord.

For those who have died this day, and for those whose loved ones and friends have moved from the missing to the dead; let us pray to the Lord.

In thanksgiving for the privileges that we enjoy, that a heart of gratitude may lead to renewed integrity in the economic and social policies of our church and nation; for this we pray.

Let us participate with God in the work of redemption as we continue our prayers either silently or aloud.

The people add their own petitions.

WEDNESDAY, SEPTEMBER 26, 2001

These intercessions are used in conjunction with "Peace before us" in Wonder, Love, and Praise #791. *Prayers were offered between each stanza of the hymn.*

May the weapons of the world be turned into food and shelter, and acts of destruction into programs of hope, and may all people, in every land, live in peace.

That the church will witness to love that overcomes fear, stretching beyond itself to proclaim, through word and action, the promises of salvation.

That the light of eternal life may spread across the souls of all who have died, and their courage burn brightly within the heart of a grateful nation.

That Christ will unbind us from our sins—our pride and hypocrisy, our greed and false judgments—and lead us into perfect freedom.

In thanksgiving for those who serve others, who release the best in humanity, and who speak for those who are too weary to raise their voices.

Appendix 2

Remarks by an Observer

Of the Community of Bishops of
the Episcopal church

THE MOST REV. DR. DAVID M. GITARI
Archbishop of the Anglican Church of Kenya

Appreciation

First and foremost I wish to thank the Presiding Bishop for having invited me to attend this gathering of bishops and spouses and to sit in your midst to listen to the theme of "God's Mission in Global Communication of Difference" expounded by various speakers so ably and discussed so freely. Thanks to the team that put together this program and the speakers who addressed us.

I was deeply moved by your warmth and kindness and your appreciation of my presence. Every person who spoke to me started by telling me: "It is wonderful to have you here."

Two Surprises

First, during and after the last Lambeth Conference, the majority of African Bishops concluded that the Episcopal Church is preoccupied with the agenda of human sexuality, as if there are no other priorities in the mission of your church. The globalization of computers and e-mails has not helped to change our attitude. When I open incoming e-mails I find 90 percent are from David Virtue of *Virtuosity*. I am surprised that since I arrived here I have not seen or heard your preoccupation with that theme.

Nine out of twelve primates of Africa met in Pretoria, South Africa, in mid-August and asked me to deliver a letter to the Presiding Bishop containing greetings and God's blessing upon this gathering. I am glad Frank [Presiding Bishop Frank Griswold] made a reference to our letter, which was written before September 11. The primates were convinced that the Episcopal Church is capable of solving its problems and we could, therefore, not accept AMiA [Anglican Mission in America] ordinations. For this reason and while not wanting to dictate to your church, the primates called upon the church here to implement the call of the primates of the Communion to provide Episcopal oversight to those who uphold traditional orthodox faith and feel neglected, even if it means making provisions for flying bishops from within your province.

Second, in 1977 I represented the Anglican Church of Kenya at the Partners in Mission Consultation held in Louisville, Kentucky, and while in the United States the external partners were invited to attend the General Convention. It was my first visit to this great country and there were many things I learned about your church. At that time, however, there was great concern that Evangelicals, some of them from outside the United States, had started the Trinity Episcopal School for Ministry at Ambridge, Pennsylvania; and a number of speakers spoke very much against that move. I told the Convention that I was surprised by the negative attitude as I thought the Anglican Church is a *via media* where believers of different persuasions, low and high, Liberals and Evangelicals, can co-exist harmoniously in the Anglican Communion. Now something that was unimaginable twenty-five years ago is a welcome reality in your church. Grant LeMarquand, the Professor of Biblical Studies and Mission at Trinity Episcopal School for Ministry, gave us a moving presentation on "The Bible and Mission," which was deeply appreciated by all participants. I assume that after such a wonderful presentation no one can ask the question of Nathaniel: "Can anything good come from Ambridge?"

LEADERSHIP IN A TIME OF CRISIS

Though this conference was planned long before the events of Tuesday, September 11, 2001, there is no doubt that this gathering has been greatly influenced by the terror of that day. The destruction of symbols of military and economic power, by pilots trained in America using American airplanes, was an incident that shocked not only Americans but also the whole world. It has brought home the negative aspects of globalization and given new lessons for all of us to learn. It reminds us how right the psalmist was when he said: "Unless the Lord builds the house, its builders labor in vain, and unless the Lord watches the city the watchmen stand guard in vain" (Ps 127:1).

On that terrible morning of September 11, the Presiding Bishop sent out an e-mail to all in which he said: "The events of this morning make me keenly aware that violence knows no boundaries and that security is an illusion. To witness the collapse of the World Trade Center was to confront not only our vulnerability as a nation in spite of our power, but also the personal vulnerability of each of us to events and circumstances that overtake us." Frank reminded us we are called to another way—to engage with all our hearts and minds and strength in God's project of transforming the world. I have been moved by the way this conference has spent much time discussing and wishing to identify with those who are suffering. I deeply appreciate time spent discussing the HIV/AIDS pandemic in Africa and the specific actions African bishops have recommended.

At this time of world crisis, bishops must exercise their prophetic ministry even more vigorously. We do not have to agree with the powers that be. The other day President Bush said: "Either you are with us or you are with terrorists." I do not agree with him, as there is another category of people who are neutral. They cannot support terrorism, but neither are they convinced you can defeat evil with evil. As St. Paul said, "Don't let evil defeat you, but defeat evil with good" (Rom 12:21).

As leaders of the church, our relationship with powers that be, should be like our relationship with fire. If you go too close you get burnt. If you go too far you freeze. We should keep a critical and strategic distance so that we can praise our political leaders when they do what is just and true before God and criticize them fearlessly, whatever the cost, when they depart from justice, which God requires.

THREE CONCLUDING REQUESTS

First, there are bishops from Africa who are longing to come to the United States for short sabbaticals and to experience the life of the Episcopal Church. Please invite them and offer them hospitality.

Second, there are ordained clergy who have come here from around the world to study and work. If they have the blessing of their respective bishops, offer them hospitality and license them to serve as priests in your dioceses.

Third, we also welcome you to come and visit us in Africa and have a taste of our situation. In Africa we say: "A person who does not travel thinks only his mother cooks well."

Thank you and God bless you as you do God's mission in the global village.

BUILD MY WORLD ANEW

REFLECTIONS FROM THE SPOUSES' GATHERING
BURLINGTON, VERMONT

KARLAH GIBBS
Diocese of Michigan

CRISTINA DANIELS
Diocese of the Virgin Islands

The community of bishops and spouses gathered in Burlington, Vermont to address the topic of "God's Mission in a Global Communion of Difference," which in light of the events of September 11 seemed prophetic. Through on-going communication after that day, the safety of all of our members had been established. Due to the far-reaching effects of the tragedy, those in attendance reflected a multiplicity of responses to the issue of traveling to this conference. As we gathered we all benefited from being in community.

The formal and small group discussions among bishops and spouses centered on the issues of difference, mission, economics, suffering, and reconciliation. The community of spouses set aside time to be mutually supportive in ways that were practical and useful in order to strengthen us for our work and daily lives. At the Saturday morning breakfast, new spouses to the community since General Convention 2000 were introduced.

The spouses program was entitled: "The World Among Us." We embodied building bridges by discussing the differences among us as a community of spouses. We reflected on our mission and the differences we could make. Building bridges between differences is something we can do when we intentionally invite people to dinner, being keenly aware that friendships formed around dining room tables are the stuff of mission and reconciliation. Some identified that a work of healing we can do is to respond to calls to join programs or to create conversations among various groups in our communities. We can create programs among our own clergy spouses to reconcile difference. When we teach children, we can be sensitive to drawing in other cultures; such as when taking them on a tour in a museum we include the art and culture of Islam and other, less-familiar cultures.

When we pray for people we do not understand and even fear, it is difficult to feel distant from them. We see our mission is to "walk towards difference." Healing can happen. We were energized by the presence, affection, and respect that we felt and were excited by the growing mission of carrying that love to the larger world.

APPENDIX 4
PRESENTERS

DENISE M. ACKERMANN

Denise M. Ackermann, D.Th., is presently visiting professor of Practical Theology at the University of Stellenbosch, South Africa. She retired from the chair of Christianity and Society at the University of the Western Cape, South Africa in 2000, where, *inter alia,* she taught courses in feminist theologies, Christian sexual ethics, homiletics, and Christian spirituality. She has also taught at the University of South Africa, the University of Cape Town, Harvard Divinity School, and has been a guest lecturer at Groningen University in the Netherlands, Rhodes University, and Stellenbosch University, both in South Africa. She is a member of the International Academy for Practical Theology, the Circle for Concerned African Women Theologians, the Council of the University of Cape Town, editorial boards of four international theological publications, a founder trustee of the Desmond Tutu Peace Trust, and an associate of the Black Sash Trust. Denise Ackermann has published numerous articles on women and theology from a South African perspective and has edited three books: *Women Hold Up the Sky: Women in the Church in*

Southern Africa (with J. Draper and E. Mashinini); *Liberating Practices: Feminist Practical Theologies in Different Contexts* (with R. Bons Storm); and *Claiming our Footprints: South African Women Reflect on Context, Identity and Spirituality* (with the Cape Town Chapter of the Circle for Concerned African Women Theologians).

She holds a Doctor of Divinity degree *honoris causa* from the Episcopal Divinity School where she was also a Procter fellow in 1996. In 1998, she accompanied Njongonkulu Ndungane, Anglican Archbishop of the Church of the Province of Southern Africa to the thirteenth Lambeth Conference in Canterbury, England, as his theological adviser. At present she is a research fellow at the Center of Theological Inquiry in Princeton, working on a book of theological reflections on post-apartheid South Africa entitled *After the Locusts*. When not immersed in academic concerns, her favorite occupations are walking in the mountains of the Cape and playing with her grandchildren.

VALERIE BATTS

Valerie A. Batts, Ph.D., is a Licensed Clinical Psychologist and a Clinical Teaching Member of the International Transactional Analysis Association (ITAA). As the Executive Director of VISIONS, Inc., she leads the consultation and training component. Dr. Batts is the originator of VISIONS' training model and the author of several articles on modern racism and multicultural organizational change strategies, including *Modern Racism: New Melody for the Same Old Tunes*. (Episcopal Divinity School Occasional Papers, 1998). Nationally and internationally, she works in the area of cultural diversity and multiculturalism and is noted for her dynamic, insightful, and compassionate approach to training around issues of oppression.

Dr. Batts has provided consultation and training since 1975 to human service providers, psychotherapists, educators, clergy, and private sector managers in a variety of areas; these include enhancing effective communication, interpersonal skill building, psychotherapy techniques, supervision strategies, lifestyles changes, and the establishment of environments that support, respect, and appreciate differences. Additionally, she specializes in relationship-oriented psychotherapy and lifestyle change counseling.

Dr. Batts was raised in a small black Episcopal church in Eastern North Carolina. She is currently an Adjunct Faculty at the Episcopal Divinity School, Cambridge, Massachusetts, where she teaches racial and multicultural courses and assists in the incorporation of an anti-racist agenda into the school's ongoing liberation theology practice. She has worked with the National Council of Churches, New York; Riverside Church, New York; and All Saints Episcopal Church, Pasadena. Dr. Batts works with several community development projects throughout the U.S. in which faith-based organizations play a vital role.

IAN T. DOUGLAS

The Rev. Ian T. Douglas, Ph.D. is Associate Professor of World Mission and Global Christianity and the Director of Anglican, Global, and Ecumenical Studies at the Episcopal Divinity School in Cambridge, Massachusetts. He also serves as Priest Associate at St. James's Episcopal Church in Cambridge, Diocese of Massachusetts.

Douglas has held positions as a Volunteer for Mission in *L'Eglise Episcopale d'Haiti* (The Episcopal Church of Haiti) and as Associate for Overseas Leadership Development at The Episcopal Church Center in New York. He is past Secretary and Chair of the Standing Commission on World Mission for the General Convention of the Episcopal Church and is currently a member of the Inter-Anglican Standing Commission on Mission and Evangelism. Douglas also serves as the Convener of the Episcopal Seminary Consultation on

Mission. He is a member of the House of Bishops Theology Committee, and Consultant to the Primates Theological Education Working Party of the Anglican Communion. Published widely in studies on mission and global Christianity, he is author of *Fling Out The Banner: The National Church Ideal and the Foreign Mission of the Episcopal Church,* and co-editor with Kwok Pui-Lan of *Beyond Colonial Anglicanism: The Anglican Communion in the Twenty-First Century* (both books published by Church Publishing, New York, 1993 and 2001 respectively).

Douglas holds degrees from Middlebury College (B.A.), the Harvard University Graduate School of Education (Ed.M.), and Harvard University Divinity School (M.Div). An Episcopal Church Foundation Fellow, he completed his Ph.D. in Religious and Theological Studies with a focus in missiology at the Boston University Graduate School in 1993.

Douglas is married to Kristin Harris and they are blessed with three children, Luke, Timothy, and Johanna. Ian and his family reside in Belmont, Massachusetts, USA.

CHRISTOPHER DURAISINGH

Christopher Duraisingh, a presbyter of the Church of South India, is the Otis Charles Professor of Applied Theology at the Episcopal Divinity School in Cambridge since 1997. He studied at the University of Madras, and the Episcopal Theological School. He received his doctorate in theology from Harvard University in 1979.

Dr. Duraisingh taught theology in Bangalore, India. In 1989 he became the director of the Commission on World Mission and Evangelism of the World Council of Churches (WCC) in Geneva. He directed a worldwide study on gospel and cultures, gathering up the results in a WCC world conference on mission in Salvador, Brazil, in 1996. He has been a consultant at the meetings of the Anglican Consultative Council (ACC). He gave a series of four devotional addresses at Lambeth 1978 and was a consultant to Section III at Lambeth

1998.

Dr. Duraisingh was the editor of the *International Review of Mission* from 1990 to 1997. His recent publications include an edited volume, *Called to One Hope: Gospel in Diverse Cultures* (World Council of Churches, 1998), entries in the *Dictionary of Third World Theologies* (Orbis Books, 2000), and *A Dictionary of Asian Christianity* (Wm. B. Eerdmans Publishing Co., 2001), an article in the Fall 2000 issue of *Anglican Theological Review* and an essay in *Beyond Colonial Anglicanism* (Church Publishing, Inc. 2001).

He is a member of the Ecumenical Association of Third World Theologians, American Academy of Religion and Society for Biblical Literature. Promoting authentic structures for greater ecumenical dialogue in theology across cultures is his professional commitment. He identifies equipping local congregations for their participation in God's mission locally and globally as his major passion.

GRANT LEMARQUAND

The Rev. Grant LeMarquand was born in Montreal, Canada. Raised in the United Church of Canada, he became an Anglican in his late teens. He received his ordination training at McGill University and Montreal Diocesan Theological College. Following ordination he was an assistant curate in a suburban parish and then an associate priest at Christ Church Cathedral in Montreal, where he also served as Anglican Chaplain to McGill. During this period, Grant completed an M.A. in New Testament studies under N.T. Wright. In the late 1980s, Grant and his wife Wendy, who is a family doctor, became mission partners of the Anglican Church of Canada in Kenya where he taught at St. Paul's United Theological College. After several years, they returned to Canada, where Grant began doctoral studies at Wycliffe College in the Toronto School of Theology, later joining the faculty of Wycliffe. He has been at Trinity Episcopal

School for Ministry for three years where he is Professor of Biblical Studies and Mission. His main area of research interest is the use of the Bible in Africa. Grant and Wendy have two children: David, who is 16, and Chara, who is 13.

LENG LIM

The Rev. You-Leng Leroy Lim, a native of Singapore, received his B.A. in Public Affairs and International Relations from Princeton University (where he met Bishop Fred Borsch), and his M.Div. (1995) from Harvard Divinity School. He has tutored Harvard undergraduates in economics. In June 2001, Leng received his MBA from Harvard Business School and also delivered the graduate student oration at Harvard's 350th commencement ceremony.

Leng served in the Diocese of Los Angeles as an assistant in an inner city Japanese parish, in campus ministry at University of California, Irvine, and as chair of the Ministry Study Year of the Commission on Ministry. He also served as a member of the Social Responsibility in Investment Committee of the General Convention. Prior to ordination, he worked as an AIDS educator to the Chinese-speaking communities of Los Angeles County and as a researcher with the Singapore International Foundation.

A convert to Christianity at age twelve, Leng was brought into the Anglican Church through the charismatic movement, and was baptized and confirmed in the Diocese of Singapore. (His parents followed his conversion, and now work as part-time missionaries for the Assembly of God Churches in Nepal.) Leng now uses Vipassana meditation from the Buddhist tradition as his contemplative prayer method of choice.

Leng has been on three expeditions to Alaska, and once traveled overland from Singapore to Beijing. He works as a management consultant with the international strategy-consulting firm Marakon Associates in San Francisco.

RICHARD PARKER

Richard Parker is Senior Fellow at the Shorenstein Center, John F. Kennedy School of Government, Harvard University.

An Oxford-trained economist, he is also a former journalist, the co-founder, editor, and publisher of *Mother Jones* magazine, and currently sits on the editorial board of *The Nation*. He has written for dozens of publications, including the *New York Times, Washington Post, Boston Globe, Los Angeles Times, New Republic, Atlantic Monthly, Foreign Policy*, and *Le Monde*. Active in environmental issues, he helped build Greenpeace from 1,500 to more than 600,000 members, as well as helping in the growth of the Sierra Club and Friends of the Earth. During the 1980s, he served as an advisor to Senators Kennedy, Moynihan, Glenn, and McGovern. The author of three books, he is completing an intellectual biography of economist John Kenneth Galbraith for Farrar, Straus & Giroux. He serves on the board of several foundations, and as a philanthropist has directed more than $30 million in support of various social justice, environmental, and peace groups. A member (and, until Spring 2001, vestry member) of Christ Church, Cambridge, he is the son of an Episcopal priest who served for 52 years in the Diocese of Los Angeles.